COLLECTED WORKS OF ERASMUS

VOLUME 83

COLLECTED WORKS OF
ERASMUS

CONTROVERSIES

APOLOGIA AD FABRUM

APPENDIX DE SCRIPTIS CLITHOVEI

DILUTIO

RESPONSIO AD DISPUTATIONEM
DE DIVORTIO

edited by Guy Bedouelle

University of Toronto Press

Toronto / Buffalo / London

The research and publication costs of the
Collected Works of Erasmus are supported by
University of Toronto Press.

© University of Toronto Press 1998
Toronto / Buffalo / London
Printed in Canada

ISBN 0-8020-4310-0

Printed on acid-free paper

Canadian Cataloguing in Publication Data

Erasmus, Desiderius, d. 1536
[Works]
Collected works of Erasmus

Partial contents: v. 83. Controversies / edited by Guy Bedouelle.
Includes bibliographical references and index.
ISBN 0-8020-4310-0 (v. 83)

1. Erasmus, Desiderius, d. 1536. I. Title

PA8500 1974   876'.04   C74-006326-x rev

University of Toronto Press acknowledges the financial assistance to its
publishing programme of the Canada Council for the Arts
and the Ontario Arts Council.

Collected Works of Erasmus

The aim of the Collected Works of Erasmus
is to make available an accurate, readable English text
of Erasmus' correspondence and his
other principal writings. The edition is planned
and directed by an Editorial Board, an Executive Committee,
and an Advisory Committee.

Contents

COLLECTED WORKS OF ERASMUS

VOLUME 83

Introduction

I

'It would be preferable to devote our energies to resolving our differences rather than to providing seed-ground for new disagreements through biased inquiries.' Erasmus made this appeal for dialogue with his colleagues, both humanists and theologians, in the last lines of his *Appendix* written to answer the criticisms of Josse Clichtove. It has a rather paradoxical ring, if one considers the 1444 quarto pages of the ninth volume of his *Opera omnia* (Froben 1540)[1] containing the texts that Erasmus wrote to deal with his various critics – and in which, whatever he says, he took a certain amount of pleasure.[2] The polemical works therefore occupy an important place in the cwe English edition.

This present volume of the *Controversies* contains, first of all, the *Apologia* that Erasmus addressed to his friend Jacques Lefèvre d'Etaples in 1517, and, second, three short treatises refuting the accusations made against his writings on Christian marriage. Before turning to them, however, the reader will find it helpful to consider briefly the different terms used by Erasmus in his own defence – a defence which can at times go on the offensive as well. The first term, *apologia*, is frequently seen in classical texts; the second, *dilutio*, is rare; the third, *responsio*, is commonplace. The noun *dilutio*, derived from the verb *diluere* (to dissolve reproaches) and connoting the act of justifying oneself, is not found in classical Latin, although St Jerome uses it.[3]

* * * * *

1 The absence there of the *Dilutio*, written as a refutation of Clichtove, should, however, be noted.
2 A 1522 edition (Basel: Froben) includes seven of Erasmus' *Apologiae* and consists of nearly four hundred pages.
3 *Contra Ioannem Hierosolymitanum ad Pammachium* 5 PL 23 375A

Erasmus wrote twelve treatises which bear the title *Apologia*, some of which likewise appeared from time to time under the title *Responsio*. The best known of these constitutes one of the prefaces to his edition of the New Testament.[4] But he also refuted under this rubric the attacks of Jacques Lefèvre d'Etaples (edited here), of Jacobus Latomus, of Diego López Zúñiga, and of others. One short, previously unedited *Apologia* has only recently been published.[5]

The term *apologia* has been made famous by such ancient works as Plato's *Apology* for Socrates and the *Apology* of the late second-century rhetorician and philosopher Apuleius, and by modern ones such as the *Apologia pro vita sua* of John Henry Newman (1864). In Greek, the term designates a pleading, and such was certainly the aim of Apuleius, who was obliged to clear himself of accusations of magic in order to marry a wealthy widow. Indeed, the most common title for Apuleius' text is *Pro se de magia liber*. Just as with Newman, Apuleius' goal was the justification of his personal behaviour, of a way of life. This personal connotation is never absent from Erasmus' mind in his controversial writings, but his main concern in them is always to defend his reputation for orthodoxy.

Another semantic component of the word *apologia* is to be sought in the writings of those Greek Fathers known as 'apologists,' who used this literary genre to defend and justify the Christian faith to their contemporaries, especially their philosopher colleagues who had remained pagan. Eusebius of Caesarea mentions Quadratus and Aristides of Athens as among the first who engaged in this exercise; but St Justin Martyr (c 100–c 165), who gave the name *Apologia* to two of his works, is the most famous of the apologists.

Nevertheless, Erasmus' model is first and foremost St Jerome, whose skill in disputing with St Augustine Erasmus so greatly admired. Did he not go so far as to compare his minor quarrel with Lefèvre d'Etaples to the disagreement over Sacred Scripture which brought the two Latin Fathers into conflict?[6] The title *Apologia* alludes above all to the work which Jerome wrote against the books of his friend Rufinus on the subject of

*****

4 *Des. Erasmus Roterodamus Ausgewählte Werke* ed H. and A. Holborn (Munich 1933; repr 1964), and *Les Préfaces au 'Novum Testamentum'* ed Y. Delègue and J.P. Gillet (Geneva 1990)

5 Erika Rummel 'An Unpublished Erasmian Apologia in the Royal Library of Copenhagen' *Nederlands Archief voor Kerkgeschiedenis / Dutch Review of Church History* 70 (1990) 210–29, a refutation of four Dominicans from Louvain who had attacked him under the pseudonym 'Taxander'; published in CWE 71 113–31, 165–71 as *Manifesta mendacia*

6 Ep 778:252–3

Origen.[7] Some manuscripts give the title as *Defensio*, but that of *Apologia* prevails. In Erasmus' *Apologia* against Lefèvre, one can discern the famous exclamations – the cries of a friend betrayed – drawn from the opening lines of Jerome's *Apologia* against Rufinus.

In addition to the patristic references, Erasmus clearly has the New Testament in mind, especially Paul's defence in the court of Agrippa (Acts 26:2–3). Erasmus indicates this in the first lines of the *Apologia* published with his edition of the New Testament, where his approach is characteristically pre-emptive: 'I want now, with my *Apology*, to anticipate objections ... But my situation is completely different from that of Paul, because, if I need an apology, it is to answer those who understand nothing of my work and its controversial subject matter and who criticize it for the one and only reason that they do not understand it.'[8] A little further on, Erasmus declares that he is perfectly ready to be corrected, but not before being heard by those from whom one expects sound judgment – in this case, the theologians.

Thus an *Apologia* (like a *Responsio*) is clearly a discourse through which one defends oneself against the accusations of others, whom one intends to refute. But its pedagogical function as a vehicle of learned dialogue, of an exchange of ideas, of a clash of opinions must not be underestimated. Certainly the tone may become sharp, vehement, and even biting, because the two dimensions of self-justification and explanation are constantly in play. The cries of dismay and lament over supposedly false accusations are likewise part and parcel of the literary style of the *Apologia*. As always happens with Erasmus, there is an element of give and take that allows even the modern reader to study with pleasure very detailed arguments which have become somewhat obscure and which can certainly be tedious. Nevertheless, in these relatively unknown works, as we shall see, Erasmus puts his finger on vital issues of theology and the Christian life.

ERASMUS V. LEFÈVRE: A DISPUTE BETWEEN THEOLOGY AND PHILOLOGY

In the minds of their contemporaries, the two humanists Erasmus and Lefèvre d'Etaples, who both died in 1536, were indissolubly linked, be it through admiration or reprobation, and were even, at times, confused with each other. Even the king of France, Francis I, fell into the latter trap. Wishing to

* * * * *

7 Already in 1498 Erasmus was reading this *Apologia* and asking Robert Gaguin for information about it (Ep 67:2–5).
8 Apologia 1.1 *Les Préfaces au 'Novum Testamentum'* ed Y. Delègue and J.P. Gillet (Geneva 1990) 128–9

promote good learning in France and urged to endow an institution similar to the Collegium Trilingue in Louvain, the king was persuaded to summon the prestigious Erasmus, who, in turn, requested a letter of safe conduct for entry into France. The king willingly granted the request. Then when he saw Guillaume Budé, the jurist-humanist whom he received as an intimate friend among the nobility at court, he told him: ' "I say, Budé ... we shall soon have Lefèvre in this France of ours." When Budé replied that Lefèvre was in France all the time, the king realized he had got the name wrong and said, "Erasmus, it was Erasmus I meant to say. For the passport is ready, so that he can get here safely." '[9] To such a sovereign, caught up in the affairs of state, the right to be mistaken should be granted; but the anecdote illustrates the generally accepted idea that the two men were engaged in the same cause of reviving the humanities. We need not postulate a total affinity to acknowledge this. Thus Geoffroy Tory in his *Champ fleury* (1529), a famous work on the proportions of elegant printer's fonts, praised those who 'eradicate the inveterate barbarisms of the unlearned, as Erasmus the Dutchman, Jacques Lefèvre d'Etaples in Picardy, and Budé are engaged in doing.'[10]

To their detractors, the two men – 'humanistae theologizantes,' as Noël Béda described them[11] – were in league with all those who encroached upon the fiercely guarded territory of the doctors of theology by commenting on the Bible and by considering and pronouncing on exegetical questions.[12] Lefèvre, an editor of and commentator on Aristotle, was certainly never a doctor of theology; and, although Erasmus received a doctorate in theology from the University of Turin on 4 September 1506, he did not take much pride

* * * * *

9 Ep 1342:607–13
10 'mortifiant les inueterees barbaries des indoctes, comme nous voions auiourd-dhuy faire trois nobles personnages, Erasmus le Hollandois, Iaques le feuure Destaple en Picardie, et Bude'; Geoffroy Tory *Champ fleury au quel est contenu Lart et science de la deue et vraye proportion des lettres Attiques* ... (Paris: Gilles de Gourmont and Geoffroy Tory 1529) book I fol VIII verso
11 'Lefèvre was once cleverly described by one of his enemies from the Faculty of Theology of the University of Paris as a *humanista theologizans*, a humanist who dabbled in theology. The phrase catches rather well the transitional character of his thought, the uneasy jostling of barbarism and classicism in his Latin style, the complex play of tradition and innovation in his work'; Eugene F. Rice, Jr 'Humanism in France' in *Renaissance Humanism: Foundations, Forms, and Legacy* II *Humanism beyond Italy* ed Albert Rabil, Jr (Philadelphia 1988) 109–22, especially 115.
12 There is an echo of Béda's influence in a letter by Zwingli dated 4 July 1521; *Huldreich Zwinglis Sämtliche Werke* VIII (Leipzig 1911) 462.

in his degree, which was not highly regarded – even if he was informally co-opted by the faculty of theology of the University of Louvain when he arrived there in 1517. Adversaries like Diego López Zúñiga were not ashamed to call him a 'factitius theologus.'

In any case, the controversies and refutations of the two humanists go together. Zúñiga and Béda linked them in the titles of their works,[13] and both were the target of vicious attacks like those of Nicolaas Baechem, known as Egmondanus, prior of the Carmelites in Louvain, who treats them as heretics and associates their names with that of Luther.[14] Frans Titelmans, another theologian at Louvain, denounced the 'curiositas' and the 'amor novitatis'[15] of the two humanists.

Luther himself regarded the two men as similar in their attitudes, but preferred Lefèvre to Erasmus: 'I fear that Erasmus does not give enough importance to Christ nor to God's grace, about which he knows considerably less than Lefèvre d'Etaples.'[16]

LEFÈVRE AND ERASMUS AS SEEN BY EACH OTHER

But what did the two great men think of each other? Before entering into the controversy that was to divide them for some time, let us first examine what they wrote about each other in their correspondence and other writings. On the part of Lefèvre d'Etaples, aside from the quarrel to be considered below, there was almost complete silence. With the exception of his own teachers and followers, Lefèvre seldom mentioned his contemporaries at all. Eager for compliments, he avoided controversial discussions.[17] Unless we are mistaken, Lefèvre never even alludes to Erasmus in any of his prefaces or in

* * * * *

13 *Annotationes Iacobi Lopidis Stunicae contra D. Erasmum . . . et in Iacobum Fabrum* (Alcalá: Arnão Guillén de Brocar 1519, 1520; repr Paris: Pierre Vidoue for Konrad Resch July 1522); and for Béda, *Annotationum . . . in Iacobum Fabrum Stapulensem libri duo et in Desiderium Erasmum Roterodamum liber unus* (Paris: Josse Bade 1526). In his letter to Erasmus, dated 29 March 1526, Béda insists, 'You have many errors in common with Lefèvre' (Allen Ep 1685:57–8).

14 Ep 1144:35–6

15 *Prologus in Collationes quinque* (Antwerp 1529) sig Aiv recto

16 'Sed timeo ne Christum et gratia Dei non satis promovet, in qua multo est quam Stapulensis ignorantior'; letter to Johann Lang 1 March 1517 WA *Briefwechsel* I 90. Luther was very conversant with Lefèvre's works and had carefully annotated his exemplar of the *Quincuplex psalterium* (Bedouelle *Quincuplex psalterium* 226–40), but was a harsh critic of Lefèvre's interpretation of Scripture; see the letter to Spalatinus of 19 October 1516 WA *Briefwechsel* I 70.

17 It is this fact of being singled out which so struck and vexed Erasmus when their quarrel erupted; see Ep 794:60–1.

the few extant letters to third parties. There is no catalogue of his letters; and even in the magnificent edition of Lefèvre's dedicatory epistles and prefaces published by Eugene F. Rice in 1974, Erasmus' name is strangely absent. Thus we know very little about the Parisian humanist's opinion of his younger colleague, who, as the years passed, became more famous than he.

We do have one short letter written by Lefèvre to Erasmus on 23 October 1514. Laudatory in tone, it gives the strong impression of being primarily a stylistic exercise: Erasmus is compared to the sun, which diffuses its light. Yet one sentiment undoubtedly rings true: Lefèvre declares that he knows Erasmus to be working not for himself alone but for the good of all.[18] This observation is too close to Lefèvre's understanding of his own vocation to be impersonal.[19]

Lefèvre chose instead to express his full esteem, affection, and admiration for Erasmus through intermediaries, as demonstrated in a letter of 5 August 1516 from Thomas Grey to Erasmus. Grey protests that, far from holding a grudge against Erasmus for his criticisms of his Pauline commentaries, Lefèvre would remain grateful to Erasmus for them. Grey adds that Lefèvre had noted them carefully but was prevented from writing by illness.[20] But Erasmus soon had occasion to observe that things were more complicated than they appeared. Just when the first signs of the disagreement were appearing and when Erasmus had mentioned in passing his bitterness, Pierre Barbier assured his friend, on 12 August 1517, that both Lefèvre and Josse Clichtove praised him to the skies and approved of all his works.[21]

Some years earlier, a more formal mention of Erasmus than that found in private letters had been made by Lefèvre's Alsatian student Beatus Rhenanus, who addressed his preface to the works of Gregory of Nyssa (actually Pseudo-Gregory) in March 1512 to Lefèvre. Here we see Rhenanus engaged in an exercise much appreciated at that time: drawing up a list of respected humanists. To be included in such a list and thus to acquire fame among one's peers was at times the only recompense for the thankless task of the scholar. There, in a text dedicated to him, Lefèvre would have read that Erasmus, this 'utriusque linguae callentissimus,' had been snatched from France by Upper Germany.[22] However trite and marginal, that is the only

* * * * *

18 Ep 315:9–12
19 Bedouelle *Lefèvre d'Etaples* 17–20
20 Ep 445:31–51
21 Ep 621:22–4
22 Eugene F. Rice, Jr *The Prefatory Epistles of Jacques Lefèvre d'Etaples and Related Texts* (New York 1974) 263 Ep 87

direct mention of Erasmus made by a member of Lefèvre's camp prior to the great debate.

For his part, Erasmus frequently mentioned the Parisian humanist in his correspondence with all those who counted – or wanted to count – in the world of learning. He did so with great warmth and persuasion up until 1516, sometimes even likening Lefèvre to Lorenzo Valla – a comparison which, coming from the editor of Valla's *Adnotationes in Latinam Novi Testamenti interpretationem* – was no small compliment: 'I have the highest opinion of Lefèvre as a scholar of uncommon erudition, I respect him as a man of high character, and I wish him well as a close friend.'[23] This also furnished Erasmus with an occasion to cite the famous phrase from the *Nicomachean Ethics*, which turns up in his writing from time to time, 'Amicus Plato sed magis amica veritas.'

Erasmus and Lefèvre met on at least two occasions, the first in Paris several times between April and June 1511,[24] and once again in Basel in 1526. Indeed, in 1511 they had 'the most intimate conversations' in the abbey of Saint-Germain-des-Prés, where Lefèvre was living at the invitation of its abbot, but nevertheless omitted to discuss the exegetical projects they had in common.[25] This was a great pity, because it was between these two occasions that the debate took place which would bring them into conflict and reveal their agreements, their differences, and their true feelings about each other.

THE DEBATE BETWEEN ERASMUS AND LEFÈVRE

A short review of the career of Lefèvre prior to this debate will help to situate and explain Erasmus' dismay at the sudden and – to Erasmus – unwarranted attack on him by Lefèvre. Born c 1460 at Etaples in Picardy, Lefèvre became a student and then a professor in the faculty of arts at the Collège du Cardinal Lemoine in Paris. One of the earliest figures of French humanism, he was eager to publish the *fontes* of philosophy, spirituality, and patristics that he considered necessary for a unified spiritual theology. On his return from Italy, where in 1492 he met the Aristotelian Barbaro, the Platonist Ficino, and Pico della Mirandola, Lefèvre began to annotate the whole corpus of Aristotle's work. Then, assisted by students and colleagues – among them Josse Clichtove – he moved on to publish hermetic and mystical authors such as the Pseudo-Dionysius, Richard of Saint Victor, Ramon Lull, Ruysbroek, Hildegard of Bingen, and Nicholas of Cusa. He gradually moved away from

* * * * *

23 Ep 326:104–6
24 See *Apologia* 8.
25 Ep 337:887–9. This is the famous letter to Maarten van Dorp of May 1515.

this set of interests to devote himself exclusively to the Bible, doing so in three stages in which he successively became a commentator, a translator, and a preacher. It was in the early stages of the last phase that his disagreements with Erasmus arose.

A brief chronology will help to clarify the debate. In 1509, Lefèvre published his *Quincuplex psalterium*, which was to be republished in 1513 and almost universally acclaimed in the intellectual world of that time.[26] In December 1512 (Paris: Henri Estienne) he brought out an important commentary on the Epistles of St Paul in which he naturally included the Epistle to the Hebrews. Erasmus, in his *Novum instrumentum* (1516), ventured to criticize Lefèvre's interpretation of Hebrews 2:7, which cites Psalm 8:6. Lefèvre, however, slipped his response to Erasmus into the second edition of his Pauline commentaries, dated 1515 but actually published in 1516. In July 1517, Erasmus noticed what he would call Lefèvre's 'disputatio.' Gripped by anger or indignation, he wrote his *Apologia ad Iacobum Fabrum Stapulensem* in two weeks.[27] This work appeared in Louvain between 23 and 28 August 1517. There would be six editions of it in Erasmus' lifetime.[28]

Let us now broach the crux of the controversy.[29] Looking first at Lefèvre, we see that in his *Quincuplex psalterium* he insists very strongly that the traditional reading 'Minuisti eum paulo minus ab angelis' ('Thou hast made him a little lower than the angels'), which was found in both the Psalter (8:6) and the Epistle to the Hebrews (2:7), should be corrected to read 'Minuisti eum paulo minus a Deo' ('Thou hast made him a little lower than God'). Lefèvre held the traditional reading to be theologically incorrect on the ground that the abase-

* * * * *

26 Bedouelle *Quincuplex psalterium* 207–15
27 In December 1517, Erasmus mentioned 'fourteen days' to Wolfgang Capito (Ep 731:4), but a month later he changed the number to twelve when addressing Johannes de Molendino (Ep 755:17).
28 Louvain: Dirk Martens 1517; Strasbourg: Matthias Schürer 1517 or 1518; Basel: Johann Froben 1518; Louvain: Dirk Martens 1518; Basel: Johann Froben November 1521; and Basel: Johann Froben February 1522 (*Apologiae omnes*). Andrea W. Steenbeek has provided a critical edition of it, 'with an Introduction, Critical Apparatus and Explanatory Notes,' ASD IX-3. In Froben's edition of the *Opera omnia* from Basel, 1540, the *Apologia ad Stapulensem* is found in volume IX 19–57 with Erasmus' annotation on Heb 2:7 and Lefèvre's *Disputatio* (59–68).
29 The controversy has been studied many times, eg by Margaret Mann (Phillips) *Erasme et les débuts de la Réforme française, 1517–1536* (Paris 1934) 16–46, and, more recently, by Helmut Feld 'Der humanisten Streit um Hebräer 2:7 (Psalm 8:6)' *Archiv für Reformationsgeschichte* 61 (1970) 5–33, and John B. Payne 'Erasmus and Lefèvre d'Etaples as Interpreters of Paul' *Archiv für Reformationsgeschichte* 65 (1974) 54–83.

ment of the Son at the Incarnation occurred solely with respect to the Father (John 14:28). To the objection that the phrase referred only to the humanity of Christ, Lefèvre replied that when Scripture speaks of the 'filius hominis' (the 'Son of Man'), as in Psalm 8:4, it refers to the single person of Christ, not to his two natures. He further asserts that, although the Hebrew word used here for God (*Eloim*) is plural, its Latin equivalent is best rendered in the singular – thus maintaining an idea important to the Christian Cabbala that the plural 'Eloim' confirms the three-person Trinity within the affirmation of a single divinity.[30]

After the first edition of his Pauline commentaries (1512) and the second of the *Quincuplex psalterium* (1513), Lefèvre maintained his position in the *Corollarium* that he added to his notes on the Epistle to the Hebrews, in spite of the observations which Erasmus had ventured to make. Erasmus then countered with Psalm 22 (21 Vulg):7: 'Ego autem sum vermis et non homo' ('But I am a worm, and no man'). This time Lefèvre, deeming the verse unsuitable for attribution to Christ, revealed his hermeneutical principle that, for the believer, the literal sense becomes spiritual. As demonstrated by the hymn in the Epistle to the Philippians (2:6–11), of which he made a verse-by-verse comparison with Psalm 8,[31] the humbling of Christ, for the Christian, goes hand in hand with his exaltation.

Erasmus had suggested that the Hebrew adverb *Meat* (Latin *paulo minus*) used by the author of Psalm 8 could have a temporal sense which would resolve all the difficulties: it was 'for a little while' that Christ was made lower than the angels. Lefèvre refuted this philological position with the argument that neither the Hebrew nor the Greek Septuagint carries this sense of duration, even if Athanasius and Chrysostom, deceived by the standard translation of the psalm, were compelled to understand it in a temporal sense. Lefèvre concludes his *Corollarium* with a defence of the Pauline authenticity of the Epistle to the Hebrews.

Thus Lefèvre's exegesis begins fundamentally with his intuition as a believer, his sense of the Christological dimension of Scripture. It is from this position that one must begin, if one is to present an interpretation worthy of Christ and of that which has been revealed to us about him. Philology and the harmony of the Scriptures have only to be brought together to corroborate, or rather manifest, the theological intuition. Every other interpretation is, according to Lefèvre, 'heretical and most unworthy of Christ and God ... contrary to the spirit and adhering to the letter which destroys.'[32]

* * * * *

30 *Quincuplex psalterium* (1513) fol 10v
31 Ibidem fol 10. Cf Bedouelle *Quincuplex psalterium* 124–6.
32 *Commentarii in S. Pauli epistolas* (1515) fol 226v

It is obviously this sentence which most unsettled Erasmus. He could not bear being treated as a heretic, for such is the implication of the word *impius*, so inopportunely applied by Lefèvre.[33] The *Apologia ad Iacobum Fabrum Stapulensem* therefore gives us Erasmus' position as he refutes Lefèvre's thesis step by step, whereas successive editions of his *Annotations on the New Testament* would clarify his arguments in a more irenic manner.[34]

The tone of the *Apologia* is that of a man appalled. This helps to explain why this very repetitive work is not exempt from cruelty. Erasmus finds a certain pleasure in noting the weaknesses in Lefèvre's knowledge of Greek, especially throughout his last section. The same accusation would be repeated by Erasmus' partisans in Louvain, who would insinuate that in Greek, as in Hebrew, Lefèvre could not have done without his young colleague François Vatable.[35]

Erasmus' method in the *Apologia* is completely different from that of Lefèvre. More 'critical' and developed, it carefully distinguishes theology and philology, traditional arguments, patristic references, and grammatical considerations – not in the design of the work, which more or less follows the disordered thesis of his adversary (69), but none the less in the intention and spirit of the polemicist. The style is brilliant and, as usual, filled with adages and with quotations from ancient authors, all of which provide some relief in a text which might otherwise be tedious.

In fact, the gist of his argument is that there is no basis for a quarrel. Erasmus had never wished to censure Lefèvre on the point in question, but simply to say that all the Fathers of the church except St Jerome followed the 'ab angelis' reading, and even St Jerome did not exclude it. Lefèvre's mistake was to be so uncompromising and to accuse him so 'atrociously'[36]

* * * * *

33 For an analysis of *pietas* and thus of *impietas* in the sixteenth century, see Massaut *Critique et tradition* 63–6, and John W. O'Malley's Introduction to CWE 66 (Toronto 1988) xv–xxi.

34 Reeve III 706–13 (on Hebrews 2). Erasmus composed the definitive text for this annotation in 1519, by going back to the *Summa*, already published with the *Apologia*, and ending up with a veritable case of fifty-seven points. This text was included in all subsequent editions up to 1535.

35 Letter of Wilhelm Nesen to Bruno Amerbach 9 August 1518 *Die Amerbach-korrespondenz* ed A. Hartmann (Basel 1943) II 121. François Vatable, a Picard like Lefèvre, was a skilled Hebraicist who studied and then taught in Lefèvre's circle in the Collège du Cardinal Lemoine. In 1530 he became the first royal professor in Hebrew named by Francis I.

36 Reeve III 708

in a matter that is equally difficult whichever side one takes. Which is easier, to say that Christ was made less than God or that he was made less than the angels, since there is no proportion between human and divine nature? The version proposed or, rather, imposed by Lefèvre on the ground that it avoids heresy (*citra haeresim*) lends itself to as many theological difficulties as the other reading upheld by tradition.

After a number of preliminary remarks in which he discusses his opponent's disagreement with St Thomas Aquinas and the Fathers of the church, Erasmus enters into an examination of Lefèvre's Christological doctrine. If one can in fact apply this psalm verse to Christ, one is equally free, he asserts, to apply it to created man. Already, the differences in the hermeneutical approaches of the two men are seen to be quite marked; but Erasmus lays claim none the less to have a view of the person (*hypostasis*) of Christ that is as orthodox as Lefèvre's, and to be as competent as Lefèvre to discourse upon an 'exchange of idioms' (*communicatio idiomatum*) which allows for the application of divine as well as human attributes to Christ, the incarnate Word of God. Aware nevertheless that there are two ways of speaking about Christ, Erasmus tells his opponent: 'You prefer to extol the sublimity of Christ; someone else may prefer to contemplate the lowliness which he assumed; and though it would be difficult to say whose zeal is more pious, it is the latter perhaps from which more profit is to be gained for the present' (35).

This is the crux of the debate. Erasmus stresses the humanity of Christ to such an extent that, for him, the mystery of Christ's incarnation and passion, which so humbled him, is the very source of our redemption. His commentary on the hymn in Philippians (2:6–11), which Lefèvre likewise cherished, is imbued with a fine theological inspiration (60–1). Lefèvre, however, leans much more towards the Platonic or Dionysian tradition, which emphasizes the divine nature of Christ. This twofold Christological approach is an integral part of Christian theology.

Compared to this issue – which is, in a way, Erasmus' defence of the reality of the Incarnation (27–8), in which what is 'most pious' is not necessarily 'most sublime' – the other points of contention are insignificant. Erasmus enters into philological discussions of certain terms, especially the meaning of the Hebrew term *Meat*, which he interprets to mean 'for a little while.' In addition, he questions the canonicity of the Epistle to the Hebrews and its Pauline authenticity. Finally, overlooking not even a single verse, Erasmus demonstrates to Lefèvre his lack of critical judgment, his ingenuous positions, and his errors in translation, all the while inviting him not to make a laughing-stock of himself. Even if this process is interspersed with protestations of friendship, and even if the theological points were weighty, it was a harshly administered lesson.

Erasmus did not doubt his victory. As soon as the *Apologia* was published, he claimed to be considered everywhere the uncontested winner. The difference in the temperaments of the two humanists, however, will become clear.

TWO KINDS OF REACTION

From July 1517 to the end of 1518, Erasmus' correspondence was virtually taken up with his dispute with Lefèvre, of whom he had no direct news other than the contradictory rumours that reached him. Even if Erasmus' first reaction was to enter not into a quarrel but rather into a debate, even if he remained more or less calm during the writing and distribution of his *Apologia*, the tension mounted with respect to his correspondents, who ventured to comment on the tone he had adopted. He had been persuaded by the numerous testimonies received from his correspondents – mostly laudatory, but some ambiguous – that the intellectual world was entirely bound up with this affair.

Generally speaking, the republic of letters watched with great consternation as its two most prestigious members proceeded to tear each other apart.[37] An exchange of lengthy missives between Erasmus and Guillaume Budé turned rather sour, and the tone of both men became bitter.[38] Few risked dealing with the heart of the issue besides Symphorien Champier, a member of Lefèvre's circle, who reckoned that both interpretations could be sustained.[39]

It is clear that the exegetical and theological debate is not without interest, even if the occasion for it is trivial. The psychological attitude of the two parties in the debate also comes to light. Erasmus churns out repetitive, almost obsessive explanations, vacillating between the distress of a bad conscience and a sense of the rightness of his cause. Lefèvre remains silent.

Erasmus did not abandon his affirmation of esteem and friendship for Lefèvre. It was indeed the thought that he was betrayed by a friend that wounded him the most. He even went so far as to reproach Cuthbert Tunstall for having been too biased in his favour and too disparaging of Lefèvre![40] The term which most often recurs is *invitus*: reluctantly, in spite of

* * * * *

37 For an analysis of the reactions, see Rummel *Catholic Critics* I 52–8.
38 Epp 744, 778, 810, 906. See Marie-Madeleine de La Garanderie *La correspondance d'Erasme et de Guillaume Budé* (Paris 1967).
39 Ep 680A 13–15 September 1517
40 Ep 675:13–15

himself, he has been obliged to defend himself. The whole business was so distressing that it had to be attributed to 'fate' or some 'evil genius,' either his own or Lefèvre's, or to some 'demon.' His correspondents sometimes echoed this theme,[41] not without bombast, in comparing this dispute to the Homeric quarrels or to the controversies between Jerome and Rufinus and even Jerome and Augustine. Erasmus himself, as we have seen, goes so far as to recall the dissent between Paul and Barnabas recounted in the Acts of the Apostles (15:39).[42]

On the whole, Erasmus believed that slandering theologians had pushed Lefèvre to criticize him;[43] but he was at times so exasperated that he did not hesitate to accuse Lefèvre of imbuing his remarks with hate.[44] He calls him vain and reproaches him for a kind of Parisian pride.[45] Still, we must recognize that he then sought to enter into dialogue with his opponent, whom he still considered his friend. Erasmus wrote three letters to Lefèvre, diminishing each time the bitterness of his tone.

The first letter, written on 11 September 1517, accompanied the delivery of the *Apologia*.[46] Undoubtedly trying to soften the blow, he entrusted the book and the letter to a theologian at the Sorbonne for personal delivery to Lefèvre.[47] As in other places, Erasmus repeats here all the remarks, or, rather, 'the monstrous accusations,' of Lefèvre that had most wounded him: ' "words most unworthy of Christ and of God," "words self-destructive from every point of view, and from every aspect exhibiting their own falsity," "words which are hostile to the understanding of prophecy," "words which support the case of those pestilent Jews and treat Christ with contumely as they do," "words worthy of Bedlam," "words which, if obstinately adhered to, would make me a heretic," and plenty more of the same kind.'[48] Yet Erasmus, having now defended himself, proposes to put an end to the polemic, which could please only those adhering to the old ignorance.[49] A pure and truly Christian sincerity has to be maintained.

* * * * *

41 See eg Budé's letter of 12 April 1518, Ep 810.
42 Ep 855:63–5
43 See Ep 800:16–21.
44 See Ep 627:18.
45 Ep 663:71–2
46 Ep 659
47 See Epp 724:2, 778:322–3.
48 Ep 659:6–12. 'Bedlam' is literally 'Anticyra,' where the cultivators of the hellebore whom the *Apologia* mentions on numerous occasions had the reputation of being touched with madness.
49 See Ep 659:26–7.

Erasmus counted the passing months while awaiting the response, which never came. On 30 November 1517, he decided to write again.[50] This time it was only a short note which, although still on the defensive, solicits a response while requesting that its tone be 'what befits' a man like Lefèvre, a man who was 'truly dear' to him.[51]

But still no response came from Paris. Rumours abounded that Lefèvre, after the publication of his treatise on Mary Magdalene and the Triduum of Christ, was much occupied in drawing up a response, which he would also have printed.[52] As the time continued to pass, on 18 January 1518 with some irritation Erasmus requested Henricus Glareanus, who had studied for a while with Lefèvre, to caution his master and convey to him, along with Erasmus' friendly greetings, his desire to receive at least a response.[53]

When yet another three months had passed, it was Erasmus who took the initiative to write to the still silent Lefèvre. This time, on 17 April 1518, Erasmus requested a private letter of reconciliation – 'I do not suggest that you recant [palinodia] ... Do just publish some letter which will make it clear that you entered the lists from zeal to pursue the truth, and that in other respects we are personally in agreement [concordia]'[54] – adding that silence could only inflame the discord.[55]

Now silence was precisely the reaction which Lefèvre chose to maintain in the matter, as he would do later in connection with more weighty issues.[56] Guillaume Budé attested that Lefèvre had never spoken to him of his quarrel with Erasmus, even when it was clearly known to everyone.[57] Certainly, Erasmus received some indirect echoes of Lefèvre's reactions through his friends and the theologian who performed the good offices of a messenger for him. Lefèvre did not withdraw his friendship for Erasmus, but he had been wounded by the vehement tone of the Apologia. Upon receiving it, however, he was reported to have remarked that Erasmus was 'inconstant' and 'not serious' (levitas).[58]

* * * * *

50 Ep 724
51 Ep 724:7
52 See Ep 775:20–1.
53 Ep 766
54 Allen Ep 814:21, 24 / cwe Ep 814:26–8
55 Allen Ep 814:25 / cwe Ep 814:30–1, and Allen Ep 826:13–14 / cwe Ep 826:18–19
     to Henry Bullock. In this last letter, of 23 April 1518, one senses that Erasmus
     has reached his saturation point.
56 See Bedouelle Lefèvre d'Etaples 120ff.
57 Ep 896:61–2
58 Allen Ep 778:297 / cwe Ep 778:229, and Allen Ep 796:25–6 / cwe Ep 796:25–6

Of a rather stubborn temperament himself and no doubt also taciturn, Lefèvre used his silence, in any case, both to defend himself and to manifest his deep desire to avoid great controversies. On the rare occasions when he did enter the fray, he was content simply to justify himself. He did not recant, but neither did he endlessly pursue the quarrel in a public forum. This was especially the case in his dispute with John Fisher and several others on the subject of Mary Magdalene.[59] The French humanist maintained that three separate followers of Jesus could be distinguished in the gospel narratives, contradicting the liturgical tradition that conflated them into the single disciple Mary Magdalene. Erasmus made no very explicit pronouncement on the subject; but, paradoxically, he believed that Lefèvre took the reproaches against him too much to heart, and considered that Fisher, for his part, took too much trouble to make this affair a question of faith.[60]

Yet to all things there is an end. In August 1518, a year after the original wound, Erasmus told Willibald Pirckheimer that he hoped it would heal over.[61] It did, and on both sides, probably because the issues no longer seemed so divisive in the face of the turbulence which Luther was unleashing in Germany. Even if the main points had been enough to elicit a debate, they did not touch upon fundamental questions. Contact was re-established between Erasmus and Lefèvre.

A REDISCOVERED PEACE
A change in tone is perceptible throughout Erasmus' correspondence in 1520. He sharply reprimands Juan Luis Vives, who had taken the liberty of criticizing Lefèvre indirectly,[62] remarking that in his current mood 'my feelings are such that I should listen impatiently to anyone who spoke of him otherwise than one would of a most upright and most learned man.'[63]

What had happened? Wearied by this quarrel, Erasmus wanted to persuade himself that he could interpret Lefèvre's silence as an admission of his guilt, and wrote in this vein to Bishop Jacopo Sadoleto on 25 February

* * * * *

59 Anselm Hufstader 'Lefèvre d'Etaples and the Magdalen' *Studies in the Renaissance* 16 (1969) 31–60; Massaut *Critique et tradition* 67–70; and Bedouelle *Lefèvre d'Etaples* 191–6
60 Ep 936 to Fisher 2 April 1519, in which he considers the English theologian the winner; and Ep 1068 to Fisher 21 February 1520. These judgments occur after the controversy between Lefèvre and himself.
61 Ep 856:73–4
62 Ep 1108:175–80 4 June 1520
63 Ep 1111:99–101

1525.[64] Admittedly, this statement came more than six years after the dispute between the two humanists. But much had come to pass in the meantime to demonstrate to Erasmus how harmful such indulgence in this type of quarrel could be to their common cause. For example, the conservative theologians, distressed by the rapid diffusion of Luther's ideas, were multiplying their attacks and associating the names of Erasmus and Lefèvre in their suspicion and condemnation. Several times, notably in a letter written on 13 March 1521 to Alexander Schweiss, secretary of the count of Nassau, Erasmus cited a sermon by a Carmelite who, in the presence of Francis I, had announced that 'the coming of Antichrist is at hand, and that he already has four precursors: some Minorite or other in Italy, Jacques Lefèvre d'Etaples in France, Reuchlin in Germany, and Erasmus in Brabant.'[65]

But the most distressing part for Erasmus was the way these adversaries used his disagreement with Lefèvre as an example of the schisms which always divide heretics.[66] In the letter to Schweiss just mentioned, Erasmus cites in this context his Louvain opponent, the Carmelite prior and theologian Nicolaas Baechem.[67] Jean Lange, a disciple of Lefèvre who lived near him in Meaux after having previously been his pupil at the Collège du Cardinal Lemoine in Paris, spoke of his sorrow when he saw this 'slight' disagreement between Erasmus and 'that excellent man Lefèvre' used by the factious 'tribe' of theologians 'as a handle for false accusations.'[68]

Certainly when faced with the disdain and criticism of Noël Béda, Erasmus did not deny his solidarity with Lefèvre.[69] Nevertheless, he took care to distinguish a difference in style that is important for any comparison between the two men. In his long letter of 15 June 1525 to Béda, Erasmus declared: 'You understand, I hope, that there is an immense difference between Lefèvre and myself: he boldly asserts his position, I merely put the case and

* * * * *

64 Ep 1555:89–91
65 Ep 1192:29–33. The Franciscan may have been Bernardino Ochino. Erasmus alludes to the same event in a letter to Louis Guillard, bishop of Tournai, on 17 June 1521 (Ep 1212:29–33).
66 Pierre Cousturier (Petrus Sutor), a Carthusian theologian, a graduate of the Sorbonne, alludes to it; *De tralatione Bibliae* ... (Paris: Josse Bade for Jean Petit 1525) fol 86v.
67 Ep 1192:56–8. Baechem's remark is echoed several times in one form or another, eg to Thomas More Ep 1162:143–6 and to Vincentius Theoderici Ep 1196:618–20. For further information on Baechem, see Rummel *Catholic Critics* I 52–8 and 135–43.
68 Ep 1407:23–8. For Lange, see Michel Veissière *L'évêque Guillaume Briçonnet* (Provins 1986) 234.
69 Allen Ep 1685:57–8

leave the decision to others.'[70] This protest in his own defence[71] reflects the two temperaments rather well.

In any case, it is clear that the combined attacks against the two estranged humanists brought Erasmus round to a friendlier disposition towards his opponent. We even have some evidence, though inconclusive and generally unnoticed by historians, for a possible intervention by Erasmus in favour of Lefèvre with the authorities in Rome.

This occurred in 1525, a year that proved especially difficult for the old man working with Bishop Guillaume Briçonnet in Meaux. After Emperor Charles v defeated French forces at Pavia in February and took King Francis i captive, the Parlement of Paris and the theologians at the faculty of theology enjoyed a freer hand to move against humanists and reformers. In August, they condemned Lefèvre's French translation of the New Testament and the collection of homilies *Epistres et evangiles pour les cinquante deux sepmaines*. Both books were strategic parts of the reform Briçonnet and Lefèvre were attempting at Meaux. With some of his collaborators, Lefèvre fled to Strasbourg under a false name – a ruse which Erasmus found amusing.[72] But a letter from Gian Matteo Giberti, bishop of Verona and *datarius* and counsellor of Pope Clement vii, furnishes evidence of Erasmus' intercession on behalf of Lefèvre. Writing to Erasmus on 27 November 1525, Giberti makes his position clear with regard to the two humanists' difficulties. He expresses pleasure with a plan, apparently disclosed to him by Erasmus, to defeat the heretics: 'I shall be with you and your friends as I have always been; I shall do what I can to let Jacques Lefèvre know, if I am approached by his agents, that your support was no less significant than his own merits.'[73] Had Lefèvre's enemies plotted to pursue him in a Roman court? We know nothing more definite about this; but the testimony of Bishop Giberti places Erasmus in a generous light.

Reconciliation between the two men was now possible. It was to take place at Basel in mid-May 1526,[74] after Lefèvre quit his exile in Strasbourg and set out again for France, where he had been restored to favour after the

* * * * *

70 Ep 1581:864–7. For the context, see James K. Farge *Orthodoxy and Reform in Early Reformation France* (Leiden 1985) 256ff.

71 A little later, on 23 June 1526, Erasmus complained to the faculty of theology in Paris that Cousturier treated it less tactfully than Lefèvre (Allen Ep 1723:38–9).

72 Allen Ep 1674:70–2. For more about these episodes, see Bedouelle *Lefèvre d'Etaples* 103–10, and Veissière *L'évêque Guillaume Briçonnet* 317–68 (see n68 above).

73 Ep 1650A:16–18

74 Allen Ep 1713:19–21. Lefèvre, having been misinformed, announced Budé's death to Erasmus.

liberation of King Francis I. The following year, on 24 March 1527, Erasmus wrote a short, very serene and conciliatory letter to Lefèvre concerning a translation of St John Chrysostom's commentaries on the Acts of the Apostles. Erasmus says that he had intended to undertake this work himself, but that, having heard Lefèvre and Gérard Roussel were to take it on at the behest of the king, he now left the field open to them. To Lefèvre, Erasmus wished the happy tranquillity which his grand old age merited.[75]

From that time on, Erasmus' correspondence mentioned only hearsay accounts of Lefèvre. In 1528, he was astonished not to have had any news.[76] That was at a time when in his *Ciceronianus* Erasmus was passing judgment on the Latin style of his contemporaries. In quest of true 'Ciceronians' of the past and present, Bulephorus, one of Erasmus' interlocutors, declares, 'Jacques Lefèvre is thought very distinguished.' His fellow, Nosophonus, replies, 'A pious and learned man, but he prefered to express himself as a theologian rather than a Tullian.'[77] There was no animosity in that.

Conversely, in the following years Erasmus repeated some disquieting gossip, which he did not however take very seriously: had he not heard a rumour that Lefèvre had been burned?[78] But he thought that there must have been some confusion with Berquin. Indeed, several months before this Lefèvre had left Blois, where he had served as the private tutor of the royal children, and found his final refuge at Margaret of Navarre's court in Nérac.

On 9 July 1533, Pierre Barbier, the dean of Tournai, wrote to Erasmus about a conversation he had had with Girolamo Aleandro: 'He spoke quite a bit about Lefèvre, whose reputation has been tarnished for several years. May it please God that it be groundless! He is a man whom I have always venerated as a father.'[79] Indeed, Lefèvre's final years, when he had retreated into silence, are shrouded in mystery. He died sometime during the first few months of 1536. Erasmus was not to survive him by much, since he in his turn passed away on 12 July of the same year.

Silence concerning the person and work of Lefèvre was to prevail, however, even after the reformers in Geneva at the end of the century named him as a forerunner of their Reformation. In contrast, the renown of Erasmus suffered hardly at all, even when the Roman Index condemned part of his work.

* * * * *

75 Allen Ep 1795:18
76 Allen Ep 2052:15–16
77 *Ciceronianus* CWE 28 421
78 Allen Epp 2362:20 11 August 1530 and 2379:466 5 September 1530
79 Allen Ep 2842:30–1. On the relationship between Lefèvre and Aleandro, see Bedouelle *Lefèvre d'Etaples* 126–7.

II
ANALYSIS AND OUTLINE OF THE APOLOGIA

Composed rapidly and in the grip of anger, the *Apologia* against Lefèvre follows no harmonious plan, despite disclaimers of Erasmus. He was in fact well aware of this, but imputes the responsibility to his opponent: 'Since your whole treatise lacked order, because you were tearing away at individual parts of my treatise as they came, and in my reply I was forced to follow your sequence, the reader may find my own presentation rather unfocused and for this reason less than clear' (69).

The reader may nevertheless find it helpful to refer to the following sequence of the *Apologia*'s principal arguments, each followed by the page reference in the present volume.

INTRODUCTION: WHY ERASMUS FELT OBLIGED TO WRITE THIS APOLOGIA

- Erasmus discovered almost by chance the second edition of Lefèvre's *Commentaries on the Epistles of St Paul* and the passage which concerned him (4).
- He complains about the hostile behaviour manifested by Lefèvre, and repeats the view of certain people that 'you seem here to be a different person' (5).
- Men of reputation like Lefèvre and Erasmus ought to avoid contradicting each other publicly (6).
- Meanwhile, there is still room for discussion 'in those matters which do not properly bear upon articles of faith' (7).
- Erasmus refutes Lefèvre only in order to redress an error and in the interest of truth (8–9).
- Erasmus has always spoken honourably of Lefèvre and wonders why Lefèvre did not respond to the sensitive points in his letters, where he warned 'that in making my emendations I would in certain places take a different view from yours' (9).
- Erasmus raises the question of the backdated edition of Lefèvre's Pauline commentaries, but prefers to see it 'as a result of an error on the part of the printers' (10–11).
- Why has Lefèvre never thanked Erasmus for his remarks, even when he has clearly taken account of them? (12).
- Erasmus was forced to intervene by Lefèvre's accusation of sacrilege (13).
- Perhaps Lefèvre's exaggerated reaction is due to the influence of his supporters, who cannot tolerate criticism of their master (13).

PART 1: DISCUSSION OF THE TRADITIONAL INTERPRETATION
- Erasmus' task is not easy because Lefèvre's treatise 'spreads out in all directions' (14).
- Nevertheless, it is possible to synthesize the debate as Lefèvre has done: 'Our friend Erasmus does not accept my opinion ... nor does he approve of St Jerome's interpretation of the sixth verse of the Eighth Psalm, namely: "You will make him a little less than God"' (15).
- But is that not an artificially fabricated disagreement? (15).
- There has from the start been a misunderstanding as to the nature of the annotations made by Erasmus: 'I simply record two opinions, neither of which constitutes a heresy' (16).
- Lefèvre claims to defend Jerome's interpretation, but does not cite his commentaries (16).
- In fact, Erasmus supports neither of the two opinions; on the contrary, he might even be closer to that of Lefèvre, for which he offers a valid solution (17).
- Erasmus discusses the reproach of contradicting Aquinas: in itself one can do it, but not without having studied what he said (18–19).
- Generally speaking, the Fathers of the church favour the reading 'less than the angels,' 'with the single exception of Jerome, though even he is ambiguous' (19–20).
- Giustiniani's eightfold Psalter, that 'heaven-inspired ... work you refer to' (20), is no great help in this matter (20–1).
- Erasmus reaffirms that as far as he is concerned, theologically speaking, 'the same difficulty remains whether you say 'than God' or 'than the angels' (22). In fact, Erasmus had said 'seems to remain' (25).
- Erasmus examines St Paul's authorship of the Epistle to the Hebrews, which he believes was not originally written in Hebrew, and his use of the Septuagint (24).
- Erasmus summarizes his personal position: 'I favoured ... the opinion which you share with St Jerome; but at the time I decided not to accept one reading if it meant that I would be repudiating the other as impious and heretical' (24–5).
- What does the exegetical preference signify in relation to Christology, with which Erasmus is as familiar as anyone else? (26).

PART 2: THEOLOGICAL DISCUSSION
- Erasmus interprets Psalm 8:6 to refer to Christ's humanity, or to 'Christ incarnate,' a mode of expression which he justifies (27–8).
- Erasmus uses the well-known and legitimate procedure of the 'exchange of idioms' only when speaking of the person of Christ (28–9).

- Erasmus discusses the vocabulary used for Christ. In Catholic tradition, it is perfectly acceptable to speak of Christ as a 'man,' as Augustine does (29).
- It is just as legitimate to speak of the 'mingling' of the two natures of Christ as to speak of their 'union' (30–1).
- What does it mean to say that 'the Son of Man was diminished'? (31).
- Erasmus holds firm to what he wrote: 'Christ, both on account of the human form which he assumed and on account of the disadvantages of the human condition, was made lower not only than the angels but even than the lowliest of men' (32–3).
- Christ 'took upon himself almost all the misfortunes of this life' (34).
- Erasmus begins to discuss the two Christological perspectives, wherein his own orientation distinguishes him from his opponent. For Erasmus, the weakness of Christ 'has more relevance for us.' 'You prefer to extol the sublimity of Christ,' he tells Lefèvre (35–6).
- In this context, the hymn in Philippians 2 assumes profound significance: the *kenosis* of Christ seems to be the condition of his exaltation: 'by employing the word "exalted," Paul admits that Christ humbled himself to the greatest degree possible' (36–7).
- This is the interpretation of Ambrose and Hilary (38–40).
- By emphasizing the abasement of Christ, Erasmus compares him to martyrs (40), who like him obtain the crown (41).
- There is no contradiction between the cross and glory: 'In the one we see what we must imitate, in the other what we may hope for' (41).

PART 3: LOGICAL AND PHILOLOGICAL DISCUSSION
- All the foregoing remarks, says Erasmus, were 'a preparation for my main point, namely, that the expression βραχύ τι is to be given a temporal reference' (42).
- How can Christ be called 'a worm and no man' (Ps 22 [21 Vulg]:7)? (42–4).
- One must never weaken the cry of Christ abandoned upon the cross (45).
- One must not fall into that heresy which says, 'Christ suffered not in reality but in his imagination' (45).
- There is 'no reason why anyone who worships his eminence should be offended by a reminder of his lowliness' (48).
- Erasmus discusses the problem of the relation between the human and divine natures of Christ. What does this term relation signify? (49).
- There is neither contradiction nor heresy in saying that 'as the Word Christ is the creator . . . while as a man he is a created thing' (51).
- Lefèvre's Christological language is not exempt from weaknesses (52–3).

- In this case, how does Lefèvre dare to accuse Erasmus of using a language 'most unworthy of Christ and God, contrary to the spirit' (54), and of being associated 'with the Jews who have an ill opinion of Christ'? (55).
- This leads us necessarily to Erasmus' solution that '*for a time* Christ was made lower than most.' That is the meaning of βραχύ τι (57).
- This solution is 'consistent with either of the two readings, "than God" or "than the angels"' (58).
- Digression on Philippians 2:7 (60–1).
- Examples from classical philology and Greek grammar (61–5).
- Discussion of the Hebrew term *Meat* (65).
- Discussion of the Latin expression *paulo minus* or *paululum* (66).
- In a digression, Erasmus refutes the presumed translation of the Epistle to the Hebrews by St Luke (67).
- Discussion of the Hebrew *Eloim* (68).

EPILOGUE: SUMMARY AND REMAINDER OF THE DISCUSSION
- 'By way of an epilogue, it may not be out of place to draw the main threads of the argument together into a summary' (69):

1/ 'There is no argument between us.' There are two readings; 'each is in its own way acceptable' (69).

2/ 'The adverbial expression *paulo minus*, or *paululum*, causes a problem, though it is one which is more acute if we choose the reading which you regard as the only possible one' (70).

3/ The true matter at issue here is Christological (71–2).

4/ The proper use of ὑποστάσεως (73).

- The discussion resumes with a development of the Christological interpretation of the prophetic texts, in particular the Psalms (74–5).
- 'Indeed, it is not at all a case of doubting whether this psalm applies to Christ, but whether it applies to him exclusively,' which seems to be Lefèvre's narrow interpretation (76).
- Erasmus embarks upon a discussion of the Pauline attribution of the Epistle to the Hebrews (79), in which he intends to respond to the triple charge that Lefèvre has laid against him.

1/ According to Lefèvre, this problem was not relevant to the matter under discussion. Erasmus' intention, in fact, was 'to offer a reminder that there had long been some dispute as to the author of this letter' (80).

2/ Lefèvre reproaches Erasmus for having declared that the Epistle to the Hebrews was accepted by the church at a late date (81). Erasmus replies, 'The only point I make is that there is uncertainty as to the author' (81), and justifies his position (82–6).

3/ 'Your final charge, that of ignorance, I hardly took seriously' (86); Lefèvre is not justified in mocking a friend (88).

In conclusion, Erasmus once again laments the damage that this kind of controversy between humanists does to the cause of *good learning*: 'We shall turn out to be the talk of the world' (90).

- Erasmus does not at all like this exercise in which Lefèvre has compelled him to engage (91), but he was forced to defend himself (92).
- In the controversies of the early church, certain hasty assertions made by some of the Fathers of the church like Augustine or Chrysostom demonstrate that one can be mistaken, yet remain sincere and devout (93–7).
- One should follow the example of Augustine *On the Trinity* 1.3, who agreed to be corrected (97).
- Lefèvre should not have been annoyed: 'I corrected your mistakes with the hope of receiving your thanks, as anyone who corrected mine would receive thanks from me' (98).
- Erasmus then recalls in detail all the minor corrections which he proposed to Lefèvre for his Pauline commentaries (98–105).
- As for the reproach made by Lefèvre that Erasmus was 'a would-be theologian' (106), Erasmus is not worried about it: 'Where in my writings do I boast of being a theologian?' (106).
- Erasmus hopes that Lefèvre will never attack him again. 'I am confident that you will do what I most dearly hope will be better for both of us and more pleasing in the end to Christ' (107).

III
CONTROVERSIES CONCERNING THE DOCTRINE OF CHRISTIAN MARRIAGE

The theology and what we would now call the spirituality of Christian marriage occupied Erasmus for almost his entire life. To this end, he used almost all the literary genres familiar to him, and showed much ingenuity in exploiting the stylistic rules proper to each. He sometimes utilized his stylistic skill to evade, as well as to respond to, the objections raised against him (see the *Appendix* written against Clichtove, 112–15 below, on what constitutes a *Declamatio*). The diversity of his approaches somewhat undermines the clarity of his position.

First, there is the eulogy, the *Encomium*, a hybrid genre which Erasmus uses frequently. His *Declamatio* in favour of marriage, later known as the *Encomium matrimonii*, was published in 1518 but had been composed around 1498 or even earlier.[80] Erasmus took up this text again in his *De conscribendis*

* * * * *

80 The *Encomium* was translated into English, as part of a program of ecclesiastical reform, by Richard Taverner in 1532 from the edition and translation which

epistolis in 1522 (CWE 25 129–45) but paired it amusingly there with *De genere dissuasorio,* an exercise in dissuasive rhetoric on the marital contract, in which some readers hoped in vain to find a praise of virginity (CWE 25 145–8). Furthermore, since comparison, if not opposition, among celibacy, virginity, and marriage is obligatory in any discourse upon the seventh sacrament, it is appropriate also to mention here the *Virginis et martyris comparatio* of 1524 (LB V 589–600).

Next come the scriptural commentaries, the *Annotationes* and the *Paraphrases* on the New Testament. Whenever the Gospels or St Paul treats the question of marriage and divorce, Erasmus enters into the discussion, giving his opinion by means of philological or exegetical remarks upon the passages from Sacred Scripture.

Then there is the formal treatise such as the *Institutio christiani matrimonii* of 1526, a work dedicated to Queen Catherine of Aragon, the wife of Henry VIII of England, whose marriage, in point of fact, would trigger 'The King's Great Matter,' with its immediate and long-term consequences (LB V 613–724). *De vidua christiana* of 1529, dedicated to Mary of Hungary (CWE 66 177–257), can also be added to this category.

Neither should the *Colloquia* be forgotten, where the characters sometimes speak in an amusing way the ideas of Erasmus himself, even if, as a matter of principle, he denies it. Among others of this kind, the *Virgo μισόγαμος* ('The Girl with No Interest in Marriage' CWE 39 279–301) and the *Coniugium* ('Marriage' CWE 39 306–27), both published in 1523, and the *Ἄγαμος γάμος, sive Coniugium impar* ('A Marriage in Name Only, *or* The Unequal Match' CWE 40 842–60) of 1529 may be mentioned.

We come finally to the polemics and controversies, which might rather be called debates were it not for the bitter remarks and even insults they contain. Erasmus is always concerned to defend his writings and his reputation for orthodoxy, especially in regard to his views on marriage or divorce. From May 1519 onwards he had to confront successively and sometimes simultaneously Jan Briart of Ath (*Apologia de laude matrimonii,* 1519, CWE 71 89–95), Edward Lee (1520), Diego López Zúñiga (Stunica) (1521–2), Sancho Carranza (1522), Noël Béda (1527), the faculty of theology in Paris, and still others.[81] The two important controversies concerning marriage involve the

* * * * *

Thomas Cromwell favoured: *A ryght frutefull Epystle in laude of matrimony,* translated by R. Tavernour; and published with *De conscribendis epistolis* (1532). This text is so rare that it is not found, for example, in the Bodleian Library in Oxford, although the British Library possesses an exemplar of it.

81 For further information on these attacks, see Rummel *Catholic Critics.*

objections raised by Josse Clichtove and Johann Dietenberger, the refutation of which takes up a large portion of the present volume of the CWE.[82]

Before examining the details of these controversies, and in order to understand them better in the light of the themes developed there, it seems desirable to explore briefly the position and, at times, the evolution of Erasmus' thoughts on the exegetical, theological, and spiritual and canonical problems involved.

THE HIERARCHY OF STATES OF LIFE

It is a theological commonplace, almost a rhetorical device in the Christian tradition, especially in the patristic and medieval periods, to classify the states of life of baptized Christians according to the degree of merit that one may acquire in each. Let us examine Erasmus' position on this matter, beginning with the texts published in this volume but also looking more broadly throughout his work, to see whether or not he departs from the received tradition. How did he rank the merit or honour of the consecrated life in comparison with that of the married life and of celibacy?

It is immediately apparent that when Erasmus criticizes Josse Clichtove for a certain semantic confusion, his own choice of words is no more rigorous. In any case, his usage differs from the modern one whereby virginity, continence, and chastity have decidedly different connotations. In the moral theology of our day, 'virginity' applies to the person who has never had sexual relations, 'continence' to whoever abstains from them, and 'chastity' to those whose behaviour is motivated by modesty, self-control, and propriety, even when marriage is involved. Thus a person may be continent even though no longer a virgin, just as one can be both married and chaste. Erasmus, though, seems to apply the word 'virginity' to a consecrated state of life which implies continence – a word which, in turn, pertains to the vocabulary of chastity. Erasmus does a better job of distinguishing three different modes of civil status: celibacy (the unmarried state), marriage, and widowhood.

In accordance with the orthodox opinion and tradition, Erasmus offers a hierarchy of the states of life which gives pride of place to virginity over marriage, and to marriage over celibacy. These three ways of living the Christian life still require some further clarification, since they are crucial to an understanding of Erasmus' position. When he uses these terms in the *Dilutio* against Clichtove, Erasmus puts in first place the state of 'virginity entered into voluntarily through love of a holy life' (117) – in other words, the

* * * * *

82 For a description of the reactions to the *Encomium matrimonii*, see ASD I-5 353–81.

monastic vocation espoused without any psychological or social pressure. He puts in second place, marriage lived in the spirit of chastity that ought to pervade even the conjugal sexual relations of the Christian married couple. He puts in third place, finally, the celibate or single state, which is not the same as consecrated celibacy lived chastely.

We must note as well that what is important for Erasmus is the way any state of life facilitates the practice of the Christian life. Only in this way can we understand what he means when he uses the word 'piety' – as we saw in his debate with Lefèvre. For Erasmus, the states of life are neutral, as it were, 'unless the purpose is that a man may have more time for piety' (128). This is how we must understand his expression 'Monachatus non est pietas,' which was so attacked by his opponents in the mendicant orders.[83] In fact, if there was an evolution in Erasmus' view of monastic life when he was experiencing his own difficulties with it, his insistence upon the distinction between *pietas* and *religio* remains essential to it. In order to be evangelical – even Christian – the monastic 'religio' must spring from an interior source, in the hearts of those who profess it out of 'piety.'[84]

Fully aware of the behaviour of certain religious in the cloisters he frequented, Erasmus considered a married life lived chastely preferable to one of monastic 'virginity' accompanied by dubious moral behaviour. As in Matthew 19:12, he would reserve the vocation of 'virginity out of love for the gospel' to 'eunuchs' who are perfectly happy to have received this gift – we would say, this 'charism' – of continence.[85]

Even then, however, Erasmus does not wish this rare gift to be so valued as to detract from the ideal he proposes to the Christian, the chaste marriage. In this he reverses the age-old vision of the superiority of the religious state over marriage, which, for example, Bernard of Clairvaux constantly preached. The allegory which Erasmus develops in his treatise *De vidua christiana* elucidates his position: 'Virginity is not to be preferred to marriage as gold is to bronze but rather as a precious stone is preferred to gold ... If you compare gold to emerald, it is possible to doubt which you should

* * * * *

83 'Being a monk is not a state of holiness but a way of life, which may be beneficial or not according to each person's physical or mental constitution' (*Enchiridion* CWE 66 127).
84 In response to his opponent, the Franciscan Carvajal, Erasmus defined *pietas* as a 'spiritual predisposition which witnesses to the love of God and one's neighbour' (LB X 1675B).
85 *Paraphrasis in Matthaeum* LB VII 104B. It is possible to understand this text with reference to those who practise chastity in every walk of life.

choose; if you surround an emerald with gold, it is wondrous how beautifully each sets the other off. In this way each of the three states has some special characteristic in which it excels the others.'[86] One can easily discern Erasmus saying here that the chaste marriage is like an emerald embedded in gold.

In fact, Erasmus seems to exalt 'virginity' to such an extent – for example, by applying to it the traditional metaphor of martyrdom[87] – that he turns it into something 'angelic.'[88] He could certainly find support for this position in allegorical and exaggerated expressions drawn from certain Fathers of the church, especially Jerome.[89] But such exaltation – which his opponents held suspect – prompted certain commentators to see this as double-talk and, finally, as 'a brilliant exercise in demonstrating the impossible.'[90] It certainly led Erasmus to disapprove of the celibacy of those priests who were unable to remain continent.[91] It should be added that, especially towards the end of his life, when faced with the radical depreciation of monastic life in the regions won over to the Protestant Reformation, Erasmus reconsidered his position. In October 1527, for example, he regretted certain excesses of expression he had fallen into earlier, and highly praised the life consecrated to prayer and study, 'provided that it is totally dedicated to Christ.'[92] In a preface of 1533, he takes care to distinguish good monks from mediocre or bad ones, all the while retaining the angelic metaphor.[93]

Meanwhile, with a certain logic too subtle for his opponents, who saw in it, above all, a depreciation of the religious state, Erasmus blamed a canonical provision that rendered the religious vow, with its commitment to continence, a potential impediment to marriage in cases where there was no carnal consummation. This regulation should be seen in the context of a time when the marriage or betrothal of minors, who sometimes deferred consummation for several years, was a common occurrence. Erasmus explains that when a man pronounces solemn vows of religion, even against the will of his spouse, the latter cannot remarry for a year.[94] He condemns this provision,

* * * * *

86 *De vidua christiana* CWE 66 202
87 *Virginis et martyris comparatio* LB V 589–600
88 *Appendix* 114; *Dilutio* 128; *Apologia adversus monachos* (*Contra coelibatum*) LB IX 1089F
89 'God dedicated paradise to virginity and the earth to marriage' (*Adversus Iovinianum* PL 33 246ff)
90 Telle *Erasme* 255
91 *Exemplum epistolae suasoriae* (*De conscribendis epistolis*) CWE 25 137
92 Allen Ep 1887:59
93 Allen Ep 2771:97–9
94 *Institutio christiani matrimonii* LB V 634D

not for the inequality of the sexes, which it assumes, but because the monastic vow, which has no obvious scriptural basis and which the church has never considered a sacrament in the strict sense, should not take precedence over the sacrament of marriage.[95] In short, Erasmus' concept of the Christian states of life is closely related to his doctrine of marriage.

MARRIAGE

It is generally known that, in his reform treatise of 1520 *On the Babylonian Captivity of the Church*, Martin Luther reacted against the conception of marriage as a sacrament.[96] In his view this seemed to be a late and abusive outgrowth of the systematization of medieval scholasticism. The following year, King Henry VIII defended all seven sacraments of the Catholic church in his *Assertio septem sacramentorum*. These instances underline the importance which Erasmus' position could assume in this area, both before and after the controversy initiated by the Protestant reformers. Already in 1516, in the course of translating Ephesians 5:32, a key text in the theology of Christian marriage, Erasmus had substituted the term *mysterium* for that used in the Vulgate, *sacramentum*.[97] For Erasmus, the text did not seem a particularly apt basis for the doctrine of marriage as a sacrament conferring grace.[98] In any case, there followed a series of disputes which we need not repeat here, but which permitted Erasmus to clarify his position.

While protesting his obedience to the church in this respect,[99] but no longer appealing to the authority of that text in the Epistle to the Ephesians, Erasmus did not personally call into question the sacramental character of marriage. Still, he saw no reason to view the opposite opinion as a cause of scandal.[100] What he could not accept was the contract, the mutual exchange of consent between a man and a woman, as the foundation of marriage, even though Catholic theology ratified this belief and practice. For Erasmus, marriage should arise from a mutual love which he so aptly calls 'the conjugal sympathy of souls.'[101]

* * * * *

95 *Institutio christiani matrimonii* LB V 647D and F
96 WA VI 550–60
97 Georges Chantraine '"Mysterium" et "Sacramentum" dans le "Dulce Bellum"' in *Colloquium Erasmianum* (Mons 1983) 33–45; 'Le mustèrion paulinien selon les annotations d'Erasme' *Recherches de science religieuse* 58 (1970) 351–82
98 John B. Payne *Erasmus: His Theology of the Sacraments* (Richmond, Va 1971) 109–25
99 *Ad notationes novas Ed. Lei ad Philippenses* LB IX 271B
100 *Ad notationes Ed. Lei ad Ephesios* LB IX 227E–F
101 'connubialis animorum consensus' (*Institutio christiani matrimonii* LB V 618A)

We can readily discern the importance of the consequences of Erasmus' view, particularly for the indissolubility of marriage. Just as in canon law there is no real marriage if there is no contract (for example, in cases where there is lack of consent or no carnal consummation to ratify it), so for Erasmus no valid union between a man and a woman could exist if the element of true affection, of mutual love, were lacking.

Erasmus considered marriage a means of salvation in which, moreover, women have a particular role to play.[102] How, in his view, did they carry out that role? By the procreation and Christian education of children,[103] by conjugal love,[104] by the piety they teach in living Christian lives,[105] and, finally, by prayer – as is revealed in a beautiful orison composed by Erasmus himself.[106]

Thus, in a time of arranged and negotiated marriages, Erasmus placed a very high value on conjugal love, the *affectus coniugalis*. In this light, one should not be astonished by his mistrust of dynastic marriages based upon self-interest. Although, in principle, such marriages were concluded in favour of a peace whose praises the humanist sang, they appeared suspect to him because they rested upon a false foundation. Their political function was equally distorted: 'It may be true what they say, that a good man is not automatically a good prince, but it is plain that he who is *not* a good man cannot possibly be a good prince.'[107]

Erasmus made no public pronouncement on the 'divorce' of King Henry VIII of England. Still, one can discern his thoughts on the subject in the words of his disciples, as, for example, in the theological and juridical counsel of Bonifacius Amerbach in 1530 that Gilbert Cousin repeated after the death of the master.[108] But it is characteristic of Erasmus, in his rare comments on what he somewhat impertinently called the affair of Jupiter and Juno,[109] to mention the lack of affection of the king for his wife, Catherine of Aragon.[110] Amerbach would reply that, in this case, any husband grown tired of his wife might simply invoke lack of true love.[111] Nevertheless, Erasmus' young friend used

* * * * *

102 *Institutio christiani matrimonii* LB V 704E
103 *Puerpera* CWE 39 606
104 *Institutio christiani matrimonii* LB V 686B
105 *De vidua christiana* CWE 66 228
106 *Precationes: sub nuptias* LB V 1205D–E
107 *De vidua christiana* CWE 66 194
108 Guy Bedouelle 'Le milieu érasmien' in *Le 'divorce' du roi Henry VIII: études et documents* ed G. Bedouelle and P. Le Gal (Geneva 1987) 299–307
109 Allen Ep 2040:41
110 Allen Ep 2256:35–44
111 Allen Ep 2267:4–6

his arguments from the annotation on 1 Corinthians 7:39 when refusing to allow non-consummation to be a decisive factor in determining the validity of a marriage. One can nevertheless well understand how the Erasmian concept of the valid marriage, which places conjugal affection at its centre, could encourage the humanist to be generous in his understanding of 'divorce.'

DIVORCE

In Erasmus' time, the word *divortium* described what canon law still calls 'a declaration of the nullity of the marital bond.' But Erasmus uses it in its modern and secular sense: the severing of a valid marriage after disagreements and conflicts.

Reviewing the scriptural texts used by the church, first, to formulate its doctrine of the indissolubility of the conjugal bond and, second, to determine cases where separation can legitimately take place, Erasmus notices two bases for 'divorce' (aside from cases of nullity, where a marriage is judged never to have taken place). The first and majority position reaching back to the authority of St Augustine envisages an actual separation of the married couple, the abandonment of their cohabitation without any possibility of remarriage. The second position, based on Matthew 19:3, recognizes the possibility of a divorce after adultery of one of the parties. In his annotation on 1 Corinthians 7:39, which, of all his editions, constitutes a veritable treatise on how to understand the indissolubility of Christian marriage, Erasmus proposes some new solutions.[112]

Armed with his concept of mutual love as the foundation of Christian marriage, Erasmus pleads for a broader understanding of 'divorce.' Grounding his opinion in Origen, Tertullian, and Ambrose, he accepts adultery as a ground for divorce because it violates the very nature of marriage.[113] But he also argues that, in certain cases, separation should allow remarriage in the church, at least for the innocent party.

In such a case, can one still speak of the indissolubility of marriage? Following his own logic, Erasmus gives his definition of it. A true marriage, a union worthy of this name which comes from the Holy Spirit, is indissoluble. 'Death breaks the chains of the marriage; but true love has no bounds and alone remains even after death.'[114] But what harm would come were the

* * * * *

112 On 1 Cor 7:39, see LB VI 692–703; cf Reeve II 460ff. The debate with Phimostomus, edited in the present work, focuses upon this text. Based upon certain patristic interpretations, the theology and discipline of the Eastern Orthodox church have maintained adultery as a ground for divorce.

113 LB VI 698

114 *De vidua christiana* CWE 66 224

church to allow divorce 'as a relief for the unfortunate parties in a marriage which has come to grief'? Such a judgment would in no way compromise the solemn nature of marriage.[115] Erasmus views in this light many more cases that would permit the separation of married couples without proscribing their remarriage: certainly that of adultery, but also cases involving deceit, sorcery, parricide, and infanticide. Anticipating the Council of Trent, Erasmus also denounced clandestine marriages.

Erasmus' approach actually contains a rather pastoral element, in so far as he regularly recommends vigilance against contracting marriage too hastily, and places great emphasis on the spouses' psychological maturity and freedom of choice. Citing the text of Deuteronomy 24:1, which allowed a man to send his wife away because he has 'found some uncleanness in her,' Erasmus demonstrates that the soul's vice is worse than the physical fault which warranted the repudiation at that time.[116]

In this way, as usual, one can discern the liberties taken by Erasmus with respect to the legal tradition or its contemporary application. He sees possible adaptations of church doctrine in matters not pertaining to definitions of faith, and above all he shows compassionate understanding of the human failures and difficulties of the Christian life. Marriage aims at personal happiness; and certain characters in the *Colloquies*, who act as 'true guide[s] to the Christian life,'[117] witness to the fact that, rooted in piety and conforming with the spirit of the gospel, Christian marriage does bring happiness. Such is the case with Eulalia, a character with a well-chosen name in the *Coniugium*. Erasmus, however, even in his most complex arguments remains completely faithful to the simplicity of his Christocentric vision as he had expressed it in the *Enchiridion*: 'If you love [your wife] above all because you perceive in her the image of Christ, for example, piety, modesty, sobriety, and chastity, and you no longer love her in herself but in Christ, or rather Christ in her, then your love is spiritual.'[118] True conjugal love resembles that of Christ for the church.[119]

It is understandable that in an age of contention about the sacraments and the authenticity and validity of the monastic life, these Erasmian ideas

* * * * *

115 Ep 1126:215–17 to Hermannus Buschius
116 The standard English translations (King James, Douai, rsv) translate the Vulgate *foeditatem* by 'uncleanness' or 'impurity.' The English translation of the Jerusalem Bible has 'impropriety.' These all connote some moral fault rather than a mere physical fault ('blemish'), as the Bible de Jérusalem's 'tare' (and Erasmus) interpreted it.
117 Franz Bierlaire *Les Colloques d'Erasme: réforme des études, réforme des moeurs, et réforme de l'Eglise au xvie siècle* (Paris 1978) 149–99
118 cwe 66 53–4
119 asd i-3 731; cf Eph 5:25–33.

would be contested by the champions of orthodoxy, who were often skilful. Erasmus refuted the objections raised against him with great zeal, by attempting in a more or less convincing way to show that his ideas on the hierarchy of the states of life, on marriage, and on divorce were in harmony with the theology of the church, and, above all, to demonstrate that he had been misunderstood.

His first refutation answers a work by Josse Clichtove, who, in opposition to the growing influence of Luther's writings, proved himself a staunch and intelligent defender of Catholic theology.

AGAINST CLICHTOVE

After Erasmus' *Encomium matrimonii* was reissued in 1522, a scathing response came from one of the most solid theologians, Josse Clichtove, a doctor in the Paris faculty of theology, who was not without humanist credentials, having been a friend and supporter of Lefèvre d'Etaples in Paris for more than twenty years.[120] Clichtove wanted, above all, to contribute to the reform of the church by promoting a renewal of discipline in the Latin church, beginning with priestly austerity[121] and celibacy.[122] He was involved in the faculty of theology's pursuit of Lutherans, and he participated in its 20 May 1525 condemnation of the French translations of Erasmus' *Encomium matrimonii* and of a mishmash of other Erasmian and Lutheran works made by Louis de Berquin, who would eventually be burned at the stake, in 1529.[123]

The title of Clichtove's treatise – *Propugnaculum ecclesiae adversus Lutheranos*[124] (1526) – was, if not aggressive, at least defensive, proposing to erect

* * * * *

120 Massaut *Clichtove;* James K. Farge *Biographical Register of Paris Doctors of Theology* (Toronto 1980) 90–104

121 *De vita et moribus sacerdotum* (Paris: Henri Estienne 1519 among many later editions); Massaut *Clichtove* II 159–71

122 Massaut *Clichtove* II 172–209. See also, by the same author, 'Vers la Réforme catholique: le célibat dans l'idéal sacerdotal de Josse Clichtove' in *Sacerdoce et célibat* ed J. Coppens (Gembloux and Louvain 1971) 459–506.

123 Le Chevalier de Berquin *Declamation des louenges de mariage* ed E.V. Telle (Geneva 1976). See also ASD I-5 354–8 and 372–4. The other two books condemned were excerpted by Berquin from the *Paraphrases* and *Colloquia* of Erasmus, but Berquin had mixed in passages from Luther and Guillaume Farel. It is important to note that the faculty condemned these works 'sic translata,' ie 'translated *in this way*': see James K. Farge ed *Registre des procès-verbaux de la faculté de théologie de l'Université de Paris, de janvier 1524 à novembre 1533* (Paris 1990) 96–7 no 94A.

124 In editions of this work, one finds indiscriminately both *adversus Lutheranos* and *contra Lutheranos* in the title. Clichtove published an *Antilutherus* in the same year, while Noël Béda wrote an *Apologia adversus clandestinos Lutheranos* in 1529.

a fortification or bastion against Luther and his supporters. In it he sets out three reproaches against Erasmus – 'accusations,' Erasmus will call them: first, against certain declarations contained in the *Encomium*; second, against certain declarations regarding Erasmus' position on ecclesiastical celibacy; and finally, against Erasmus' attitude towards the practice of abstinence in the church.

The first book of the *Propugnaculum* considers only Luther and his innovations in the mass. But the second harshly analyses the *Encomium matrimonii* and Erasmus' *Apologia de laude matrimonii* of 1519 (CWE 71 85–95), with which chapters 31–4 are entirely concerned. First having asserted that Erasmus minimized the glory of *coelibatum* only to exaggerate his praise of marriage, Clichtove launches into a long discussion on whether the sexual appetite (*stimuli libidinum*) pertains to human nature itself or to the concupiscence introduced by original sin. However, in the dedicatory preface to Bishop Louis Guillard, Clichtove had clearly stated that the aim of the book was first and foremost a refutation of Luther, and had omitted all reference to Erasmus.

Erasmus quickly answered Clichtove in that same year, although he cites the title erroneously, and declares he has been able only to flip through it in haste. In fact, however, even in the few pages which constitute this *Appendix*, one can discern the major points of the reply to Clichtove which Erasmus was to develop some years later. Erasmus asserts that Clichtove has misjudged the literary genre: the *Encomium matrimonii* was a *Declamatio*, not a theological discourse; one cannot submit a fictitious, persuasive speech to the rigours of a theological examination. Moreover, the question put forward was not a general one, involving the superiority of marriage or celibacy, but a particular one, touching upon an individual case. Besides, the kind of marriage he advocated was chaste to a degree approaching continence. Finally, if he made some unfavourable comparisons to the monastic life, he was concerned only with the glaring abuses that anybody can see, and not with the very purpose of a life consecrated to continence.[125]

Having announced, at the end of the *Appendix*, a fuller response based upon a closer reading of Clichtove's objections, Erasmus fulfilled his promise

* * * * *

125 Erasmus, in fact, does not change his assertions. Already in 1526 he had written, 'It is true that I prefer a chaste marriage to an impure celibacy,' and again, 'I am not recommending that priests and monks should marry, but I do say that in this crowd of priests and monks, marriage should be allowed to those who cannot live a continent life'; Erika Rummel 'An Unpublished Erasmian Apologia in the Royal Library of Copenhagen' *Nederlands Archief voor Kerkgeschiedenis / Dutch Review of Church History* 70 (1990) 226–7. See n5 above.

in 1532 with his *Dilutio*. As discussed above, the term indicates simply the action of clearing oneself of false accusations. With no attempt to avoid repetition, this text develops the answers which had arisen in response to his first reading of the *Propugnaculum*.

Straight away Erasmus insists upon the fact that he had not wished to make a systematic comparison between the state of celibacy and that of marriage. He will argue repeatedly that Clichtove got all worked up over nothing, and that he mistook the literary genre. What Erasmus had wished to do was to engage in a rhetorical exercise, an example of persuasive discourse, with the text aimed at a particular case: someone sincerely pondering the problem of whether or not to marry. From this point of departure, Erasmus displays the different facets of the argument. His discourse is not general but particular, and he does not express himself absolutely, or *simpliciter* (a word that turns up frequently), but in response to an individual situation which is that of the person addressed. Furthermore, since a literary fiction is in question, there is no justification for identifying Erasmus himself with the person arguing the case. One should never, he argues, attribute to an author the opinions of his characters. In this regard, the *Colloquies* and even the *Moriae encomium* spring to mind: amid so many paradoxes and quips, it would be very difficult to determine exactly who speaks for Erasmus.

To put it in more modern terms, Erasmus reproaches Clichtove for lacking a sense of humour. Twice he tells him that he should put some distance between himself and the text, and that he has taken it too seriously (116, 128). Erasmus had been engaged in a literary game, a *declamatio*, which, in the manner of a lawyer's argument, ought to embrace all the possible arguments, but which Clichtove submits to a rigorous theological examination.

Then Erasmus demonstrates with considerable irony how one ought to maintain this distance even when engaged in the most serious and dialectical genre possible, the scholastic question. Could one not make St Thomas Aquinas say practically anything, if all the objections which he proposes, in order the better to refute them, were to be imputed to him? 'That is no more fitting than if one were to combat the arguments of Thomas or of Scotus in which they impugn vows or defend fornication, while neglecting to mention the rebuttal that follows' (121). Obviously, Erasmus' argument is weak, because the very structure of the scholastic question – the objections, the *sed contra* arguments against each, and their rebuttals – offers no ambiguity concerning the final position. But the idea is amusing.

Erasmus cogently summarizes his arguments concerning the literary form he employed: 'that it is a declamation; that it is the first part of a set theme to which an opposing argument must be made; that these things are said not by Erasmus, but by a young layman; . . . that a virtuous action is being recommended and one that in a certain way is necessary for him; that there is not a licentious word in the whole speech; that even in theological disputations it is permitted to use false reasoning in order that the listeners may learn how to refute it' (143).

With regard to the substance of the problem – its theological or, more precisely, its moral and spiritual implications – Erasmus uses his *Dilutio* to reassure Clichtove of his deep-seated orthodoxy: yes, in absolute terms virginity is preferable to marriage, as Catholic tradition affirms; yes, marriage is a sacrament; but all this must be considered with moderation and, above all, with a precision of vocabulary and a feel for words which Clichtove does not have. He confuses continence with celibacy, a term to which he attributes a whimsical, arbitrary, even ridiculous etymology.

As to the controversial question of ecclesiastical celibacy, Erasmus feels that his position was distorted by Clichtove. He thus takes up the issue again by stating more clearly than in his *Appendix* of 1526 what he had really wanted to say there: 'In view of the present status of those who profess celibacy, Erasmus wonders whether it would be a lesser evil for the church to permit wives for those who after making every effort still do not lead continent lives' (*Appendix* 112). He does not repudiate the law of the western church, but faces up to the reality that the law has always been violated by certain priests and monks. The historian senses here a hint of Erasmus' personal bitterness about his own birth as the illegitimate son of a priest.

Without questioning Erasmus' orthodoxy (as a whole tradition of commentators has done)[126] the reader nevertheless cannot fail to notice in the *Dilutio*, as Clichtove surely did, a series of little attacks, none essential to the central question; these were sure to unsettle the conservative theologian of the sixteenth century. Scholasticism is not attacked head on but by way of its rhetorical questions or, worse still, by presenting those questions as useless and indiscreet.[127] Its syllogistic form is subjected to ridicule (136); and

* * * * *

126 See Telle *Erasme* and Telle *Dilutio*.
127 '. . . a certain Parisian theologian of some renown wonders whether the mother of Jesus felt the first stirrings of nature, especially before she gave birth to Christ, although in my opinion it would have been more seemly not to raise this question' (*Dilutio* 134). Undoubtedly this question, superfluous in fact, should be understood in the context of the quarrel over the Immaculate Conception of the Virgin Mary (Massaut *Critique et tradition* 37–45).

Erasmus cannot resist slight cutting remarks against theologians who rely too much on Aristotle. But even here, Erasmus would warn us not to take his subtly ironic barbs too seriously.

We can perhaps detect a slight hint of anti-Semitism in this tract. We can likewise wonder whether, after Luther's *De votis monasticis*, written in the wake of the great Reformation treatises which began to appear in 1520, Erasmus' descriptions of violations in clerical continence, or even his simple investigations into Catholic discipline, did not do a disservice to the church. The assaults of the reformers explain the lively sensitivity of theologians like Clichtove amid this great hodgepodge of ideas.

Erasmus seems not to have realized, however, that in this *Dilutio*, as in several of his works, regardless of the way he saw it, his positions could appear harmful. In fact, in placing virginity on such a pedestal ('perfection belongs to the few,' *Dilutio* 129) or in calling it 'angelic,' even if he is using traditional vocabulary ('I compare virginity to the angels while I attribute marriage to men,' *Appendix* 114), was there not a danger of reducing it to a practically unattainable ideal? Did Erasmus not in this way risk calling consecrated celibacy into question while, conversely, idealizing Christian marriage, for which he prescribed continence?

All these discussions notwithstanding, the emphasis of this text, so engaging and so characteristic of Erasmus' manner and concerns, is placed on the truth of the Christian life experienced as much in the married state as in the celibate. Affirmations of this *pietas* are found in the body of the discussion: 'Neither celibacy nor virginity nor continence is praiseworthy in itself unless the purpose is that a man may have more time for piety' (128). This appeal for *pietas* is repeated at the end, when Erasmus warns his reader against placing too much importance on exterior things while neglecting 'what is more directly concerned with evangelical piety' (147).

From this attitude also arose Erasmus' rejection of verbal injury and the clearly excessive language to which Clichtove had resorted in demanding that texts like those of Erasmus be burned (144). 'Were you sober when you wrote this, Clichtove?' And what are we to say, he continues, 'if similar impartiality is used in making judgments by those whose verdicts determine whether men are to be burned at the stake?' (144). Far better to seek unity and further the practice of understanding differences than to yield to these petty attacks, Erasmus insists: 'It would be preferable to devote our energies to resolving our differences rather than to providing seed-ground for new disagreements through biased inquiries' (last lines of the *Appendix*). But was this fault to be imputed only to the theologians?

The following analysis may facilitate the reading of the two texts.

An Appendix on the Writings of Josse Clichtove (1526)[128]

– Erasmus was able only to skim through Clichtove's *Bulwark of the Faith.* In this work, Clichtove misunderstood some of Erasmus' statements.
– How could Clichtove, no stranger to the literary arts, fail to grasp the genre to which a declamation belongs?
– If it be permitted to speak 'as a philosopher,' as theologians concede to their beloved Aristotle, can one not speak as an orator?
– Erasmus has been using the example of continence since 1498, when he wrote his *On the Writing of Letters,* which has nothing to do with theology.
– Scholastic disputation likewise uses preliminary arguments which do not limit the author to those positions.
– When the orator says that it is better for incontinent monks to marry, he thinks that these monks can be released from their solemn vows as readily as from their simple vows.
– Erasmus returns to the distinction between rhetoric and theology.
– He has already replied to the objections raised by Jan Briart and Noël Béda to the *Encomium matrimonii.*
– Erasmus concludes with a declaration of his own orthodoxy and recalls that he has also responded to the questions of abstinence and fasting.

Dilutio: Refutation of the Accusations of Josse Clichtove (1532)[129]

1/ A Misunderstanding of the Literary Genre (116–23)

– Erasmus was amused by reading Clichtove's book, in which the latter enters the fray armed with the entire arsenal of theological weaponry against a fictitious theme.
– Clichtove is an honest man, but Satan can use everything, even devotion, to his own advantage.
– In order not to take what was a mere diversion too seriously, Erasmus does not intend to respond to all the arguments at this time, but only to those which seem truly excessive to him and which do no honour to the renowned faculty of theology in Paris.

* * * * *

128 The Latin text is found in LB IX 811–14.
129 The Latin text is edited in Telle *Dilutio* 69–100, following Froben's 1532 edition and constituting the second part of another text: *Declarationes ad censuras Lutetiae vulgatas* ... The *Dilutio* is found neither in the *Opera omnia* of 1540 nor in the Leiden edition (LB). A modern French translation with an introduction exists: Erasme *La philosophie chrétienne* ed Pierre Mesnard (Paris 1970) 359–99. A single allusion to the *Dilutio* (Telle 57) is found in Erasmus' correspondence in a letter written on 8 February 1532 to Viglius Zuichemus: 'I also responded to Clichtove's empty old phrases' (Allen Ep 2604:38–41).

- Clichtove reproaches Erasmus for not having repudiated – as did Pope Pius II – or at least amended a work written as a youth; but does one have to reject an encomium of chaste marriage?
- Although better informed than others among Erasmus' opponents, Clichtove does not really understand the literary genre of the *Declamatio*, which is not to be debated as before a judge.
- Furthermore, Erasmus did not intend to measure the state of marriage against that of celibacy, but merely to pose a clearly determined question in a genre which the art of rhetoric would call the *Suasoria*.
- Against Clichtove's reproach that he had not exhorted the reader to that which is best, Erasmus points out that in several places he did just that.
- Why is Clichtove interested only in the second part of the declamation (arguments against marriage) and not in the first (arguments in favour of it)?
- It is not a question of a real case, but of an example, as Aristotle recommended for use.
- Clichtove, having misunderstood the genre employed, accumulates arguments of a general nature. To make Erasmus say more than he said, even when he does apply common arguments to a specific case, is the basis of a false accusation.

2/ Celibacy and Continence (123–9)
- Celibacy must be carefully distinguished from continence. One can be celibate and not at all continent. Erasmus prefers marriage to celibacy, not to continence. Monks take a vow of chastity, but, according to Erasmus, the same is demanded of all Christians.
- Some of Jerome's etymologies and scriptural citations in defence of celibacy cannot be trusted.
- As for himself, Erasmus prefers to use Latin precisely and to distinguish his terms, as he demonstrates with several citations from his text.
- Why does Clichtove not recognize the similarity between his methodology and the scholastic disputation? Have not many authors praised the vices in jest?
- One ought not reproach Erasmus for using false arguments in the same way theologians themselves do, since their approach is as much a work of artifice as the declamation.
- In the text, one layman attempts to persuade another, who has a weak character, that a chaste marriage is better than celibacy. There is no question here of continence.
- As for virginity, Erasmus praises it as a heavenly state for a chosen few.

3/ The Consecrated Life (129–39)

- In the declamation, a layman ventures a simple, personal opinion that in certain circumstances priests and monks ought to be able to marry as a lesser evil.
- Erasmus cites examples from the Old Testament and from the early days of the church, and also less edifying examples in his own time.
- Moreover, a religiously motivated celibacy, which can lift someone above the human condition, must be distinguished from a renunciation of marriage on account of grief.
- But a religious motivation does not imply the impossibility of living a holy life in the state of marriage. Is marriage not a sacrament?
- One can struggle against nature for the sake of the kingdom of God, but what has that to do with someone who is influenced by purely human sentiments?
- Does the stimulus to procreate not belong to nature, even if corrupted?
- To counterbalance Clichtove's idealization of the religious life of the day, Erasmus gives a few examples of its depravity. In this he is in the tradition of St Jerome and St Bernard.
- In what way and manner can one say that the celibate person sins against the propagation of his race?
- Erasmus argues against certain statements and citations used erroneously or in too absolute a manner by Clichtove.

4/ Marriage and Nature (139–43)

- Sexual instincts are natural, even if the corruption of nature sometimes makes them rebellious to the spirit; but indecency is a function more of the human imagination than of reality. Yet Erasmus admits that this is not a very convincing argument.
- Nature's role is to preserve and propagate itself. The example of the incest of Lot's daughters is used in the declamation only to demonstrate this instinct.
- To this end, Erasmus justifies his use of so-called prurient language.

5/ Conclusion (143–8)

- Erasmus summarizes his argument once again and vigorously refuses to allow his 'little treatise' to be compared with the works of a Poggio or a Valla.
- Final summation of Clichtove's reproaches and Erasmus' answers concerning ecclesiastical celibacy, fasting and abstinence, and the laws of the church. Erasmus' aim is to bring about a rediscovery of true, spiritual, and

evangelical piety; he suggests that counsel can sometimes be more effective than obligation, but always avoids accusations of Lutheranism. Since Clichtove once repented of his impudent words against the *Exsultet*,[130] he would do even better to retract the slanderous things he wrote against a friend.

Do we have here an anti-monastic treatise? A manual on naturalism or on the Epicureanism for which Jerome attacked Jovinian? Praise of the sexual impulse, relativization of ecclesiastical celibacy, freedom from the hierarchical view of the states of life sanctioned by tradition? All of these can be found in the *Dilutio*, where they seem to worsen Erasmus' case rather than justify it. What is more, does Erasmus not emphasize nature over grace? Could not the accusation of Pelagianism made against him by Luther in his *De servo arbitrio* be taken up again by the Catholic theologians? By presenting the consecrated life as something exceptional, heroic, even unattainable, did not Erasmus minimize the role of divine grace?

In fact, the faculty of theology in Paris did condemn the *Dilutio*. Although Clichtove had not attended sessions there since 1526, the solidarity of the doctors with him was assured by the leadership of the faculty's syndic Noël Béda, who was as active in 1532 as he had been in 1525, when Berquin's translations were condemned. The debate is mentioned in the conclusions recorded between 3 April and 2 May 1532.[131] The book was proscribed because it did not furnish 'a declaration of truth but a cover for and defence of error.' The term *involutor*, used here against the author, gives the impression that the theologians felt caught in a web of Erasmian dialectic.

AGAINST DIETENBERGER

In September 1532, Erasmus joined to his *Epistolae palaenaeoi* (Freiburg im Breisgau: Emmeus) a short work entitled *Responsio ad disputationem cuiusdam Phimostomi de divortio* (LB VIII 955–65). Erasmus drew the name 'Phimostomus' from the title of his antagonist's polemical work[132] proposing to impose a *phimostomus* – a bit or bridle, or more precisely a muzzle – of Catholic rectitude on the new commentators on Scripture, whom he called 'Scripturalists.'

* * * * *

130 Clichtove recanted in his *Elucidatorium ecclesiasticum* of 1516. See Massaut *Critique et tradition* 101–5.
131 Farge *Registre des procès-verbaux* 263–4 nos 339A–342A (see n123 above)
132 *Phimostomus scripturariorum*

The opponent, Johann Dietenberger (c 1475–1537), a German Dominican and friend of Johannes Cochlaeus, was just beginning to teach at Mainz in that same year.[133]

Dietenberger's text, presented as having been originally produced (*aeditus*) in Augsburg at the imperial diet of 1530, is made up of fifteen chapters written for the use of Johann von Metzenhausen, legate of the archbishop of Trier at that diet. We know it, however, only by Petrus Quentel's 1532 Cologne edition. Like the majority of Catholic works dealing with the controversies of the time, it consists of short accounts of questions disputed between Catholics and Protestants – for example, the interpretation of Scripture, prayers to the saints, free will, and the celebration of the Eucharist. A supplement in the form of a sixteenth chapter is a special (*specialis*), brief treatise on divorce which attacks Erasmus' interpretation of 1 Corinthians 7:39. This addition is dedicated to Valentin von Tetleben, coadjutor of Albert of Brandenburg, the archbishop of Mainz, for whom Tetleben acted as vicar *in spiritualibus* in 1532. Tetleben was to become bishop of Hildesheim in 1537, a date which corresponds with that of Dietenberger's death.

Dietenberger cites and refutes the 1519 edition of Erasmus' *Annotationes*, and ignores the lengthy addenda of later editions.[134] Erasmus maintains here his usual position that, in certain circumstances, the remarriage of a divorced person is legitimate. Jacob of Hoogstraten had already criticized him for that position in his *Destructio Cabalae* of 1519, written in the course of the Reuchlin affair. By August of that year, Erasmus had responded to his critic in a personal letter,[135] and he developed a more elaborate defence in his additions to the *Annotationes* published in 1522 and 1527, which Dietenberger appears not to have known.

Just as Erasmus, adhering to the convention of the time, follows the order of the objections raised by his opponent, so shall we here examine Erasmus' response to Dietenberger point by point.

Addressing himself to a doctor in canon and civil law like Tetleben, Erasmus informs him that he has read the treatise on divorce written by a certain Phimostomus. It seemed to him that this text was not without merit, although the style of it may have been a bit hard on the 'Scripturalists.' After

* * * * *

133 Hermann Wedewer *Johannes Dietenberger (1475–1537), Sein Leben und Wirken* (Freiburg im Breisgau 1888; repr Nieuwkoop 1967); Nikolaus Paulus *Die deutschen Dominikaner im Kampfe gegen Luther (1518–1563)* [Freiburg im Breisgau 1903] 186–9
134 Rummel *Catholic Critics* I 25–6, and on this point II 163 n95
135 Ep 1006:52–3

all, other theologians hardly even mention Scripture or, worse still, they apply philosophical criteria to it.

The Reply to the Disputation on Divorce (1532)
1/ Considerations of Vocabulary (152–60)
– Dietenberger wants to refute Erasmus' annotation on 1 Corinthians 7, where he took up the question of marriages contracted without discernment. Unlike Erasmus, the Dominican understands the words *divortium* and *repudium* in the Bible as the separation of the married couple, whose marriage has been consummated, without a dissolution of the marriage bond. But can one alter the meaning of the words in this way? In 'sending Mary away privately' Joseph had resolved to seek a divorce (Matt 1:19).
– It is the same for *foeditas* (foulness) in Deuteronomy 24:1. Who told Phimostomus that this text necessarily implied the wife's adultery? It might instead be a question of a 'hidden blemish of body and mind.' According to the Jewish law, the 'bill of divorce' was not concerned with a woman who was adulterous, but with one who was specifically permitted to remarry. This proves that divorce is not merely a termination of the couple's cohabitation.
– The divorce for which Scripture provides must be considered a benevolent law. In the New Testament, Christ explains only the meaning of the Mosaic law and not the interpretation which the Pharisees make of it. Unlike human law, divine law does not permit a lesser evil in order to avoid a greater one. Thus one cannot imagine how the Mosaic law could stipulate adultery as ground for divorce when in fact it legislates a stoning for it.
– A ground for divorce in the Old Testament could be a strong aversion felt by the husband at a given moment for his wife, which permits him to dismiss her. If Dietenberger can cite Paul of Burgos, Erasmus can refer to Cajetanus! Does not the great Dominican theologian believe that remarriage was permitted to the Jews only because of their polygamy? Jesus, however, does not interpret the law in this way (Matt 19:9). The time of the patriarchs must be distinguished from that of the Law.

2/ The Question of Divorce in the New Testament (161–76)
– Christ prescribes a stricter law than that of Moses by allowing divorce for one reason only, adultery. This astonishes the disciples (Matt 19:10). In fact, Jesus' recommendation not to 'put asunder' that which has been joined by God goes even further if one interprets it strictly: it would not even allow their living apart. The position taken by Phimostomus on Romans 7:2–3 cannot stand because the context is different.

- The next passage (Rom 7:10-11) demands further explanation, since it does not recognize adultery as ground for divorce, even if Ambrose (Ambrosiaster), to whose authority Dietenberger had appealed, presupposes that it does. In Erasmus' opinion, Paul proffers here a counsel of perfection: the husband will not resort to divorce, even in the case of his wife's adultery. That is how Ambrosiaster and Pseudo-Jerome also understood it. Erasmus notes that, on the question of divorce, Paul gives more rights to the husband than to the wife, even though he considers the couple to be equal in the married state (1 Cor 7:4).
- After a syntactic discussion of Matthew 19:9, Erasmus confronts Augustine's opinion head on by distinguishing a remarriage after a divorce caused by adultery (and not permitted by church discipline) from a divorce 'in accordance with the law.' Certainly canon law details all that; but does not Dietenberger claim that his arguments are based upon Scripture?
- Gratian's *Decretum*, while firm on the principle of no remarriage, seems to admit exceptions on the ground of the infirmity of the flesh. The *Decretals* contain contradictory opinions. After all, the apostles had their disagreements, just as the church has its hesitations and reversals – as, for example, over the *filioque* or sacramental theology. It is therefore not inappropriate for Erasmus to turn his attention to a disputed question.
- Furthermore, both the pope and the church enjoy great latitude in their power to interpret Scripture, even in such matters as these, as exemplified by the exceptions in canon law known as 'the Petrine privilege.'
- Erasmus then explains his way of understanding the prescriptions given in 1 Corinthians 7. He demonstrates that, in fact, the church grants separation for many reasons other than merely divorce. For example, is separation not permitted when one spouse becomes a heretic, because it is interpreted as 'spiritual adultery'? What about the dissolution of the marital bond when the husband makes a profession in the monastic life? Is that mentioned in Scripture? The evangelical call to perfection also exists in the married state. Such practices are admissible, but Phimostomus is mistaken in thinking that they are contained in Scripture, taken in its literal sense.
- In his epilogue, Dietenberger wishes that Erasmus would accept the current practice of the church concerning the separation of a married couple as founded upon Holy Writ. He rejects the analogy which Erasmus drew from pagan customs. Erasmus then cites some of his opponent's contradictions.
- Finally, because Phimostomus has aligned him with Arius, Luther, Karlstadt, and Zwingli, Erasmus devotes a few words to refuting the accusation that he had called the sacrament of penance into question (176–7). Perhaps, he hopes, his correspondent will be able to act as a mediator.

It is clear that Erasmus, as is customary in his controversial or justificatory treatises, makes no effort to organize his discourse systematically. Instead he responds point by point to the objections raised by his opponents, which more or less follow the order of his original discourse. If one adds to that the subtlety, skill, and artful parrying and ironic thrusting that are the hallmarks of the Erasmian style, then the humanist's thought revealed to us in these polemical treatises might appear not only complex but also susceptible of new interpretations. Thus, by way of a conclusion to the introduction of these texts, rather than catalogue manuscript exemplars and ancient editions, we shall highlight some impressions which the modern reader is likely to get from reading them.

IV

Although separated in time, these four texts – the *Apologia* addressed to Lefèvre d'Etaples (1517), the two refutations of Clichtove (1526 and 1532), and the treatise on divorce against Phimostomus (1532) – all demonstrate the pugnacious nature of Erasmus' theological opinions and show that he expressed them in a consistently argumentative manner throughout his career. Modern readers' reactions to Erasmus the theologian and exegete, who is justifying his positions to Lefèvre on issues that hardly matter any more, will be different from their reactions to Erasmus the moralist, who is reflecting upon marriage in ways that seem quite current.

    In the polemic triggered by Lefèvre's interpretation of Psalm 8, Erasmus had a more nuanced and flexible vision of biblical hermeneutics than his opponent. He was more sensitive than Lefèvre to the different levels of interpretation that a biblical text may carry. Thus a psalm need not always be applied directly to Christ, but may be legitimately related to the psalmist or the reader. This contradicted the strictly Christocentric hermeneutic of Lefèvre, which shackled him to such a degree that he was at times obliged to twist the texts to make them fit. Nevertheless, Lefèvre, basing his exegesis upon the 'harmony of the Scriptures,' attached a much greater importance than Erasmus to the concordance between the Old and the New Testaments – as shown in the manner in which the two authors treated the relationship of the hymn in Philippians 2 to Psalm 8.

    Underlying this hermeneutical debate and at stake in the quarrel between the two humanists is, in fact, their Christology. Erasmus, careful to guard the equilibrium between the two natures of Christ, refuses to sacrifice his humanity. Beyond exegetical methods or varieties of interpretation among the Fathers of the church, it is this view which Erasmus defends against the 'sublimity' of Lefèvre's interpretation. For Erasmus, the abasement of Christ the man is the logical end of the Incarnation, whereas Lefèvre, without deny-

ing that humiliation, wants to minimize it in order to preserve the divine dignity of Christ. Did Erasmus detect in Lefèvre a sort of latent monophysitism?
If he did, he did not accuse him of it, because he was not one to root out
and systematically denounce heresy as did, to his dismay, his theological
opponents. For all that, he could not abide a charge of impiety against himself.

This notion of *impietas*, for which not only Lefèvre but also Luther
reproached Erasmus, is crucial because it touches upon the very heart of
the Christian vision of humanism, either denying or misapprehending that
which is its exact opposite, *pietas*. We need not repeat here the analysis of
Erasmus' concept of *pietas*, of which John W. O'Malley has so aptly revealed
the components, connotations, and sources;[136] but, following him, let us agree
that 'Erasmian *pietas* might then also be described as "principled" rather than
"prescriptive," to use an old distinction ... Erasmus was not trying to reduce
affairs to lowest common denominators, but rather to moderate prescriptions
that inhibited the full flowering of *varietas* and the manifold expressions of the
Spirit in the life of Christians of all states and conditions.'[137] One can see how
essential Erasmus' notion of *pietas* was to debates on marriage and divorce.

The modern reader may be astonished to discover how close the problems that preoccupied Erasmus are to his or her own concerns today. With
regard to the validity of marriage, the separation of the married couple,
and the indissolubility of the marital bond, the Roman Catholic church has
maintained canonical prescriptions more akin to those of Clichtove or Dietenberger than to those of Erasmus. In his debate with Lefèvre, Erasmus shows
how audacious he can be and how much freer he is in regard to ecclesiastical tradition – certainly where the sacrament of marriage is concerned, but
above all in its canonical prescriptions – than in the strictly dogmatic domain
of Christology.

One might aptly designate his approach as 'pastoral.' The Erasmian doctrine of marriage is founded upon the love and reciprocal affection which
grounds the sacrament (which he has no difficulty in accepting as such) in the
very heart of the New Testament. His 'matrimonial evangelism' ('évangélisme
matrimonial,' in the words of Emile V. Telle, who pushes his interpretation to
extreme conclusions) is inspired by his reading of the Pauline Epistles. More
generally, it is consistent with his 'philosophy of Christ.' Erasmus has in mind
the good 'of the greatest number'[138] when, reacting to problems of his day, he
proposes solutions, supports them, and explains them to his correspondents.

* * * * *

136 CWE 66 xv–xxxiii
137 CWE 66 xix–xx
138 *Institutio christiani matrimonii* LB V 651D

Another striking element is the lucidity, indeed the severity and irony with which Erasmus judges the customs of his time, as much when he considers the monastic life and its infidelities as when he reflects upon the marriages of his contemporaries. This, too, constitutes an aspect of his pastoral vision – this making use of an analysis of the society and church that encompass his contemporaries' weaknesses. One must intelligently recognize their faults, and, in the spirit of the gospel, denounce them and work to blunt their force. With a realism that one could call 'theological,' Erasmus reminds us repeatedly that state of life – whether the consecrated or the married – is valuable only to the degree to which it fosters virtue. This is precisely the stance of Rabelais, who often treated the question of marriage by endowing it with the comic aspect of an existential question – as, for example, in the case of Panurge.[139]

Certainly Erasmus was conscious of the canonical and even theological difficulties which his positions raised. With a certain relativism or distance afforded by his culture and familiarity with the texts – above all the patristic ones, so keenly assimilated by him – he believed that change within the church was possible, since the history of Christianity attests to many developments. Erasmus was always careful to distinguish between matters of faith that were defined and theological opinions that can vary. For him the folly of the scholastics was their desire to pose questions on every topic and reach a verdict on everything in the most definitive possible way.[140] One can understand how his relativism stirred so much indignation and unrest among his contemporaries at a time when church dogma and traditions were being called into question.

The subtlety of style, rhetorical devices, ironic allusions, and constant recourse to paradox – above all when deployed in a genre as distinctive as the *Apologia* and the austere polemical treatises – do not make these works a route of easy access to Erasmian intuitions. The intuitions are displayed more felicitously in the great treatises like the *Enchiridion militis christiani*. But they are indeed present in the battle waged step by step, verse by verse, and phrase by phrase against those who had the misfortune to question Erasmus' *pietas*, for in that *pietas* lay his real commitment to Christ.

GB

* * * * *

139 M.A. Screech *The Rabelaisian Marriage: Aspects of Rabelais' Religion, Ethics, and Comic Philosophy* (London 1958) 126
140 Allen Ep 1976: 64

ACKNOWLEDGMENTS
Special thanks to Janet Ritch of the University of Toronto for her translation
from the French of the introduction to this volume and of the notes to the
Apologia ad Fabrum. For their advice and assistance with various matters
the following are acknowledged gratefully here: James K. Farge, H.J. de
Jonge, John Langlois, James K. McConica, and Nelson Minnich, and the staff
of the Toronto Renaissance and Reformation Colloquium, E.J. Pratt Library,
Victoria University, University of Toronto. We are indebted to Mary Baldwin,
Lynn Burdon, Penny Cole, Theresa Griffin, and Philippa Matheson for their
indispensable contribution of preparing the text for publication and bringing
it into print.

APOLOGY AGAINST
JACQUES LEFÈVRE D'ÉTAPLES

Apologia ad Iacobum Fabrum Stapulensem

translated by HOWARD JONES
annotated by GUY BEDOUELLE

The controversy between Erasmus and the Parisian humanist Jacques Lefèvre d'Etaples, which culminated in the publication of the *Apologia ad Iacobum Fabrum Stapulensem*, had its origin in a critical comment by Erasmus on Lefèvre's interpretation of St Paul's reference to Psalm 8:6 in the Epistle to the Hebrews 2:7. At issue was whether the meaning should be 'You have made him a little lower than God,' as Lefèvre contended, or 'You have made him a little lower than the angels,' as Erasmus maintained. Lefèvre first declared his view in his annotation on Psalm 8:6 in his *Quincuplex psalterium* of 1509, and he repeated it in 1512 in his annotation on Hebrews 2:7 in his translation of and commentary on the Epistles of St Paul (*Epistolae* XIV *ex Vulgata, adiecta intelligentia ex Graeco, cum commentariis*). Erasmus' criticism of Lefèvre's position came in his annotation on Hebrews 2:7 in his *Novum instrumentum*, which appeared in March 1516. Lefèvre responded with a note of some eight folio pages which he included in the second edition of his commentary on St Paul's Epistles, which was published sometime between November 1516 and July 1517 but bore a date in the colophon of 1515. It was not until July 1517 that Erasmus' attention was drawn to Lefèvre's 'disputatio,' as Erasmus called it. Incensed by its harsh tone, and dismayed by what he regarded as a betrayal of friendship on Lefèvre's part, Erasmus lost no time in striking back, composing the present *Apologia* in a space of two weeks or less.

The first edition was published by Dirk Martens at Louvain. It bears no date, but appeared sometime between 23 and 28 August 1517.[1] Four more editions were published before the death of Erasmus (and Lefèvre) in 1536. Corrected copies of the *editio princeps* were sent by Erasmus to Matthias Schürer in Strasbourg and to Johann Froben in Basel. Schürer published what was the second edition between the end of October 1517 and February 1518, indicating on the title page that the edition incorporated revisions by the author. In addition to the text of the *Apologia* the edition contained Erasmus' annotation on Hebrews 2:7 and Lefèvre's 'disputatio.' Froben followed with a third edition in February 1518, which contained only the *Apologia* and a brief prefatory letter by the publisher outlining the history and nature of the dispute. A fourth edition was published by Martens in Louvain between February and 6 March 1518. This edition contained, in addition to the text of the *Apologia* and a commendatory letter from the publisher, a summary of Lefèvre's 'disputatio' together with refutations of its main points, and an

* * * * *

1 The translator's brief account of the history of the printed text of the *Apologia* is indebted to the comprehensive and detailed treatment given by Andrea W. Steenbeek in ASD IX-3 46–58.

explanatory letter by Erasmus addressed to Guillaume Budé. A fifth edition was issued twice by Froben – in November 1521 and in February 1522. Each formed part of slightly differing editions of Erasmus' apologetical writings. In each case the text of the *Apologia* was followed by an adaptation of the prefatory letter which Martens had included in the *editio princeps*. A sixth edition of the *Apologia* appeared in 1540 in volume IX of Erasmus' *Opera omnia*, published by Froben in Basel. Martens' original prefatory letter was appended, as were Erasmus' 1516 annotation on Hebrews 2:7 and Lefèvre's 'disputatio.' This sixth edition also contains a few additions to the text of the *Apologia* prepared by Erasmus prior to 1536, which make it 'the most recent edition of the apologia for which Erasmus was responsible.'[2]

The present translation is from the text of the *Apologia* in the Leiden edition (LB). It appears in volume IX, columns 17–66 (with columns 65/66 wrongly numbered 49/50) and reproduces the 1540 Froben text.

HJ

* * * * *

2 ASD IX-3 57

APOLOGY AGAINST
JACQUES LEFÈVRE D'ÉTAPLES

DESIDERIUS ERASMUS OF ROTTERDAM TO JACQUES LEFÈVRE
D'ÉTAPLES, RENOWNED PHILOSOPHER,[1] GREETINGS

My most learned Lefèvre, just when I was boarding the coach for my journey to Louvain, for I preferred to go there to live rather than accompany the Prince [Charles] to Spain,[2] one of my close friends[3] apprised me of the second edition of your *Commentaries on St Paul*, in which you have entered upon a lengthy dispute with me, and at the same time he pointed out the text in question, namely, the second chapter of Paul's Epistle to the Hebrews.[4] I was delighted to be able to secure a copy from the bookseller on the spot. In the meantime, since I never fail to take an interest whenever some new point is raised, especially if it concerns myself, I spent the journey eagerly reading your *Apologia*, though polemic would be a better term,[5] since such is the intensity and fervour with which you fight for hearth and home[6] that you are not satisfied with recovering the possessions taken from you, but carry out a raid of your own against mine; and such is your manner of protecting your forces that you do not stop at destroying my front line, but exulting in the very moment of victory you storm forward into my camp in a wild

* * * * *

1 Lefèvre was known for his commentaries on and editions of Aristotle. In October 1515, Thomas More designated him 'instaurator verae dialecticae veraeque philosophiae, praesertim aristotelicae'; E.F. Rogers *The Correspondence of Sir Thomas More* (Princeton 1947) 36.
2 Erasmus left Bruges for Louvain at the beginning of July 1517 (Ep 596), responding to an invitation from the theologians (Ep 551). He had declined the invitation of Charles v to accompany him to Spain (Ep 694:6).
3 According to Allen, it was Gerard Godfrey (Garret Godfrey) from Graten in Limburg who apprised Erasmus of the second edition (Allen Ep 777:29–30).
4 The edition dated 1515, fols 225v–229v. See ASD IX-3 206–39.
5 Erasmus contrasts *apologia* with *pugna*.
6 *arae* and *foci* (Cicero *Philippicae* 8.8)

orgy of plunder, glorying in a twin triumph, your own standards recovered
and mine captured. Still, my good sir, I read your comments not with any
feeling of anger, but, to be frank, with some regret, not because I would be
aggrieved at receiving advice, or even a rebuke, from a friend, especially so
learned and sincere a friend as yourself, but because I would have wished
that in this dispute with someone who is, as you write, a dear friend you
had behaved in a somewhat more friendly fashion, and this not so much for
my own sake as for yours, or rather for others'.[7] For I personally have no
doubt whatsoever that whether it was on your own initiative that you undertook this business or at the prompting of some other party,[8] you have
pursued it with sincerity and conviction. But, ready as most people are to
suspect the worst, there may perhaps be those who will infer that we have
been spurred on by rivalry, and they may hurl against us Hesiod's observation that 'craftsman envies craftsman,'[9] the more so since we have chanced
to light upon the same topic, and more especially since in your writing they
will read certain things expressed in a tone more bitter, more strident, and
more dramatic[10] than either the topic itself or our friendship warranted, together with some remarks, and these I shall point out in their proper place,
which go beyond the matter in hand and have all the marks of obsession.
Indeed, I am even now assured that there are some who are offended because in the section concerned they claim to find quite lacking that genuine
frankness for which you are known and for which you have so often earned
my praise, a quality which up to now has complemented your learning in
singular fashion and protected you in very large measure from that envy
which always seems to assail the highest excellence. To these people you
seem here to be a different person, and, as the saying goes, they fail to
find the craftsman in the craftsman.[11] For since in your many books to date
your pen has been free from spite and venom, they are surprised that you

* * * * *

7 The disputes between the humanists go beyond personal attacks to the very
principle of *les bonnes lettres*.
8 Was Lefèvre inspired by the theologians? Cf Ep 800:16–21.
9 Hesiod *Works and Days* 50; *Adagia* II ii 25: *Figulus figulo invidet, faber fabro*.
This citation permits Erasmus to introduce a wordplay on the name 'Faber.'
Such corporate rivalry plays into the hands of the humanists' enemies (Ep
724:9–10).
10 Erasmus uses the word τραγικώτερον, which constitutes one of the points of the
debate. For Lefèvre, the Christological debate is dramatically significant.
11 Here is a fine portrait of Lefèvre's *humanitas*. Erasmus is still playing on his
family name, Faber (see n9 above), and thinks that Lefèvre has failed to live up
to his own reputation.

should have regarded me in particular as an appropriate victim for the first stab of your pen, and that it should be with my blood that you stain for the first time the weapon of your intellect, especially since you not only have never been mistreated by me but actually have been commended on so many occasions.[12]

But since true Christian love, which Paul calls unselfish,[13] is such that it is moved more by the discomforts of one's friends than by one's own, I would rather that no excuse at all should have been given for even a single person to think the worse of Lefèvre. If in accordance with Paul's teaching we are always to keep free not only from wrongdoing but also from all appearance of wrongdoing,[14] as far as is possible, it is especially incumbent upon us when we are discussing the mysteries of the Scriptures, which should be approached by minds which are as like as possible to those which recorded them.[15] Nor is it proper that the din of human passions should obtrude where all is divine and heavenly; or fitting that we should appear less than temperate and impartial in our treatment of these Books which alone make us truly virtuous and worthy. This is something to which we of all people should have paid attention, considering our years, when to strive for the victory like young warriors in the battle[16] is a sign of bad taste, and given both the renown which your works, so many times republished,[17] have deservedly long established for your name and the more slender reputation, far greater though it is than my merits deserve, which my humble industry has lately gained for me. Both of us together, therefore, whether we wish it or not, stand at centre stage, as it were, with the eyes of almost the entire world upon us,[18] and we are well aware how scornful is the judgment of the multitude, no less so indeed than the look of the theatre-goers whom even the finest performances barely satisfy. It is all the more important, therefore, that we accommodate ourselves to the theatre in which we find ourselves,

* * * * *

12 This alludes to the controversy over Mary Magdalene.
13 Erasmus uses the Greek word ἀνυπόκριτον (Rom 12:9; 2 Cor 6:6).
14 1 Thess 5:22
15 There ought to be a sympathy between Holy Scripture and the mind of the reader (Augustine De doctrina christiana 2.7.9–11 CCSL 32 36–8).
16 Erasmus uses two Greek verbs meaning 'to show ambition' and 'to behave like a juvenile.'
17 Lefèvre's philosophical, spiritual, and, later, biblical works were republished on a regular basis; Eugene F. Rice, Jr The Prefatory Epistles of Jacques Lefèvre d'Etaples and Related Texts (New York 1974) 535–68.
18 The world of letters is also represented as a theatre. It is Lefèvre who, according to Erasmus, gave it this dramatic dimension (see n10 above, and 90).

and that we make no unseemly or juvenile slip that could get us hissed or laughed off the platform. I cannot help thinking that it would have been best if we had avoided this particular production. But since some divine will has brought us here, it remains only to accommodate ourselves to the script which we have taken on.

But you will say that it was I who provoked you by taking issue with you over so many points.[19] If disagreement amounts to insult, then I offer no defence and, however harsh may be your demand that I make amends, I have nothing to say. But if in every area of discussion there has always been room for disagreement,[20] at least in those matters which do not properly bear upon articles of faith, then it should not be counted a fault or an offence in my case either. What is more, I would have you note how I have not acted from any zealous motive;[21] to the contrary, I have been drawn in unwillingly,[22] but have acted respectfully even so. For what do you think I ought to have done, when you had already brought out your work beforehand, and when I realized that you had emended several passages wrongly, and when I was aware of the degree of authority which you commanded in the eyes of both the church hierarchy and the mass of the learned? The matter was too open to be overlooked, and your book had by this time already been published. What was I to do? Was I to allow you to be free to lead your reader into error? Was I to permit the error to become fixed? I do not think that you yourself would have recommended that, especially since the benefit given to the public would not have been at the price of any disgrace to your reputation. Indeed, to fall into error and stray on occasion in matters of this kind is so much a part of being human that no mortal has yet escaped it, except for those very few whose writings we do not scrutinize as human products but venerate as divine.[23] Again, it was not your publication which inspired me to take up this task, in case anyone should jeer that my criticisms of you were a deliberate plan. In fact, I had already completed my work and submitted

* * * * *

19 It was in point of fact Erasmus, in his *Novum instrumentum*, who had called Lefèvre's interpretation of Heb 2:7 into question, but he continues to cite the Parisian humanist frequently (ASD IX-3 87:117n).

20 This is Erasmus' typical stance on theological matters which had not been defined by the church and thus were still open to interpretation.

21 At this point, Erasmus emphasizes his scientific and even theological responsibility. He did not seek the polemic and must insist upon friendship, truth, and the public interest (ASD IX-3 84:91; 86:100, 113; see n413 below).

22 *Adagia* III ix 33: *Quod aliis*

23 Biblical commentaries do not benefit from the inspiration which underlies Scripture: they are human not divine works.

it to the printer before yours was published.[24] As soon as yours appeared,
I wondered more than once how it happened that in the many lengthy and
intimate discussions and arguments which we had at Paris there had not been
even a chance mention of what my study or yours might finally give birth
to. If I had realized at the time, I would perhaps have abandoned what I had
started, and if I had chanced to have anything prepared which might have
contributed to your work, I would have passed it on as a colleague; not that
your talent stands in need of assistance from me when it is exercised in its
own field; but the fact is that when you were engaged in those 'examinations,'
as you call them, you were out of your own arena and in territory where
I myself, however much I am inferior in other spheres, have your respect,
if I am not mistaken.[25] But now that the affair had reached this point, I
do not think that you would have demanded that so much notice be taken
of your name that in scriptural matters feeling for a friend should weigh
more heavily with me than truth itself, and that I should place the public
good lower than one person's reputation, though, as I have said, your name
was not at stake. Rather, such was my judgment of your talent and your
character that I believed that your friend Erasmus would become a dearer
friend still if with my humble work I too should have assisted the public
good for which you had taken so much care, especially since I was coming to
the aid of truth in such a way as not to harm in the slightest the reputation
of a friend, and far from slighting his reputation was adding to its lustre
wherever I could. For you know yourself, if you have read my works, what
an amicable form my disagreement with you takes: in places I hide my true
opinion, I overlook certain mistakes, I do as much as possible to excuse
and minimize others, I refrain entirely from harsh criticism and sarcastic
comment, I press no point with insistence, even though there were some
glaring errors, and though some other person, more wedded to his own glory
than to Christian tolerance, might well have abused you soundly, especially
since your pronouncements carry such great weight. Nor is this all, as you
well know. For how often do I mention Lefèvre with some expression of
honour? How often do I appeal with respect to your authority to support

* * * * *

24 Erasmus' chronology is hard to justify since he had already revealed his knowl-
    edge of the Pauline commentaries in March 1515, well before the publication of
    the *Novum instrumentum* (Epp 326:95–6, 334:173–5, 337:879).
25 This courteous assault does not mask the fact that in Paris in 1511 the two
    humanists did not tell each other about their respective work on the New
    Testament. In his *Examinationes circa litteram*, Erasmus believes himself more
    qualified than Lefèvre with respect to Greek philology.

my views? I pay to you while you are alive the kind of respect which some do not enjoy after they have died, though the grave is supposed to bring all malice to an end.[26] And I do this in some places where I have no need of the patronage of your name; for example, in the foreword to my commentary on Paul's letter to the Colossians, where, although I had demonstrated from so many authoritative sources that the Colossians to whom Paul writes were not on the island of Rhodes, I none the less added you as an authority quite gratuitously.[27] Again, in the very passage under discussion, you go out of your way to pick a quarrel with me, while I go out of my way to bring in your name with great respect. I would rather be seen leaning in this direction than the other, which for some reason has appealed to you more.

Beyond all this, take note how I have neither done nor undertaken anything in a false or deceitful fashion but have been at all times open and candid. First, when I was in the preparatory stages of my edition, and then later, when I was in the midst of composition, I wrote to you to give advance warning that in making my emendations I would in certain places take a different view from yours, though I would do so in a friendly manner. That you sanctioned my intention is clear from the fact that in your reply you repeatedly commended my efforts but made no reference to this particular aspect. Second, in a further letter, and again in a third, I gave you an account of what I had done, and assured you that wherever in your second edition you were prepared to change what I had brought to your attention, then in the next edition of my notes I would in turn omit mention of the passage; but that wherever you refused to comply, I would gladly accept your reason if it turned out that you were justified in disagreeing with me, and if the mistake was mine, I would regard your reproof as a benefit.[28] But while so many people have earnestly clamoured for your letters to me, including that excellent and noble champion of the faith Etienne Poncher, bishop of Paris, as well as the renowned dean of learning Guillaume Budé, there has been no indication at all on your part as to what you approve and what you do not.[29]

* * * * *

26 Ovid *Amores* 1.15.39
27 ASD IX-2 218:880–4. The words 'no need' and 'gratuitously' reveal the annoyance which this whole passage expresses.
28 These letters seem to have been lost, but Josse Bade, the Parisian printer who was a close friend of Lefèvre, attests to their existence (Ep 434:18). Lefèvre himself mentions them at the end of his *Disputatio* (ASD IX-3 224 Appendix IV).
29 No trace of these procedures seems to have survived. Etienne Poncher, to whom Erasmus will refer again (33), was consecrated bishop of Paris in 1503. In 1505, Lefèvre had written the preface for one of Guillaume Budé's editions.

Meanwhile, naïvely trusting that we were of one mind, I could only assume that your talents were being devoted to weightier matters. Moreover, in the matter of your second edition as well there has been a silence on all sides that is remarkable, seeing that the edition has been circulating widely now for a year and a half, and with me the only one unaware of it despite being the very person with the greatest interest in knowing of it. One could almost apply to me that well-known quip about the house being the last to know of its own disgrace.³⁰ For quite without concern and trusting that all was well, I was being made a fool of without knowing it, like someone going about with a tail pinned to his back,³¹ and would be a helpless laughing-stock even now had it not been for a certain bookseller, not a scholar but a friend, who happened quite by chance to put me in the picture.³² I assure you, I suffered the same kind of shock as those who read their names on a blacklist when they have had no inkling that a list even existed. In war, perhaps, it is a matter for congratulation to swoop swiftly upon the enemy, to overpower him unexpectedly, to take him unawares, to engage him before he has any idea that a battle is upon him.³³ But the rule in military matters is one thing, the rule in scriptural studies quite another. Anyway, the best generals do not even sanction deception against an enemy who is waging war by force of arms. Not that I would say that there has been any manoeuvring on your part; I suspect rather that we may look for the hand of someone who is less open than we are.

Yet mention of your second edition does prompt me to say that I am quite at a loss to imagine how it has happened that though my own edition was published by Froben at Basel in 1516, yours bears the date 1515. If yours came out first, or if the two came out simultaneously, how could yours cite mine? If yours came out later, in what way could it anticipate mine, when mine was already off the press? To be sure, it must have happened as a result of an error on the part of the printers; they make mistakes so frequently that they cause us to make them responsible for our own slips as well. Or it may be that someone with your interests at heart thought he should make

* * * * *

30 Juvenal *Satires* 10.342. That Lefèvre would not answer the personal letters which were addressed to him is one thing, but that he did not warn Erasmus of his attack against him, which had been circulating in print, is quite another. The words 'for a year and a half' announce the following discussion of the date when the second edition of Lefèvre's Pauline commentaries appeared.
31 Horace *Satires* 2.3.53
32 See n3 above.
33 This military analogy is taken up again, in relation to the same controversy, in a letter written by Erasmus to Fisher, Ep 784:40–2.

sure in advance that you not appear to have included in your work anything borrowed from mine. Thus, while he was conscientiously looking out for your reputation, he either did not remember or did not notice that in your edition you made mention of my earlier one.[34] But however all this may have come about is not of great importance to me. For my reputation is not so vulnerable or insecure that I would care to haggle in this fashion.[35]

As to your charge that it was I who gave you cause to keep the argument going,[36] I admit that I encouraged you to disagree freely on any point which seemed to you worthwhile, but on the understanding that your disagreement would take the same form as mine, that you would plead your case in courteous, not contentious fashion, free from sarcasm and rancour. Even if I have not always set the example despite my desire to do so, it was still your responsibility to exhibit what I could but aim for, seeing that you are so much the better person, and not only better but a little more mature in years, even though I have myself just seen my fiftieth birthday. If you thought the responsibility was shared by us, at least your sense of what is fitting, which I regard as not the least part of your reputation, required that you not only match my politeness but give more than measure for measure, in accordance with Hesiod's demand for 'better still'; nor could you excuse yourself with Hesiod's 'would that I were able,' since for you it would be the simplest matter. To be surpassed in learning and fine speaking is not always a disgrace, since these are things which are inborn; but to be bested in the things which civilized behaviour demands is a disgrace indeed, while to excel is especially fine, since here each person excels only to the extent that his mind wills it, and what is required is not ability but the right spirit.[37] Accordingly, I introduce a mention of my friend Lefèvre so that I might be seen to have sought the opportunity of honouring your name and to have been as lavish in praising you as I have been sparing in rebuke, so that it is quite clear that when I offer you advice it is out of good will, and when I take issue it is because I have no choice. So, even if through human neglect something has crept into your work which might cause me offence[38] (if Christian love allowed for such a

* * * * *

34 Steenbeek believes that the hypothesis of a pure and simple misprint is the only plausible one (ASD IX-3 60–2).

35 The Greek word used by Erasmus, μικρολογεῖν, signifies to haggle, to make a fuss about nothing (*Adagia* II x 33: *Praemansum*).

36 This is what Lefèvre claims in the final lines of his *Disputatio*.

37 Thus Erasmus gives Lefèvre a lesson in *civilitas* and *humanitas* with the aid of a citation from Hesiod *Works and Days* 350.

38 The Latin expression *nasum corrugare* comes from Horace *Epistles* 5.23.

feeling), not only do I refrain from all reproof, but as far as possible I have been careful not to blurt forth any remark which could be taken as a sign of ill feeling or malevolence on my part. But if the fact itself that your name has been mentioned at all in my books gives you offence, you may be sure that such mention shall be erased as soon as possible if you cannot endure to be named by just any writer, in the same way that Alexander refused to be drawn by any painter but Apelles or sculpted by anyone except Lysippus.[39] Perhaps the most charitable interpretation one might put on your action is that you simply sought an opportunity to honour my name by way of returning a favour. But if something like that was in fact your intent, there were so many places where I pointed out a mistake on your part, and if you have corrected them (for I have not compared more than one or two), then it was a matter of simple gratitude, not to say duty, not only to give acknowledgment but to make a special point of doing so; if you have not altered these places, though some of them ought to be changed completely, then it is either a mark of disdain not to read what concerns you, or a sign of stubbornness to refuse to correct what you know stands in need of correction. If in these places you accept my advice, why do you neither acknowledge the fact nor change them? If you reject my advice, why do you not offer a refutation of someone who disagrees with you and is correcting you openly and candidly? If it was your intention to mention Erasmus, this was the time, when the matter itself offered the opportunity. If any thanks is owed to one who either names another with respect or offers advice in a sincere and friendly fashion, there is certainly a fine reward stored up for me, while you in turn have handed on to posterity a magnificent remembrance of our friendship.[40]

Why in one place only does the name of Erasmus, a friend and more than a friend, come to your mind? Is it that I disagree with you in the one place only? Why this incessant, urgent, and persistent seeking and striving to show that the opportunity was not presented, but sought after? To come to the point, why do you fabricate a quarrel where there is no quarrel, where indeed, as I shall soon make clear, I am working on your behalf? Where you have made undeniable errors I smooth them over or cover them up altogether, while you

* * * * *

39 Apelles and Lysippus are among the greatest artists of Alexander the Great's period. The suggestion that Lefèvre might be compared with them is highly ironic.
40 Lefèvre was not generous in compliments to his contemporaries in any of his writings. Nevertheless, in his 1515 edition he had accepted a correction proposed by Erasmus concerning a note on 1 Cor 5:4, with a word of thanks (see Ep 607:2–9, and n410 below).

with your language stir up a mighty storm where there is calm. Nor do I have
any doubt that you are well aware in your own mind of my politeness. Though
I would rather my politeness go without others' recognition than risk losing
some part of their commendation by striving too earnestly to substantiate it
myself, since a good part of politeness rests in not claiming it. And I swear
by God who knows all that I would willingly have overlooked this matter
too, except that you imputed certain things too offensive for me possibly
to ignore, things which will soon be brought to light. To overlook insults
is a mark of tolerance and moderation; but there is a limit to everything,[41]
as the saying goes. To remain silent against a charge of sacrilege is itself
sacrilege. Not that you have acted with open intention; all the same, you do
cast certain aspersions which might give a less than partial interpreter reason
to think that you are making me out to be not only foolish and illiterate, but
sacrilegious as well.[42] While the first two imputations I can tolerate, the last
I do not think it right for me to ignore. There is the added disadvantage that
in this I myself cannot speak in your defence, however much I might wish to.
For if I were to begin to put too positive an interpretation on those of your
comments which seem to be rather harsh, I could not help but appear to be
deluding myself. See in what a quandary you have placed me. But, I repeat,
we shall soon demonstrate that these things are so.

Yet, my dear Lefèvre, despite the fact that I have not found this business
altogether pleasant, it has not mattered enough to cause me to change the
opinion I have always had of you as someone who is second to none in
learning and loyalty, though it has taught me that you are also human, and
made me wary of saying anything in too discourteous a fashion. You have
yielded to the passions of your supporters, and I cannot be angry with you
for that. For the highest and humblest natures alike are sometimes given to
falling into the mistake of allowing themselves to be led along by instincts not
their own. For I am well aware how many there are who are greatly devoted
to you and are bound to you as if they had sworn allegiance, and who honour
your pronouncements as though they were oracles.[43] These people, perhaps,

* * * * *

41 *Adagia* III ii 10: *Usque ad aras*
42 Erasmus mentions two of the worst accusations which could be made against a
   Christian humanist – those of illiteracy and disloyalty, which would amount to
   impiety. It is true that Lefèvre had also referred to impiety.
43 Throughout his career, Lefèvre knew how to earn the trust, esteem, and admiration of circles of disciples, whom Erasmus will call the Lefèvrites (*Fabristae*)
   further on. Some of these followers reacted very negatively to Erasmus' attacks
   upon their master in the *Apologia* (ASD IX-3 93:251n).

regard it as a crime even to disagree with you and would go so far as to offer combat to anyone who challenges what you say. Yet I am quite prepared to forgive their enthusiasm, which has its roots in love and affection. But unless I completely mistake you, I believe you are too sensible and fine a man to demand that greater deference be paid to your *Commentaries* than Augustine, Ambrose, and Jerome demanded for theirs, especially since, whenever it is a matter of enquiring after truth, you would refuse to rely upon any support which rested on human authority.[44]

Now it is time for me to reply to your *Apologia* with one of my own, which I must frame in such a way as to protect my good name by making sure that as far as is possible I do no harm to the reputation of a friend or cause him distress. Although it would be an easy matter to give an answer where there is barely any disagreement in the case, in this instance your treatise has presented me with a considerable problem, since it spreads out in all directions with loose threads everywhere, whether this is your usual custom or whether you thought it a good idea to display on this particular occasion your powers of eloquence and the richness of your style. So, since it is no small task even to review your general argument, how much more difficult it is to refute you point by point, so much do you expand and amplify every one, for each making a mountain out of a molehill, as the saying is.[45] For who would not at the outset be anticipating some magnificent tragic production when in the prologue he hears you so piously invoking the aid of the heavenly spirit, and again at the end so scrupulously bringing your prayer to a close, right up to the 'for ever and ever'?[46] Then, following the approved rhetorical procedure, for I do believe that you think you are dealing with a rhetorician, you lay out what common ground you have with your opponent and what remains in dispute, as though drawing up the battle lines on this side and that. Then, as if a capital charge were being tried before the Areopagus, you set down against each article of the charge my own words. One would think you were Demosthenes submitting evidence against Aeschines![47]

* * * * *

44 Erasmus uses the same idea, also with respect to this matter, in a letter to Budé, Ep 778:310–14.

45 *Adagia* I ix 69: *Elephantum ex musca facis*. In any case, Lefèvre's *Defensio* or *Disputatio* is much less prolix than this *Apologia* of Erasmus.

46 It is true that Lefèvre's text, which was known for its liturgical piety, ends like a prayer, but Erasmus overdoes this characteristic somewhat.

47 The Areopagus of Athens was the supreme court. Demosthenes (d 322 BC) had pleaded against Aeschines (d 314 BC), who supported Philip of Macedon.

If I may be allowed to spare the reader trouble and save myself having to spend more than the minimum of energy on this necessary but distasteful business by replying selectively and by touching upon only a few points rather than all, and those in particular which someone less favourably disposed to me than to you might turn to my discredit, you set out the crux of your case as follows: 'Our friend Erasmus does not accept my opinion in this place, nor does he approve of St Jerome's interpretation of the sixth verse of the Eighth Psalm, namely, "You will make him a little less than God, you will crown him with honour and glory."' Now I beg you, in the name of truth,[48] are you not creating, I might almost say completely fabricating, a disagreement where there is harmony, are you not stirring up a battle where there is peace, preparing a defence when nobody is summoning you to court, putting yourself on trial when there is no accuser? Read again that entire section in my *Annotations*, search it through, try to detect a single word rejecting either St Jerome's opinion or your own: I merely point out that there are two readings – St Jerome's, which you accept, and that of the Septuagint and, as some assert, of the Chaldaeans,[49] a reading which the Greek church long ago accepted, which now the Roman church follows by universal consensus, and which so many orthodox theologians of our faith accept, men distinguished and respected as much for their learning as for the holiness of their lives. I thought it legitimate, especially in 'annotations,' to rehearse the different views of different people, and I chose to introduce my own on the principle that each person should be free to make his own judgment and that nobody's opinion should be condemned in advance. For since I saw that this freedom is given to commentators and is a freedom to which St Jerome himself appeals again and again and uses to defend his own practice, I thought the same right was owed to me all the more in a work which professes nothing beyond some modest little notes which are hardly more than grammatical points, particularly since I avow not once, but again and again, that I am writing annotations not doctrine.[50] St Jerome repeatedly surveys the opinions of heretics without rejecting them or naming the author:

* * * * *

48 The expression is in Greek.
49 In his 1515 edition of the Pauline commentaries, Lefèvre had praised the eightfold Psalter of Agostino Giustiniani, which was published in Genoa in 1516, especially the Chaldaic version. A little further on, Erasmus is going to ridicule the whole eightfold collection (21). In a new Latin edition of the Psalter published in 1524, Lefèvre would still refer to the Chaldaic version, which he consulted in Felice da Prato's edition (Venice and Bamberg 1515).
50 Here is the first indication of the literary genre of Erasmus' *Annotationes in Novum Testamentum*.

let him be the first to be brought to court if it is not allowed to relate what others have thought.[51] For my part, I simply record two opinions, neither of which constitutes a heresy; indeed, both have been approved by orthodox persons. And I record them without seeking to diminish or discredit either, merely pointing out what obstacle seems to stand in the way whichever of the two readings is adopted, namely, that Jesus Christ, as far as his human condition is concerned and the manner of life he lived on earth, would seem to have been diminished not only below God, but below the angels and most of mankind as well. Then I put forward some of the arguments which have been used to remove this difficulty, maintaining throughout a neutral stance and doing for the reader what a commentator, and even more an annotator, ought to do by supplying him with the material for his own evaluation.

Therefore, not only do I not reject either of the two opinions, but contrary to your claim, I seem in fact to favour yours, in as much as I record it first and strengthen it with the authority of St Jerome, pointing out where someone might look for further elucidation, if he so wished; while the second opinion, which you do not favour, I bring forward quite on its own and without support. In fact, I am in danger of appearing at this point to have introduced your name with rather too much enthusiasm. For what was the point of naming you as the author of this opinion when I well knew that so many years ago St Jerome had translated thus from the Hebrew text and had annotated the passage accordingly in his commentaries?[52] If, that is, you credit these commentaries to Jerome, seeing that, surprisingly, you make no mention of them in your own, even though you were there most eager to teach that the reading 'than God' should be adopted.[53] For I do not believe that you are so negligent that when you were writing on the Psalms you did not take care to find out what so renowned a writer had said. In the circumstances, my dear Lefèvre, I beg you to see that you must acknowledge how wrongful your denunciations are when you are not content with claiming that I have rejected your opinion, but add the still more offensive charge that I do not approve of the Jerome interpretation when, in fact, I show it favour, or at least do not oppose it.

This, however, was not enough; you add something even more distasteful. 'Meanwhile,' you say, 'we append what Erasmus has written on this

* * * * *

51 Jerome *In Hieremiam* prologue CCSL 74 1:9–11
52 Jerome *Commentarioli in psalmos* 8 CCSL 72 191
53 In his biblical commentaries, Lefèvre is guided by the principle that Scripture ought to be interpreted in itself (*sui interpres*), and thus cites few patristic authors (Bedouelle *Quincuplex psalterium* 81–92).

passage in his *Annotations* in order that the reader may more easily understand his mind and my defence of my assertion and of St Jerome's interpretation, nay, his prophetic understanding.'[54] The result of this, of course, is that you stir up against me not only all those who are your supporters, all the Lefèvrites,[55] I might call them, but also all those who regard St Jerome's authority as sacrosanct, indeed all Christians everywhere who support a defender of prophetic understanding against an enemy. But to be a defender of St Jerome's interpretation and prophetic understanding, you must have an enemy. So in this place you make me fit the bill, even though I am as far as possible from being one.

This is the beginning of your argument, in which I think you see how little, to use your own words, you deal in friendly fashion with a friend. You make me your opponent when, in fact, I defend your opinion. For suppose, as you wish, that the only possible reading is 'You have made him a little less than God.'[56] Is it 'a little' that he descends who comes down as God to man, when human nature is by infinite degrees lower than divine nature? And, though you do not have the decency to admit it, this is the difficulty which I remove, and without insult to you, because it appeared to stand in the way of your interpretation. Yet in spite of this you make out that I am an opponent and that I impugn prophetic understanding. Having thus informed the reader of the main point of your case, you challenge and assail the separate parts of my annotation as though I had offered each one as an authoritative statement, when in fact I include some things merely in passing and, as it were, gratuitously, while others I add for the sake of argument and do not claim that they are definitive. This kind of attack may seem clever and shrewd, especially if the reader is not very well informed on the issue in question. But if the same thing happens in debates as generally happens in the lawcourts, that the one who brings a false accusation loses his suit, then my case has already been made for me.[57]

Let me now proceed to show how the rest is in line with this friendly opening. You frankly admit that I advised you that the reading in the Hebrew version was 'You have made[58] him a little less than God.' Yet you make the

* * * * *

54 This citation is taken from Lefèvre's *Disputatio* ASD IX-3 207:31–3.
55 On Erasmus' use of the term *Fabristae*, see Epp 653:15–16 and 794:39–40.
56 Here the term used is *minorasti*. Cf Jerome *Commentarius in epistolam ad Galatas* 2.4 PL 26 407D.
57 In the passage which follows, Erasmus adopts the vocabulary of a legal action, brought against him by Lefèvre.
58 *minuisti*

admission as if I had brought a charge against you. If you had been the first to point it out you could have taken the credit, and I would willingly have granted you the honour. And yet, what frankness was there in admitting something which, since it was published and known, you could not deny? Then you admit, again as if it were another charge brought against you, that what I had cited from the Jerome commentaries is indeed to be found there, except that Jerome had made the point more clearly and the reader ought to have been aware of this in passing. Here too you wish to appear not only frank, though you are admitting only what is in open print, but also polite and friendly by writing, 'This too we grant to our friend; it is a fact.' What compliment to our friendship is there in this? If you were dealing with an enemy of the faith you would have no choice but to admit as true what is undeniable. Next, you treat as a third accusation my statement that in bringing forward many arguments to support the reading 'than God' over 'than the angels' you were contradicting Aquinas.[59] Splitting my statement up, you acknowledge the one part, but plead that you were justified; the other part you deny. 'I acted properly,' you say. But who is charging that you acted improperly? No denial was called for, nor was any possible, since your published writings stood ready to contradict you. I say that you brought forward many arguments, not bad ones, with no thought of discrediting your opinion or assailing your arguments; I simply point out to the reader where he might find arguments should he desire them, at the same time declining to offer the kind of lengthy review which is not in keeping with the role of an annotator. As for the other part of your defence, you adopt a twofold stance, as lawyers do. You first deny that you contradicted Aquinas, then, on the assumption that you did, you argue that it is legitimate to do so. Now in the first place consider whether someone contradicts when he adopts a position different from someone else's without being aware of what that other person's position is. Am I to be regarded as not different from Peter just because I do not know what he looks like? Am I not to think that Plato sometimes contradicts Cicero even though he did not know what opinion Cicero would hold? To my mind, you certainly contradict Aquinas every time you hold an opinion different from his and when I see that your views do not coincide. There was no point in your straining to excuse the fact that you disagreed with Aquinas, other than that it was meant, I suspect, to win you points with his followers and to turn these same people against me. Personally, I have never held it a fault in a man to disagree with anyone,

* * * * *

59 St Thomas Aquinas does indeed comment on the reading 'a little less than the angels' in Heb 2:7; *Super epistolas S. Pauli* (Turin and Rome 1953) 361–2.

no matter how great that person's name, provided he pay a proper respect to those who deserve it; and I certainly place Aquinas among that number, first because of his learning, and second because of his holiness. You claim that at the time you had not consulted his opinion or his pronouncements on the point. This is what you say. Yet at the time you were preparing your commentaries it was of great importance for you to discover what his opinion had been, a writer who was surely not to be ignored. I myself disagree with him often, but always in a far more polite and respectful way than you imply when you say, 'Neither does Erasmus agree with him, who assails him on so many occasions,' just to make it sound more violent still.[60] It does not make sense that you should have failed to consult Aquinas on the meaning of sacred texts when it might have been of benefit to your writings.

I repeat, I had no intention of causing offence or arousing mistrust when I said that you contradicted Aquinas. Had I wished to do anything like that, I would have been more inclined to declare that you disagreed with Augustine, and Hilary too, I am sure, except that that part of his commentaries has been lost. Had I wished to heap ill will upon you, I would have added Chrysostom, and Theophylact, and all orthodox writers, with the single exception of Jerome, though even he is ambiguous; in short, the general opinion of the entire church, publicly accepted and approved through so many centuries.[61] I did none of this. I merely pointed out that just as your opinion coincided with St Jerome's, so it contradicted that of Aquinas. I mentioned that Aquinas' opinion agreed with that of Chrysostom and Theophylact,[62] except that they take the reference to be human nature in general, while he takes it to be the body which Christ assumed, only to show the reader that neither opinion was unsupported by authorities. In pressing your case against Aquinas you are prepared to see him acquitted only if you are persuaded that he made a genuine mistake and truly believed that the reading he adopted is found in the Hebrew texts. But I cannot think that Aquinas was so careless and negligent that in preparing his commentaries on this passage he failed to take note of St Jerome's interpretation or to

* * * * *

60 For the ways in which Erasmus differs from St Thomas in the *Novum instrumentum*, see *Apologia* ASD IX-3 101:394n.
61 In point of fact, Lefèvre's argument is different, because he starts from the position that the authors who do not agree with St Jerome did not know Hebrew (*Disputatio* ASD IX-3 217:350–9 and 220:457–76).
62 The passage from Theophylact recalled here is taken from his *Commentarius in epistolam ad Hebraeos* PG 125 208B–C.

search out his comment on this psalm.[63] What is close to the truth is that in this particular he attached greater weight to the general consensus among all the churches and the remarkable agreement among orthodox authorities than to Jerome's annotation derived from an unknown and foreign language, especially since Jerome indicated the reading in the Hebrew only briefly and in such a way as not to reject or impugn the alternate reading, as you strongly imply. And would that you had found Jerome's example more appealing.[64] For if you had been willing to imitate his modesty, you would have done your reputation a more proper service, my dear Lefèvre, and avoided visiting this present disturbance upon a friend.

Now if Aquinas had seen that heaven-inspired eight-part work you refer to,[65] he would perhaps have ventured to change the accepted reading; for you cite this new author, for want of a better word, with such great pomp, you might be producing an oracle delivered right from the tripod at Delphi.[66] Not that I would wish to disparage the man's zeal. By the same token, however, I would not wish to be completely overwhelmed by the weight of his authority. For as far as the usefulness of his work is concerned, there has already been published at Basel a Psalter in three languages, a timely and excellent work, in my opinion.[67] And apart from these three languages there is nothing else to turn to for assistance if something in the Psalms puzzles us.[68] For as no one is able to belittle the value of original sources, so all the Septuagint translators have always enjoyed the weightiest authority, and the church has not rejected what Jerome translated into Latin from the Hebrew, even if it is not publicly used.[69] What does it matter, then, if at some time

* * * * *

63 This sentence must be connected with the reproach made against Lefèvre of having failed to consult St Thomas when he was preparing his commentaries.

64 Lefèvre ought to have imitated Jerome and left the question open.

65 'heaven-inspired': *e caelo delapsum* (*Adagia* I viii 86: *Terrae filius*). The author is Giustiniani (see n49 above). On Erasmus' position with respect to the Dominican humanist, see Epp 878:2–3 and 906:530–1.

66 Pythia, the prophetess of Apollo at Delphi, delivered her oracles from a tripod (*Adagia* I vii 90: *Ex tripode*).

67 This is the edition of Jerome's Psalter which Erasmus published in Basel in 1516, assisted by Conradus Pellicanus. The three languages are Greek, Hebrew, and Latin, along with two other Latin versions.

68 This is rather unkind to Lefèvre, the author of the *Quincuplex psalterium*, which was published in 1509, republished in 1513, and reprinted in 1515.

69 Jerome's 'Gallican' Psalter, which follows the Septuagint, was incorporated into the Vulgate and used in the liturgy. It was therefore significant in this controversy.

you bring before us a Psalter decanted into six hundred languages? For as far as authority is concerned it does not make much difference whether you offer me a Psalter in Suevian, Gaelic, Gothic, Arabic, or Armenian.[70] As a curiosity it may have a good deal to offer, but I see hardly any profit in it, except, perhaps, that we might learn so many languages from it and be prepared to declare Christ among those peoples. Yet if we are anxious for the Christian faith to be spread and published abroad in this way among the pagans, it would be more to the point to produce a history of the Gospels or the Apostolic Letters in as many languages than to produce a Psalter. A word too about the annotations which he brings forward out of Jewish, cabbalistic, talmudic, and rabbinical authors: in the first place, they are few in number, and in the second, most of them are feeble. I shall not take the trouble to wrangle over them at length at this juncture, save only to say that whatever I have so far seen derived from Jewish apocryphal writings for the most part either is regarded as doubtful or appears insignificant and having very little relevance to our Christ. Further, a word about the man's learning. His level of proficiency in the Greek and Latin languages may be discovered from his prefaces by anyone versed in both; how proficient he is in the other languages I leave to others to judge. What point was there, then, in our reading his preface in so many languages?[71] So that we might have instant faith in his proficiency in Greek and Latin? But, you say, two brethren of his preaching community not only approve his work, but esteem it and hold it in wonder.[72] That is an argument better left on the street corner – a clear case of one scratching the other's back.[73] It would carry more weight with learned people if there were some assurance that those who have commended the work understand what they have commended. For I do not think that we should admit into the republic of learning the kind of arbitrariness that would allow this man or that to give a book a white mark or a black one just as he pleases,[74] even though he understands nothing of

* * * * *

70 See n49 above. This is an ironic and gratuitous attack upon Giustiniani, whose eightfold Psalter includes texts in Hebrew, Greek, and Arabic with a Latin introduction to each, and the two Targums (Bedouelle *Quincuplex psalterium* 215–16).

71 Giustiniani's preface (sigs Aii recto–Aiv recto) is printed in Latin, Greek, Hebrew, Arabic, and Armenian (Chaldaean).

72 The two inquisitors who granted the *imprimatur* (sig Aiv recto) were Bernardus Granellus and Gaspar de Varazzo.

73 *Adagia* I vii 96: *Mutuum muli*

74 *Adagia* I v 54: *Creta notare*

it. For what else is authority without judgment except a form of tyranny? Yet I do not condemn the zeal of your Augustine, for anyone who tries in any way at all to illuminate the Holy Scriptures deserves encouragement. Likewise, my dear Lefèvre, I admire and approve your frankness, though I do wonder why you have shown it to all but Erasmus, especially since he has been so often your friend and has been brought into this affair quite against his will.

But I have pursued these matters further than perhaps is necessary. As to your saying that it is wrong to claim that angels cannot be touched by any evils, seeing that they have been guilty of sin and are afraid of punishment, I quite fail to see what this has to do with me. As though I would compare Christ with fallen angels, or when I use the word 'evils' I am thinking of sins or punishment for sins. I am referring there to the evils to which human nature is exposed: an angel cannot die, or experience thirst, or be crucified; these examples are enough. Indeed, I repeat, I do not think that Christ is to be compared with fallen angels, but rather with those whose happiness is already assured, and of whom it has been said with perfect truth, I believe, that they cannot be touched by any evils.

Up to this point, our skirmish has not drawn much blood, but now you rush to the attack and give no quarter and spare your opponent nothing. So, in what follows, there is no truce between us, the war trumpets sound, the fighting gets bloody, I am beleaguered by weapons of every sort, and I am in desperate straits.[75] Where am I to turn? Upon whom of gods and men am I to call – helpless, defenceless, a raw recruit to this kind of warfare, when such a powerful and veteran warrior is bearing down upon me? This is no fight over a donkey's shadow, as the saying goes;[76] it is a matter of life and death, the sword is aimed at the heart, and I am scampering to save my bacon.[77] You assail my statement that the same difficulty remains whether you say 'than God' or 'than the angels' as though I have committed a great sin. What difficulty remains, you say, if it is agreed that the proper reading is 'than God'? If that reading is so widely agreed upon, my most learned Lefèvre, and if the other reading is false, impious, heretical, and contrary to divine Scripture, why aren't you persuading the Christian world of this? Why aren't you imploring the synod to erase so great an error from all the writings of

* * * * *

75 Here Erasmus takes up his military metaphor again. See n33 above.
76 *Adagia* I iii 52: *Non de asini umbra*
77 The expression is in Greek. See Liddell-Scott *Greek-English Lexicon* under κρέας.

the church?[78] Why aren't you lamenting the fate of St Ambrose,[79] St Hilary,[80] Augustine,[81] Chrysostom,[82] Theophylact,[83] in short, all the theologians, with the exception of St Jerome, in as much as they have adopted this reading throughout the ages and incorporated it into their writings and teachings? Christ, you say, was made lower than the angels neither by a little nor by much. Yet this is what is heard and repeated in all the churches, all the schools, and all the sacred assemblies throughout the Christian world. If I had rejected your opinion and adhered to this reading, I would still not have deserved your abuse simply for preferring to the unsupported annotation of Jerome the authority of the Septuagint translator, which Hilary, Ambrose, Augustine, and all theologians have long held in the highest respect, and which even the Apostolic Fathers themselves often think worth following, as does the Chaldaic edition, if this adds anything of importance, as well as the general consensus of both the Greek and the Roman world on this point, a consensus, in short, strengthened by the authority of so many centuries. If, on the other hand, I had dared to go against universal and official opinion and followed the isolated judgment of Jerome, weighty though it is on other occasions, would I have been viewed as impious? No, respectful. Certainly, St Jerome's translation and comment have not escaped the notice of the foremost men of the church, and yet they have for so many centuries chosen a different reading, and they do so publicly and in solid agreement. I fail to understand what it means that in expounding this psalm you are as insistent as if you were sounding the battle-cry and urging us forward to expunge errors from the text.[84] For I do not believe that you think this reading has been introduced into the text as a result of a copyist's error, with the consequence that it deserves to be called a corruption. Whatever the reading in the Hebrew, the Septuagint has certainly handed down 'than the angels,' and to this date the church has consistently adopted this, a thing which I think it in no way likely to have done had it not determined that both readings are free from impiety,

* * * * *

78 Erasmus is referring to a general council (called ecumenical). The Fifth Lateran Council drew to a close on 16 March 1517.
79 See 38.
80 See 19 and 39.
81 See 24–5 and 37–8.
82 Chrysostom *Enarrationes in epistolam ad Hebraeos* hom 4 PG 63 38
83 See n62 above.
84 This is what Lefèvre had asserted since 1509 in his *Quincuplex psalterium* at the end of his interpretation of Ps 8.

something which you persist in challenging.[85] Unless, perhaps, there is no impiety in speaking falsely concerning Christ in the open and in earnest, and in reciting publicly and in temples things which are diametrically opposed[86] to prophetic understanding and divine writings (which for some reason you always refer to with the unusual term 'declarations').[87] Even if there were such agreement, as you constantly maintain, that in the Hebrew version the only possible reading is 'than God,' still, if the Holy Spirit has revealed something different, either through the Septuagint translators, as most agree, or through the church, then whatever it may be I do not think it should be rejected in a hostile fashion by any Christian person. Certainly, St Jerome himself did not do so, since he indicates in only two words what the Hebrew text reads and does not condemn the Septuagint version.

But there is agreement, you say, that St Paul understood 'than God.' First of all, I cannot agree that this letter of Paul was written in Hebrew, even if the majority think so.[88] Second, if Paul nowhere follows the Septuagint edition, I shall perhaps acknowledge that it does not seem likely that he intended to follow it in this instance. However, if it is known, as it is, that in other places Paul does adopt the Septuagint version, it would not be miraculous if he had done so here, especially since in the Acts of the Apostles, in examining a passage of Isaiah with the Jews, he cites the following according to the Septuagint edition and not the Hebrew version: 'Go to that people and say to them, "You will hear with your ear and you will not understand,"'[89] and so forth. But we shall examine this more closely in its proper place. Meanwhile, let me continue what I had begun. I see no reason, my most learned Lefèvre, why you should have thought that I ought to be attacked because I make note of both readings without rejecting either; for you are able to make no other complaint against me. I favoured, as I still do, the opinion which you share with St Jerome; but at the time I decided not to accept one reading if it meant that I would be repudiating the other as impious and heretical, which it has not appeared to be to the holy teachers of the church,[90] St Augustine in particular, who does not hesitate to translate this passage accordingly. For

* * * * *

85 Erasmus is insinuating that, in any case, the church's consistent adherence to one translation saves it from the accusation of being heretical.
86 *Adagia* I x 45: *E diametro opposita*
87 Lefèvre is using the word *eloquia*, which is often repeated in the long Ps 119.
88 Erasmus calls into question the authenticity of St Paul's authorship of the Epistle to the Hebrews (LB VI 1023D–1024F; CWE Ep 1171:9–12). See also n245 below.
89 Acts 28:26, citing Isa 6:9 according to the Septuagint
90 This is a very good summary of Erasmus' position.

in case you require it, I shall cite his own words: 'Seeing that the angels too are the works of God's hand, we accept also that the only-begotten Son has been placed even above the angels, whom we have been told and believe was made a little lower than the angels through the meanness of his physical birth and suffering.'[91] Furthermore, in many places Jerome, upon whose authority alone you rely, does not hesitate to follow this reading, as when he discourses as follows on a chapter of Paul's letter to the Galatians: 'In as much as he says, "You have received me as you would an angel, you have received me as you would Christ Jesus," he shows that Christ is greater even than an angel, Christ whom the Psalmist sang was made lower through his corporeal nature, saying: "You have made him a little lower than the angels."'[92] So Jerome's authority could be refuted from Jerome himself, who devoted a mere three words to his note that the reading in the Hebrew is 'than God,' and that in a work whose authenticity scholars seriously question.[93] Yet in those works whose authenticity is not in question, the same Jerome embraces that reading which you demand be rejected as unworthy of Christ.

Meanwhile, I pass over the fact that in presenting my comments, in place of my mere statement 'The same difficulty seems to remain,' you substitute 'The same difficulty remains,' as though there is no difference between doubting or questioning, and asserting, between an inquirer and a dogmatist.[94] My procedure is to leave the reader free to choose between the two readings according to his own judgment while pointing out a difficulty which seems to defy understanding. For though it is clearly a true statement that Christ was diminished, this must be understood either with respect to his divine nature or with respect to his human nature. If the former, he was not diminished in any of those respects in which he has always been equal; if the latter, I regard the gulf which exists between the happiness which angels enjoy and the wretchedness of human existence as being considerable. For I do not think that he is said to have been diminished through assuming human form as such, but through assuming all the disadvantages of this life, a point which we shall discuss somewhat more fully in due course. You have said other things too on this point which I regard as careless, but it is not worthwhile to refute them at any length. For instance, the fact that you proceed as though I thought the problem resides simply in whether we are

* * * * *

91 Augustine *Enarratio in psalmum 8* 11 CCSL 38 54
92 Jerome *Commentarius in epistolam ad Galatas* 2–4 PL 26 407D
93 This refers to Jerome's *Commentarioli in psalmos* 8 CCSL 72 191. Cf Allen Ep 778:184 and note.
94 By citing Erasmus, Lefèvre has erased the nuance of doubt.

to read 'than God' or 'than the angels,' when I make it abundantly clear that the difficulty lies in this, namely, how the Son of God can be said to have 'been made a little lower than God' when there is no relation between the human nature, by assuming which he is said to have been made lower, and the divine nature which assumed; or how he can be said to have been 'made a little lower than the angels' when there is a considerable gulf between angels, who are immortal, and flesh, which is subject to destruction and by becoming which Christ is said to have laid aside his glory.

Furthermore, when you bring in the following, 'Who in the heavens will be equal to the Lord, who among the sons of God will be on a level with God?'[95] this does not prove, as you erroneously deduce, that the angels are *much* lower than God. For when someone is said not to be equal or on a level with another, he is not thereby *much* lower, since it can happen that someone be next to first and still be only slightly inferior. For example, someone who is thirty years of age is admittedly not equal with someone who is thirty-one, but he is not *much* behind. There remains the absurdity of the conclusion which you then draw when you say, 'It makes a clear difference, therefore, whether we read "a little lower than God" or "a little lower than the angels."' Your entire treatise abounds with little gems of this kind. For I did not say simply that it makes no difference which reading is adopted, but that the reading makes no difference in the context of the distinction between 'for a little while [*paululum*] lower' and 'a little [*paulo*] lower.' If this opinion failed to meet with your approval, it should have been refuted by stronger arguments before you brought forward a counter-opinion with such authority. But there are countless things of this kind which I must pass over if I am not to burden the reader with an excess of discussion, and if I am not to appear more interested in being clever than in being sincere.

Yet, my dear Jacques, you assault me in places in a manner which may not be altogether unjustified, but which is really too severe, if indeed your words reflect your feeling. For you condemn and reject as impious my statement that with respect to the attributes which belong to Christ as God and as man something can be predicated of Christ incarnate which need not be predicated of him in his other form. Indeed, in this regard you rehearse many things concerning the essential oneness of the substance of Jesus Christ. Yet I cannot be persuaded that you think so poorly of Erasmus as to believe I am so dull-witted or ignorant that I have never read in the theologians that Jesus Christ is one person, the same as God and man; and that while he has certain attributes

* * * * *

95 Inspired by Ps 89:7

by reason of his divine nature and others by reason of his human nature, yet they are predicated of him under either title, on account of the oneness of his hypostasis (if you allow me to employ the expression), to the extent that he may be called God when he is said to have wept, and sorrowed, and died, and been crucified as the Lord of glory, and in turn may be called man when he is said to be equal to God the Father.[96] Even if the holy Doctors Jerome, Hilary, Ambrose, and Augustine had not taught me this, I would certainly have learned it from the third book of the *Book of Sentences*, a work as widely published as any, unless perhaps you think that I have never read it.[97] So, you judge me to be exceedingly ill informed if you believe that I have failed to learn what every neophyte in theology knows. Moreover, you regard me as exceedingly impious if you believe that despite my awareness of all this I wish to undermine the oneness of the person or hypostasis which is Jesus Christ. If you do not believe this, why do you go on wrangling at such length and assailing me in almost theatrical fashion? We refute you, you say, and the same again a little later. Accordingly, if I were to ignore the consensus of the divine Scriptures and the understanding of the spirit, and in that passage in Psalms were to take the words 'Son of Man' and what the passage itself says to refer to Christ incarnate and not to his substance, I would be acting irrationally, which must be avoided at all costs.

I have no doubt that upon reflection you are not so pleased with the things you said as when your first enthusiasm and eagerness for writing prompted them. For it is only human that the things which spring to mind as we are writing have a great attraction as the offspring, as it were, of our genius; for it is not given the same person to be both parent and critic. In the first place, I was at that point not engaged in declaring the reasons for what I was saying, and although I realize that in divine matters one should speak scrupulously and with due care, I do not think that one should use a contrived and affected manner, especially in discussion with you, who generally despise that kind of sophistical language and logical hair-splitting.[98] Yet you must have understood clearly enough from what had gone before what I meant when I said, 'Aquinas takes this passage to refer to the humanity of Christ, who was made lower than the angels not with respect to his spirit but with respect to the bodily form which he

* * * * *

96 This is what Christology calls the 'exchange of idioms' (*communicatio idiomatum*): in theological and liturgical terms, one can speak of either divine or human attributes when referring to Christ, the Incarnate Word. The epithet 'Lord of glory' is reminiscent of 1 Cor 2:8.
97 The reference is to Peter Lombard's *Sententiae*.
98 λογομαχίας (1 Tim 6:4)

assumed.'[99] Now a little further on I use a different expression, and instead of saying that the passage 'is taken to refer to the humanity of Christ,' I say that it 'is understood of Christ incarnate.' For what else does the expression 'Christ incarnate'[100] denote if not the humanity of Christ, so that we may sometimes employ the term 'humanity' if it helps to make the matter clearer? What else is understanding the passage in the psalm to pertain to Christ's humanity than, as we have said, taking it mentally to refer to Christ's humanity? If you are determined not to allow me to speak in this manner, why were your ears not offended earlier, when I say 'is taken to refer to Christ's humanity'? For to say, 'Christ's humanity was made lower than God,' is in no way more proper than to say, 'Christ incarnate was made lower than God.'

To take another point, when we ascribe something to one or the other of Christ's natures, we do not do so as though this were his only nature, but with the understanding that it is joined, or rather united 'substantially,'[101] with his other nature (if I may speak in this way for the time being). Yet in ascribing various things to the same Christ we do focus upon them each in a different way without at all dividing his oneness into several parts, but by virtue of the diversity of his attributes we do not always refer to his same aspect. For example, Nepotianus, with respect to one and the same Heliodorus, loved him as his uncle, revered him as a bishop, and followed him as a monk, not making several persons out of one, but isolating different aspects of the one man.[102] Why then are we prevented from making a pronouncement concerning one or the other of Christ's natures just because the same thing applies to him taken as a whole? Come now, I ask you, would anyone's ears be offended if I were to say, 'Christ's humanity has taught us to despise the affairs of man, his divinity will raise us up to things eternal'? Or again, 'From Christ incarnate let us learn humility and endurance, from Christ divine let us hope for life eternal'? Indeed, by the same token, what prevents us from using something which belongs to Christ as a whole to apply to one or other of his hypostases separately (for Augustine has employed the word 'hypostases' in this context)?[103] For example, 'The body of Christ was afflicted with blows for our sins, the spirit of Christ sorrowed for our misfortunes, the

* * * * *

99 See n59 above.

100 *homo assumptus*, an expression of which Lefèvre disapproves. See *Disputatio* ASD IX-3 209:95.

101 ὑποστατικός

102 Nepotianus would venerate his uncle Heliodorus, Jerome's friend. See Jerome Ep 60 CSEL 54 548ff.

103 *substantiae*. See Augustine *De Trinitate* 2.11.20 CCSL 50 107:4–20.

divine nature of Christ conquered death.' I think that I will have spoken with no less piety, and perhaps more succinctly, than if I were to say, 'With respect to his body Christ was afflicted, with respect to his spirit Christ sorrowed, with respect to his divine nature Christ conquered death.'

Nor should anyone distress you by saying 'Christ incarnate' rather than referring to his 'humanity' or 'his taking on human form,' since common usage by Latin writers lends approval to this mode of expression, the church does not hesitate to employ it ceremonially, and the holy Doctors do not reject it. For why should we say, 'He assumed Man,' and equally 'He laid aside Man,' in place of, 'He began to be a man,' and 'He ceased to be a man'? I admit that 'Christ is humanity' is not a suitable expression, since 'a man' would be more correct, on the ground that 'humanity' is the designation of his nature, while 'man' is that of his substrate,[104] this being a word which more recent theologians favour, though unheard of among the older ones. You, it appears, are extremely fond of the term 'hypostasis,'[105] a word which was mistrusted long ago by Jerome through hatred, I think, of the Arians, with whom it seems to have originated. But you will find the term 'man' frequently used by the most approved writers in both senses. For example, 'Christ as man is the son of the Virgin' or 'Christ as man is mortal,' as well as 'Christ as man assumed,' meaning 'Christ in his human nature.' As well, there is the ecclesiastical chant 'You are ready to assume man in order to set him free.'[106] What St Augustine says in book two, chapter six of *On the Trinity* is even more straightforward: 'As the Son of Man was assumed . . .,' meaning, as his human form was taken up.[107] If 'Son of Man' is the name of Christ, then St Augustine has clearly committed what you regard as a sacrilege by employing it of Christ in one form rather than of his substance. St Augustine again, in his third epistle to Volusian: 'Likewise, certain persons demand to be given an explanation how God was so joined to man as to become the one person of Christ.'[108] Has he not said 'man' in place of 'human nature'? Again, in epistle fifty-seven: 'For on the very day he was about to be in heaven, the man Christ Jesus did not . . .'; did he not say 'the man Christ,' meaning 'Christ in his human form'? And a little later in the same letter: 'It remains to know, therefore, whether it was of Christ as man that it was said, "Today

* * * * *

104 *suppositum*
105 'hypostasis': the word was canonized by the Council of Chalcedon in 451.
106 This citation is taken from the *Te Deum*, which had been attributed to Ambrose and Augustine since the ninth century.
107 Augustine *De Trinitate* 2.6 CCSL 50 93–4
108 Augustine Ep 137 CSEL 44:15–16

you will be with me in paradise.' '[109] Furthermore, the expressions 'as man' and 'as God' are found again later in the same work. And this manner of speaking has been given such formal acceptance among theologians that you will scarcely find them speaking otherwise.

Yet all that we have argued so far has no real bearing upon my meaning, since in the place in question it was not Christ incarnate that I called the human form in Christ as much as the very assuming of human form itself. And I think that this manner of speaking is recognized by all those who know Latin. I shall give an example to clarify what I mean. If someone praises another because he has acted wisely, and some other person explains this to someone else who does not quite understand it, and says, 'He has in mind the war that has been averted,' he does not mean that the averted war is wise, but that the praise for wisdom which he was granting him was rooted in the fact that he had avoided war. Again, when we say, 'He complains at the emptied flagon,' he is not finding fault with the flagon itself but with the emptying of the flagon. Again, 'The lost book pains him,' meaning 'The losing of the book pains him.' So when the Prophet says, 'Christ was made lower than God,' I point out that this making lower was nothing other than the taking on of human nature. And it was in this manner that St Jerome spoke in his interpretation of chapter 4 of Paul's Epistle to the Ephesians when he said, 'Thus we confess one Son of Man and God, lest by believing in part the dispensation of Christ incarnate, by which we have been saved, we cut it off in part.'[110]

I think that it has been sufficiently proved that there is nothing in my words to offend pious ears in any way. Yet even if I had said something too candidly or with too little caution, it was not in keeping with your usual fairness to attack me with such a storm of abusive language, especially since I was writing only annotations; for, as Hilary neatly put it, 'What is meant, not what is said, should bear the blame.'[111] Besides, consider how many things we could find in the works of Ambrose, Jerome, Augustine, and Gregory[112] which one could cavil at on those grounds. For, to give but one example, who now would be prepared to tolerate it if someone were to declare that there is a mingling or a joining together of natures in Christ? Yet how many times does Augustine do this in his third epistle to Volusian? 'How God is mingled with man,' he says. And again, 'In that person there is a mingling of soul and

* * * * *

109 Ie Augustine Ep 187 CSEL 57 84:13–14 and 85:13–14
110 Jerome Commentarius in epistolam ad Ephesios 2.4 PL 26 531D
111 Hilary De Trinitate 7.38 CCSL 62 305:13–14 (this is not a literal citation)
112 The four Doctors of the Latin church, the fifth one being St Leo

body, in this a mingling of God and man.' And below, 'For when the Word of God has been joined to a soul having a body, it takes on both the soul and the body at once.' And yet again a little further on, 'And for this reason it ought to be easier to believe in the intermingling of the Word of God and a soul than of a soul and a body.'[113] Would it not be unfair to create a commotion over the use of the word 'mingling' when we understand that Augustine's meaning was correct, even if he used the word 'mingling' instead of 'union'? If the theologians of old spoke rather clumsily, there are some today who speak perhaps too subtly, while the clumsiness is in their lives and understandings. Unless perhaps we idolize the man who is particular and sophistical and similar to certain people the likes of whom nobody cares to do business with, the kind of person one finds it almost impossible to mention without giving offence and without being taken to task. For those who are truly pious it ought to be a simple matter to agree in matters of terminology as long as there is no dispute over substance, especially since St Hilary also allows more than once for the fact that human discourse is inadequate for explaining the sublimity of things of this kind;[114] the older commentators do not quibble over terms in this way, and even today there is far from total agreement on them among theologians. Augustine, in his commentaries, had called Christ 'a divine man,' an expression which he later corrected and avoided.[115] If this happened to so great a man as he, then in my case you should have offered instruction rather than criticism, especially since mine was an incidental slip and you knew all along what in fact I meant. For with respect to the hypostasis of Christ my position is no different from yours. I would have been prepared to overlook even something which really did deserve criticism.

Let us pass on to other matters. You say that the point at issue between us is not, to quote your own words, 'whether Christ as servant, or Christ incarnate, was diminished in comparison with God to a small degree or to a large degree, but whether the Son of Man was diminished in comparison with God even to the slightest degree.'[116] You are quite correct. There was certainly no dispute between us on this. I did not say that Christ incarnate was diminished in comparison with God. The claim is yours, as I have pointed out time enough. For if you regard the word 'diminished' as an element in the

* * * * *

113 Augustine Ep 137 CSEL 44 110:16–18
114 Hilary *Liber de Patris et Filii unitate* PL 10 885A–C
115 Augustine *De sermone Domini in monte* 2.6.20 CCSL 35 110 and *Retractationes* 1.19.8 CCSL 57 59–60
116 *Disputatio* ASD IX-3 210:120–4

verb, then it is the divine nature, which came down to man, that can better be
seen as having been diminished than human nature, which was raised up into
partnership with the divine. However, if you regard it as an adjective and
as the equivalent of 'lower than God,' then I am sure you will admit that the
human nature which Christ assumed was far inferior to his divine nature. If
you grant this, then it follows that Christ, to the extent that he was a man, was
far inferior to God the Father, indeed, as Augustine goes so far as to say, was
'far inferior to himself as God.'[117] Now if he was far inferior, it would seem
right to reject the Prophet's statement that he was 'just a little diminished.'

Again, if you grant that human nature, in so far as it is subject to sorrows
and death, is far beneath the greatness and blessedness which belongs to the
angels, then it follows that Christ, to the extent that he was a man and subject
to the misfortunes which afflict a mortal nature, was to some degree inferior
to the angels, at any rate with respect to his body. If this is true, the two
readings pose an equal problem, which I attempt to resolve for you by taking
the Greek words βραχύ τι to pertain not to the degree of greatness but to
the length of time. If we accept this, and several distinguished and orthodox
theologians have done so, there will be nothing incongruous arising out of
either reading, and you will have an open choice as to which of the two
you prefer to adopt. In this I am not forcing an opinion on anyone, nor
am I approving or rejecting this opinion or that, as you repeatedly accuse
me of doing. 'Alternatively,' you say, 'there is the secondary reading, which
Erasmus seems to approve, namely, "You have made him a little lower than
the angels."' And again, 'For according to the Septuagint version he says,
"You have made him a little lower than the angels," a reading which Erasmus
also approved.'

Now it seemed to me that, when the words βραχύ τι, if taken as referring
to a measure of time, could solve all difficulty, you were acting with too
little prudence in claiming a triumph and in taunting me as though such a
reference was impossible. Yet with what success you later try to attack my
position we shall soon see. Certainly, since you had left this point up in the
air, there was no reason for you to hurl at an opponent who was already
lying virtually prostrate at your feet such taunting comments as 'since the
Prophet will be undermined in one way or the other, whether we read "than
God" or "than the angels," this opinion of Erasmus destroys itself and shows
itself false in every part.' Then you make a great commotion over my writing
that 'Christ, both on account of the human form which he assumed and on

* * * * *

117 Augustine *De Trinitate* 1.7 CCSL 50 45–6

account of the disadvantages of the human condition, was made lower not only than the angels but even than the lowliest of men.' And at this point you say with remarkable arrogance, 'We shall refute this opinion with vigour as heretical and most unworthy of Christ and God, as contrary to the spirit and adhering to the letter which destroys.'[118]

Your remarkable and friendly treatise contains many things of this sort, my dear Lefèvre, which forced me to take steps to clear a reputation which you have so savagely attacked. I hope that I may be prevented from knowingly paying you back in kind. But if through human weakness I let slip anything out of keeping with the teaching of Christ, it was your responsibility to give friendly advice to a friend in error. As it is, you wanted everyone to be made aware of these things before me, to whom you did not think fit to give so much as a hint, either by letter or through some close friend. Yet the bishop of Paris, when he was fulfilling a commission here on behalf of his king, mentioned in conversation that he had heard from you that although you admitted to having received sound advice from me on many points, you were preparing to take issue with me in print over several others.[119] But if the publisher's inscription is correct, your work had already been issued.[120] Now I could easily allow myself to be charged with ignorance, or error, or any human failing, but to be accused of heresy, irreverence towards God, and other such things is something which I cannot endure, nor should I have to. I shall make sure that mine appears 'the voice of Christian modesty, not resentment,' as Cyprian said with an elegance equal to his piety.[121] For the present, I shall be satisfied to have cleared myself of the charge of so enormous an impiety. I shall not trade mud for mud, but be happy enough to have washed it off myself. I shall avoid being arrogant; otherwise, in the process of removing one stain I should gain another, and by giving insult for insult make the insult seem justified. I thought that it would redound to the glory of Christ if I stressed as much as possible the lowliness which he assumed of his own accord for our sakes. Paul, after all, went so far as to say that Christ 'made himself desolate' [*exinanivit semetipsum*],[122] and the

*****

118 Citations from Lefèvre's *Disputatio* ASD IX-3 210:137–40, 144–5, 146–8, 132–6. Here, 'heretical' is a translation of *impium*. It is the only accusation which Erasmus cannot endure. Cf 34 below.
119 Etienne Poncher. See n29 above.
120 See n34 above.
121 Cyprian Ep 59 CSEL 3 part 2 679
122 Phil 2:7. This hymn in the letter to the Philippians (Phil 2:6–11) arises frequently in Lefèvre's commentary. It will be cited later on by Erasmus in support of his argument. See 36.

Prophet called him 'a worm,'[123] or, as some, among them Ambrose, translate, 'a beetle';[124] and he is so depicted by Isaiah,[125] and in the Gospel when Christ himself says, 'Foxes have their dens, and the birds of the sky their nests, while the Son of Man has nowhere to rest his head.'[126] Elsewhere too he compares himself with a mustard-seed buried in the ground,[127] and there are many other expressions of this sort which make clear to us the extreme lowliness of Christ. I repeat, whatever stress is laid upon this serves only as testimony to the unspeakable love which he had for us.

Nor do I think, as you seem to conclude, that Christ was lower than God in every way, or that he was lower than angels or men in the sense of being worse than they; rather, that he was lower in some respect. Certainly, he seems to have descended and cast himself down far below the angels to the extent that he took on a body and a soul that were subject to death and torture and pains. If this opinion is 'heretical,' if it is 'most unworthy of God and Christ,' if it 'clings to the letter which destroys,' as you declare, then I confess my error. It is what I have believed up till now, though I shall be prepared to change my view when I have been instructed in a better one. Further, in that the Son of God was not content simply to take on our nature, but took upon himself almost all the misfortunes of this life – toil, pains, sweat, hunger, thirst, tears, weariness, insults, bonds, whippings, and the cross – misfortunes which most men escape, even though they might deserve them, he seems to me to have descended to some degree far below even the lowest of men; and not because he ceased for a while to be the highest and most blessed, but because as a man he took these misfortunes of ours upon himself of his own accord. You may pile up as many illustrations of Christ's dignity as possible; there is no point in my trying to refute you.[128] The amount of space required to note down all the things which demonstrate the sublimity of Christ would be enormous, and on the other side, to recount all those which testify to his lowliness, or, as St Paul expresses it, his desolation.[129]

* * * * *

123 Ps 22:7
124 Ambrose *Expositio evangelii Lucae* 10.113 CSEL 32 part 4 498 and *Expositio psalmi 118* verse 3 (Vulg) CSEL 62 45. Cf *Apologia* ASD IX-3 117:777n.
125 This undoubtedly refers to the songs of the Suffering Servant in Isa 42 and following.
126 Luke 9:58
127 It is not Jesus himself who is described thus, but the kingdom of heaven (eg Matt 13:31) or the faith (Matt 17:19).
128 On the principle of dignity in Lefèvre's hermeneutics, see Bedouelle *Lefèvre d'Etaples* 207–10. See 37 below.
129 See n122 above.

You know that there are several places in the Scriptures which proclaim for us the boundless excellence of the Word of God; but if there were far more even than these, we could still never comprehend in speech or thought his loftiness. There are countless places as well which make exceedingly plain the low estate into which the Divine Word[130] cast himself down for our sake, and this role too it is beyond the power of any human mind to fathom and any human thought to grasp. Yet though Christ is wondrous in both these respects, I am inclined to think that it is the latter which has more relevance for us, in as much as wonder at his greatness seems to bear more upon the life to come. You prefer to extol the sublimity of Christ; someone else may prefer to contemplate the lowliness which he assumed; and though it would be difficult to say whose zeal is more pious, it is the latter perhaps from which more profit is to be gained for the present.[131] Moreover, I am inclined to think that Christ himself would prefer that we concentrate upon that aspect of himself which he exhibited for us most, waiting to display the glory of his majesty for the time to come. St Paul, certainly, takes pride in knowing only Jesus Christ the crucified,[132] that is, not the Christ who was raised on high, but Christ in his humble state. I do not suggest that in this regard you will be an enemy of St Paul because he looks upon Christ in this way, or St Paul an enemy to you because you are held rather by wonder at Christ's sublimity. Both of you revere one and the same Christ, each from a different perspective. You on your part, in admiring Christ's loftiness and majesty, do not shut out the praises of his lowliness; Paul on his, by focusing upon Christ's humbleness, takes nothing away from his sublimity: both things belong to Christ through his divine nature, in which he was always God, and through his human nature, which he thought it worthy to assume for a while. Others before me, men of proved holiness and learning, have not hesitated to say that Christ was accorded a nature lower than that of the angels through assuming a body subject to anguish and death, and you are the first and only

* * * * *

130 *sermo divinus*. In his 1516 edition of the *Novum instrumentum*, Erasmus had modified the famous opening of the Gospel according to John by replacing *Verbum* in 'In principio erat Verbum' with *Sermo*. Confronted with the general outcry which ensued, he had to defend himself and retreat to the traditional translation in subsequent editions.

131 Christology will always exhibit two tendencies, one more sensitive to the divine nature of Christ as Lefèvre is, and the other to his human nature. According to Erasmus, however, the most pious approach and that which is most faithful to the gospel is not necessarily the one which exalts his 'sublimity,' a term which recurs several times.

132 1 Cor 2:2

person to be in disagreement with them, except that in their case, though you are willing to allow that they have made a slip, you do your best to excuse them, while abusing me savagely, even though the case is similar, not only because I have dared to say the same thing but also because I have added, 'He was made lower than even the lowliest of men.'[133] This remark seems to have given you real offence, as though it detracted from Christ's loftiness, when in fact it makes his sublimity all the greater by exalting the goodness and wisdom which make him great in our eyes no less than does his power.

You protest that Christ as the Son of God is greater by infinite degrees than every creature. Though I would myself admit and hold to that, I do say that the same Christ as son of the Virgin at one time descended for our sake to a condition inferior to that of the angels; and not only this, but that he descended to a condition inferior even to that of many men, since he took upon himself not only a nature that was subject to thirst, hunger, weariness, insults, pains, and death, but also so many of the injustices of human life; in short, he took upon himself the penalties of our sins. Moreover, it is St Paul who gives me the confidence to speak in this way, for he seems to point to such levels in Christ in his Epistle to the Philippians when he says, as an example of Christ's humility, 'When he was in the form of God he did not think it robbery to be equal with God, but made himself desolate by taking on the form of a servant, was made in the likeness of a man, and being found in fashion as a man . . .'[134] To this point Paul shows that Christ descended below the angels; but he goes on to reveal that Christ lowered himself even below men: '. . . he humbled himself and became obedient unto death, even death on the cross.' Few men humble themselves to the point of death, fewer still, death on the cross. You so love Christ that you refuse to accept that he was cast down any more than a little, and only below God; but Paul says that he was 'made desolate,' an expression which allows us to understand immediately that he was cast down a great way. Then, by employing the word 'exalted,' Paul admits that Christ humbled himself to the greatest degree possible: 'On account of this God exalted him and gave him the name which is above every name.' He was exalted to the extent that nothing could approach his divine glory; he was humbled to the extent that nothing could reach so low; yet truly he was humbled and truly he was exalted. If someone humbles himself, he casts himself down; and he who has been humbled is at some

* * * * *

133 *Disputatio* ASD IX-3 210:132–6
134 See n122 above. Erasmus contrasts 'desolate' (Phil 2:7) with 'exalted' (Phil 2:9) and demonstrates that the two terms are linked (see 41). The entire passage gives the impression of a theological and remarkably spiritual inspiration.

point lower, otherwise he will not be said to have been humbled; and if he is said to have been humbled for this reason, namely, because like a servant he has been obedient unto death, even death on the cross, and has stooped to receive those afflictions which no one among mortals has suffered, or could perhaps suffer, then what impiety is there in saying that Christ degraded himself below even the lowliest of men? Poverty is a heavy burden, yet he was willing to be the poorest of all. Pain is harsh, yet he took upon himself the severest tortures. Death is the most painful of things, still more death at the hands of others and such a death as his, yet he took this too upon himself. More bitter still than death is disgrace, yet he was willing to be spit upon and be showered with insults. To the extent that he took on human form, he was on a level with other men; to the extent that he was poor, that he lived in dire hardship, he was beneath many men; in being mortal, he was equal with us; in choosing to die such a death on our behalf, he cast himself down beneath the great mass of mankind. All of this in no way detracts, I am convinced, from the dignity of Christ, in which he is equal with the Father, any more than his willingness to endure extreme tortures in mind and body takes away from his happiness or, as some express it, his enjoyment of blessedness.[135] Assuredly, we do not regard Christ as unhappy because he was willing to do without the advantages which the mass of mankind takes as the criteria of happiness, because he was prepared to suffer the misfortunes of our state and tolerate those things by which we measure unhappiness, even if these are the things in which your Aristotle places the greater portion of happiness and its opposite.[136]

Now since most recent commentators relate the humiliation or desolation of Christ to his assuming human nature, not to the pains which he took upon himself,[137] you may object perhaps that I have added this latter point with absolutely no authority but my own. In case you do, I would have you recognize that Paul himself makes a clear distinction between the form which Christ took on and the misfortunes which he suffered, not only in the passage which we have just cited, but also in the Epistle to the Hebrews, when he says, 'But we shall see Jesus, who was made a little lower than the

* * * * *

135 According to St Thomas Aquinas, the Incarnate Word never lost its beatific vision of the Father – *visio Dei* or *beatitudo*. Here, Erasmus is referring to *beatifica fruitio*. The term *fruitio* is Augustinian, but it was also used by Aquinas.
136 Here and further on, Erasmus refers to Lefèvre's work on Aristotle. The doctrine mentioned here resembles that of the *in medio stat virtus*. On Aristotle's conception of happiness, see the *Nicomachean Ethics* 1.7.8.
137 See eg Peter Lombard *Sententiae* book 3 dist 6 c 6.

angels, crowned in glory and honour on account of the death which he suffered'; and a little further on, 'For in that he was tempted and suffered he can help those who also are tempted.'[138] You hear mention here not of his nature, but of his suffering. Further, if one were to examine with particular care the interpretation of St Ambrose, one would discover that he too relates Christ's humiliation not simply to the nature which he assumed but also to the abuses of this nature which he sustained. Witness what he says in commenting on the passage which I cited a little earlier: 'Christ, therefore, knowing himself to have the form of God, showed himself equal with God, but in order to proclaim the way of humility he not only did not resist when the Jews arrested him, but debased himself, that is, withheld his power so as to appear weak and helpless in his humiliation, taking on the form of a servant while he was seized and bound and whipped; and making himself obedient, even unto the cross, to the Father, with whom he knew he was equal, he did not claim his equality but subjected himself. He teaches us to imitate this endurance and humility so that we may not only not place ourselves ahead of our equals but also lower ourselves following the example of our maker.' And a little later on he says: 'Christ is said to have assumed the form of a servant while he was humiliated like a sinner. But servants are made so because of their sins, like Ham, the son of Noah, who was the first to deserve the name of servant.'[139] In all of this you hear Ambrose unequivocally agreeing with me. He stresses the humiliation of Christ in order to make clearer the model which Christ held before us in himself and which he expressly commanded us to follow when he said, 'Learn from me that I am meek and humble in heart.'[140]

In wanting Christ to have been humiliated to only a small degree you are, I think, a man of compassion who would not wish for him a harsher treatment. What follows in Ambrose makes it clearer still that he agrees with me. 'I do not think,' he says, 'as others do, that Christ received the form of a servant simply by being born a man.'[141] I have related the diminution of Christ both to his assuming human form and to the abuses he suffered in this human life; Ambrose is prepared to relate it solely to the latter. St Augustine, though he seems to focus more upon Christ's assuming human form, none

* * * * *

138 Heb 2:9 and 2:18
139 Erasmus is referring in this passage to Ambrosiaster, a name which he himself proposed when he called into question the attribution of these Pauline commentaries to Ambrose (Ambrosiaster *In epistulam ad Filippenses* 2 CSEL 81 part 3 140).
140 Matt 11:29 (with a variant provided by Erasmus: 'that')
141 See n139 above: CSEL 81 part 3 140.

the less adds mention of his suffering when he says, 'We have heard and we believe that Christ was made a little lower than the angels through the humiliation of his mortal birth and suffering.' By 'mortal birth' he means his assuming human form, by 'suffering' he means the abuses which this form sustained. A little earlier he says, 'On account of the weakness of the flesh, which the wisdom of God thought it right that he should bear, and on account of his humiliation through suffering, it is rightly said of Christ, "You made him a little lower than the angels." '[142] Again he links together the form which Christ assumed and the affliction which he suffered, and his 'humiliation,' which you wish to be called his exaltation, he equates with his suffering.

Now I do not deny that Christ's humiliation is a mark of his glory; as Hilary said, 'Christ's humiliation is our nobility, his abuse is our honour.'[143] Do you see that on this point I enjoy the support of illustrious writers? Even if I were completely without their support, I do not think it a crime to have suggested something new, especially since it could reasonably be inferred from the words of St Paul and contributes to Christ's glory, not his abuse, and to our salvation, not our destruction. Accordingly, if I have demonstrated support for my opinion, I do not think it right that you should take offence at my saying that Christ 'degraded himself below even the most worthless of men.' Perhaps the word 'degraded'[144] has the ring of abuse. Yet when commentators have employed terms like 'descended,' 'humiliated,' 'diminished,' 'inferior,' 'lesser,' and St Paul 'desolated,' why should 'degraded' or some similar word offend us? Nor do I believe that you are so inexperienced in the Latin language as to think that the terms 'worthless' and 'degraded' are applied only to those who are subjected to misfortunes through their own fault. For when Ovid says, 'however worthless and inferior to you I may be,' he is not finding fault with his own conduct, but making known his harsh and grievous lot.[145] I beg you, therefore, not to imagine that I or any Christian has sunk to such a degree of impiety, nay madness, as to ascribe imperfection, unworthiness, or disgrace to Christ, and in terms of conscious misdeeds to compare him with the most worthless, that is, the wickedest, of men. Do we not call the burdened poor despised and worthless in the eyes of the world, and are they not to some

* * * * *

142 Augustine *Enarratio in psalmum 8* 11 CCSL 38 54
143 Hilary *De Trinitate* 2.25 CCSL 62 61:16–17. Erasmus is referring to the use which Lefèvre makes of John 12:32; *Disputatio* ASD IX-3 214:253–4.
144 *dejicere*
145 Ovid *Tristia* 5.8.1–2

extent truly lowly and worthless? When I compare Christ with worthless men it is because he was worthless in this same way, except that their suffering is often brought upon them through necessity, while his was borne willingly on our account. I do not compare him with thieves, but with martyrs. And even if I were to compare him with the thieves who were with him, because he suffered more undeservedly than they, since they were not abused, even though their offences were real, while he suffered insult upon insult despite his innocence, I do not think that I would be guilty of impiety.

Now you protest that the things which Christ took willingly upon himself are not evils, and render him not worse, but better. And you openly desert your Aristotelians for the Stoics on this point when you say, 'If we were to ask the philosophers whether a man who knowingly and willingly subjected himself to beatings, wounds, and even death itself in order to secure victory and safety for his people would be considered brave, or rather inferior and more worthless, without any doubt they would say that it increased his stature and made him far more worthy of honour.'[146] You would argue likewise in the case of martyrs. Now first of all, it makes no difference to me to what class of evils those belong which, according to your Aristotle, prevent a man from attaining true happiness;[147] it is sufficient for me that they belong to some class. Socrates was in no way a worse man when he was drinking the hemlock and wearing chains in the prison than when he stood in all his brilliance in the market-place,[148] though I admit that in the former state he was to some degree degraded and in the latter raised up and held in honour. If some king were to clothe himself in a beggar's rags and submit willingly to starvation, exile, or prison in order to serve his state, would one not be right in saying that he laid aside his royal privilege and lowered himself beneath even the most worthless of men? But, you say, he is greater through the very fact that he has sunk to these depths. Yet if you so much as admit that he has sunk, then by this token you must admit that he has become inferior. The truth is that in one respect he is inferior, in another better and more distinguished. If you focus upon his lot and his suffering and compare these with his former glory, then he has debased himself considerably; if you focus upon the excellence of his spirit, he is far better than his former self. In the case of the martyr, in as much as he offers his neck at a ruler's command and yields himself up to a tyrant, he is below

* * * * *

146 *Disputatio* ASD IX-3 214:261–4. The Stoics emphasized the nobility of man when subjected to testing.
147 See n136 above.
148 *Adagia* I viii 15: *Aureus in Olympia*

him, but in devotion he is far above. And just as the martyr humbles himself to tortures through love of Christ and following Christ's example, so like Christ he is crowned with glory and honour,[149] since he who has been Christ's ally when he was cast down is his companion when he has been raised up and received his kingdom.

Now, in fact, we have never spoken of Christ as worthless, or more worthless, as you keep repeating at this point in your argument, nor does anyone reproach him with worthlessness, something which is the habit, as you say, of the unbelievers and the Jews. To the contrary, we admire and applaud the fact both that he was raised up above all things and that he cast himself down as he did for our sake. In the one we see what we must imitate, in the other what we may hope for. We adore him sitting on high at the right hand of the Father, and we adore him crying in the cradle; we adore him when he was spit upon, we adore him when he was condemned to an infamous sentence; we adore him then too when he bore the marks of the cross and the blows which he received on our behalf. Why is the word 'exaltation' the only one that pleases you, since he cannot be exalted who has not been in some way inferior? If a man of the highest worth is rightly said to be lower than a completely worthless person simply because the one is seated at the lowest bench at a banquet while the other is reclining on the foremost couch, is he not in some way lower who took upon himself so many of the misfortunes of human life? For whoever is lower only in some degree is not thereby lower in a pure and absolute way.

'I do not speak of Christ incarnate,' you say, 'but of Jesus Christ who is God and the Son of God.'[150] I too speak of the same person, the Son of Man, the man who was crucified and suffered so many misfortunes for our sake. If Jesus Christ is only the Lord and the Son of God, how is he understood to have been diminished? If the same person is the Son of Man, and is to this degree lesser than his former self, what incongruity is there in referring his diminution to this? Moreover, I am inclined to think that 'Christ,' or 'the name of Christ,' to use your expression, though it signifies two natures, is better taken of one only at a time, not two, as you wish, or, which is more ridiculous, of Christ as an aggregate of his two natures; though when the Son of Man is said to be 'diminished,' where a comparison is being drawn between two states, the expression seems to be applicable to both natures, the one which assumes and the one which has been assumed. Moreover, when I say, 'Christ assumed human nature,' does the appellation 'Christ'

*　*　*　*　*

149 Heb 2:9, citing Ps 8:6
150 *Disputatio* ASD IX-3 209:96–7

seem to have been employed to cover both his natures, or one of the two, that is, his divine nature? And when Augustine says, 'The Son of God has assumed the Son of Man,'[151] though both appellations are designations of Christ's substance,[152] none the less each is clearly taken of one of his two natures respectively. Accordingly, you must admit that such terms as may signify two things in some manner do not do so regularly when they are used in statements. Unless, perhaps, you think that when I use the word *album*, since it may denote a substance as well as the colour contained in it, it will properly be said to be taken of the one as well as the other; or because in the Scriptures the word *Pater* may signify two persons, the one when it is used literally, the other when it is used figuratively, it may be taken of the two; or because the word *caecus* may mean 'blind' as well as 'hidden,' it will be taken to mean both.

Yet all that I have said so far has been no more than preliminary ground-work and a preparation for my main point, namely, that the expression βραχύ τι is to be given a temporal reference. Yet you attack this preliminary section as though it were the crux of my argument. All the same, it is worthwhile hearing with what effort you excuse the fact that in the Psalms Christ called himself 'a worm' and not a man, as well as 'a reproach upon mankind' and 'an outcast from the people.'[153] For I had happened to make reference to the text in question. As though, indeed, there were a danger that Christ might be thought to have been truly a worm if you had not come forward as the guardian of his reputation! In no way does it offend the ears of the devoted to hear him called a worm, any more than a stone, a lamb, a lion, a vine, a mustard seed, or the like.[154] You imagine that you have found the two-edged axe of Tenedos[155] with which to cut all knots of this kind, if all things which are said of Christ in this way in the Scriptures have to do not with fact but with the judgment or, as you say, 'the estimation of the Jews,' and if almost that entire psalm which speaks of Christ's abandonment, his degradation, and his helplessness is understood in the light of the 'estimation and judgment of the priests, the Scribes, and the Pharisees.'[156] Now if such an interpretation was legitimate, why did you not interpret my words in that

* * * * *

151 Augustine *De Trinitate* 2.6 CCSL 50 93–4
152 *hypostasis*
153 Ps 22:7
154 Stone (eg Matt 21:42); lamb (John 1:29); lion (Rev 5:5); vine (John 15:1 and 5); mustard seed, see n127 above.
155 *Adagia* I ix 29: *Tenedia bipennis*. Tenedos was a small island on the coast of Troy.
156 *Disputatio* ASD IX-3 211:165–7

way, that in the estimation of the Jews Christ was made lower than the most worthless of men? Is it a lesser thing to be more worthless than men than to be called a worm, a reproach, an abomination? If a pious interpretation can be put on these expressions, why do you look for impiety in what I say?

In fact, however, you must admit that it is not the case, as you claim, that that entire psalm has to do with the estimation of the Jews, unless perhaps you are prepared to accept that when he says, 'They will pierce my hands and my feet,'[157] and likewise, 'All who look upon me will scoff,'[158] and so forth, these statements too relate not to fact but to the estimation of the Jews. Furthermore, what about the fact that even modern theologians say that Christ would not have died had his divinity not in some way abandoned his human body? If this is true, then he was forsaken in fact, not in opinion. But since it is agreed that Christ's being called a worm signifies nothing other than his utter humiliation, and this humiliation took the form of the evils which he took upon himself for our sake, if he took these upon himself and suffered them in fact, then he was humiliated in fact, and was to this extent a worm in fact. Assuredly, that he was flayed with whips, spit upon, bound, accused, condemned, abused with insults, and crucified between two criminals, does all of this not belong to the realm of fact, not the estimation of the Jews?[159] Is it not on account of these things that he is called a worm, humiliated, degraded, and desolated? But he did not deserve to suffer those things, you say. I admit it. That they should happen to one who does not deserve them makes them all the more unworthy.

A little further on you try to make out that the term 'worm' does not refer to Christ but to us, because a worm is an earthly creature, whereas in Paul Christ is called heavenly.[160] In his interpretation of the passage, however, St Augustine does not hesitate to refer the word to Christ: 'Why is he called a worm? Because he was mortal, born of the flesh, and born without union.'[161] Since these were attributes of Christ in fact, not just in the judgment of men, how is it that for you his being called a worm is a matter only of 'estimation'? At the same time, I do confess that with respect to this passage I do not much approve of what follows in Augustine, where he argues that Christ was not called a man because he was God: 'Why is he not called a man?

* * * * *

157 Ps 22:17
158 Ps 22:8
159 Erasmus is demonstrating that, in this controversy with Lefèvre, he upholds the realism of the Incarnation.
160 1 Cor 15:48
161 Augustine *Enarratio* II *in psalmum* 21 CCSL 38 125

Because in the beginning was the Word, and the Word was with God, and the Word was God.'[162] This seems to me to contain more cleverness than truth. It was not because he was God that Christ was not a man, nor was he called 'not a man' in a figurative sense, although Ambrose, commenting on Peter's denial in Luke, argues pretty much in such a way when he suggests that in saying, 'I do not know the man,' Peter meant that he did not know God.[163] But to return to the matter at hand, Augustine again, in his commentary on the first chapter of the Gospel according to John, says: 'For if the Lord himself says, "I am a worm and not a man," who can doubt that he is saying what was written in Job, namely, "How much more is man a thing of rottenness and the Son of Man a worm"?'[164] St Augustine is referring the terms 'rottenness' to us and 'worm' to Christ. Paul does not call Christ heavenly because he did not have an earthly body, but because he was free from the earthly stain of Adam. Indeed, in that passage he created two Adams, one the source of sin, the other the source of innocence.[165] Furthermore, in letter 147 to Consentius, Augustine does not hesitate to refer to Christ as earthly when he says, 'The Lord, although he was heavenly, was made earthly so that he might make heavenly those who were earthly.'[166] If Christ alone is heavenly, then all others are earthly; therefore, the appellation 'worm' belongs to martyrs not through an estimation of their misfortunes, but literally, in accordance with your own interpretation. But if here too you wish to take refuge[167] behind your principle of 'opinion,' why do you add 'of the Scribes and Pharisees'? Did the martyrs suffer only at their hands, were they despised only by them?

Let us now consider the nature of the fallacy which you introduce concerning the expression 'not a man' when you add, 'For there is one God, and one mediator between God and men, the man Jesus Christ, who is thus a man because of all men he is most of all and truly a man.'[168] If you were dealing with a logician, see how you would be able to defend the statement that Christ is most truly of all a man by following your Aristotle, according to whom 'more' and 'less' do not fall in the category 'substance,' so that Christ may be called 'more' a man even though he ought to be called 'better' than

* * * * *

162 Ibidem
163 Ambrose *Expositio evangelii Lucae* 10.84 CSEL 32 part 4 487. The passage on which Ambrose commented is Matt 26:72.
164 Augustine *Tractatus in Ioannem* 1.13 CCSL 36 7–8, citing Job 25:6
165 1 Cor 15:45
166 Augustine Ep 205 12 CSEL 57 333
167 This passage uses the Greek word κρησφύγετον.
168 *Disputatio* ASD IX-3 212:196–8

all men.[169] I shall not give like for like on this point, arguing with you to the utmost letter of the law, as they say; nor shall I cavil over details, once it is sufficiently clear to me what you meant. But why are you afraid to take the expressions 'reproach upon mankind' and 'outcast from the people'[170] as referring to Christ, but transfer them to other men, when St Paul is not afraid to say that Christ was transgressed against and slandered?[171] If it is not impiety to say these things of Christ, what impiety is there in saying that Christ was diminished below men, provided that it is understood that by this we mean something which it is eminently pious to say concerning Christ? If it is words that trouble you, then these ought to have caused you greater offence; if you are concerned about intention, there is nothing impious here unless someone interprets it so. If I had said that Christ humbled himself beneath the most humble of men, I do not think you would be shocked; why do you cry impiety because I have said he was made worthless beneath the most worthless of men? For he who has humbled himself is rightly called humbled, and worthless is no different from humbled. If it is only the novelty of the language that offends you, St Augustine used it of Christ before I did in his exposition of this passage in the psalm: 'Wherefore did he thus make himself so worthless as to call himself a worm?'[172] But, you say, Christ made himself worthless only in speech. I admit that; but what he said was true, not empty or imagined, so that it follows that he was in actual fact made worthless.

Now when you write that it was in the estimation of the Jews that Christ was abandoned by the Father,[173] not only is this feeble, it differs from the view of all the ancient commentators. As though Christ is there complaining to the Father that the Jews, for whom he had prayed a little before, thought evil of him! I am inclined to think, my dear Lefèvre, that it would be better to avoid touching this sore spot[174] involving 'estimation' altogether; otherwise, someone may find less to quarrel with in the heresy of one Marcus, or Marcion, I think, which taught, so Augustine tells us, that Christ suffered not in reality but in his imagination.[175] As for your asking

* * * * *

169 Aristotle *Categories* 5 (3b33–4)
170 Ps 22:7
171 2 Cor 5:21; Gal 3:13
172 Augustine *Enarratio* II *in psalmum* 21 7 CCSL 38 125:3–4
173 *Disputatio* ASD IX-3 211:168 and 214:248
174 *Adagia* I vi 79: *Tangere ulcus*
175 Erasmus found in Marcus the Gnostic a heretic to whom he could, with the usual precautions, compare Lefèvre. Cf Augustine *De haeresibus* 14 CCSL 46 296.

me how it is right that 'he who is the first-born of every creature and above every creature' should be called a worm, and that he of whom the Apostle says, 'For there is one God, and one mediator between God and men, the man Jesus Christ,'[176] should be said to be not a man, you would be better to enquire of the Prophet himself, or rather Christ himself, who said through the mouth of the Prophet that he was a worm. Moreover, I am not afraid of Christ being angry with me if I employ his words in the sense in which, if we may rely upon so many orthodox interpreters, he said them. Among these is St Jerome, and he is one example out of many, who, commenting on the second chapter of Paul's Epistle to Titus, clearly calls Christ a worm, and who is with even more boldness prepared to say that Christ was transgressed against and slandered.[177]

As for your instructing us that Christ is called a man on St Paul's testimony, I admit it, and I am amused at your officiousness, as though there would have been a danger of someone denying that Christ was a man had you not brought your single passage from Paul to our attention, even though in the Gospel Christ so many times calls himself the Son of Man![178] Furthermore, the passages which you cite from the Scriptures in your attempt to instruct us that Christ was not truly abandoned work as much on my behalf as they do on yours: 'God neither rejected nor disdained the appeal of the wretched man': but he who makes an appeal, since he is asking for help, seems to have been to some degree abandoned; otherwise, what would he be appealing for if he lacked nothing? Again, 'And when I called to him, he heard me':[179] why would he cry if he were in no way abandoned? Finally, since I have no wish to prolong the matter by going through every one of your citations, the passage 'For Mary the mother of Jesus was there, and his favourite disciple, and Mary Magdalene, and the woman who followed Jesus, and with deep sorrow and thankful devotion they wept to God and the angels over him; but the heart of the Virgin was struck by his suffering as by a sword and her soul was pierced through':[180] this passage too works on my behalf. Whose suffering do they share? To whom do they direct their pity? For this is what is meant, I think, by 'devotion,' in common, if not in learned, speech. Were they weeping over the Word of God who is always equal to the Father, or a man who was suffering terribly for the sake of us all? Was he the one who

* * * * *

176 Lefèvre is citing Col 1:15, then 1 Tim 2:5.
177 This is not in Jerome's *Ad Titum* but in his *Ad Ephesios* 1.2 PL 26 501D.
178 Eg Matt 8:20
179 This citation and the preceding one are taken from Ps 22:25.
180 *Disputatio* ASD IX-3 212:189–92

is higher than all creatures, or a man who was abandoned and lower than the robbers? Moreover, if Christ is one and unchanging, to whom do such divergent references as these apply? You must admit that the passages which you cite, far from standing in the way of my view, actually support it, not to mention the fact that the passage in Luke where Christ calls himself a 'green branch' speaks more of his innocence than his majesty.[181] I am surprised that you thought it necessary to introduce it, unless perhaps you thought there was a danger that someone might judge Christ to be a criminal. If it was your intention to collect whatever passages declare Christ's majesty, why, when there are so many, did you bring forward just a select few? If you wanted to refute all the passages which seem to speak of Christ's humiliation, why do you touch upon barely one or two? In short, I am justified in ruling the whole of this section out of court.

You proceed to examine where Christ's descending to suffer these misfortunes means that he was 'diminished in himself.' In heaven's name, a fine proposal – as though I had ever suggested that 'he was diminished in himself,' though what you mean by 'in himself' I am not at all sure! If by 'in himself' you mean 'in reality,'[182] then I am prepared to say that 'he was diminished in himself.' You admit that in assuming human form and taking tortures upon himself Christ was diminished. But since he did both these things in reality, it was in reality that he was diminished. If, on the other hand, when you say 'in himself' you mean it in an absolute sense, I admit that in this absolute sense Christ is the highest. Indeed, in case you think that I have derived nothing from your writings, he is more than infinitely the highest. Further, I do not altogether understand your purpose in saying that in the Gospel Christ does not call himself a worm, but the light of the world, a green branch, and other things which are a mark of majesty, unless you are intimating perhaps that the words of the Prophet do not have sufficient weight with us, and that it is reasonable that they should give way to the authority of the Gospel.[183] Does the fact that Christ was called a worm by the Prophet really not give us sufficient grounds for believing that he is rightly

* * * * *

181 Luke 23:31
182 The two expressions *in se* and *vere* are then contrasted with *absolute, simpliciter,* and *per se.*
183 If they are not contradicted by the New Testament, the words of the Old Testament have a prophetic value. In the case of Christ's humiliation, furthermore, the New Testament abounds in passages which reveal the suffering of Christ. Here, Erasmus is recalling Matt 21:18–19, John 11:33–5, and the passion narratives.

called a worm? As if a good part of the gospel story does not speak again and again of Christ's lowliness, and as if the Prophet does not elsewhere venerate and express wonder at the sublimity of him whom here he calls a worm and an outcast from the people. When you read of the crib and the stable, of the babe crying, of his being circumcised, when you read of Christ worn tired, driven by hunger to eat from the fig-tree, led up to the mountain and tempted by the devil, when you read of the Son of Man with nowhere to rest his head while the foxes have their dens and the birds their nests, when you read of Christ weeping and groaning, his ears ringing with insults, when you review the whole tale of his suffering, tell me of what else you are reading than the Son of God made lower than all men so that he might be exalted above all things. When you read that he was dishonoured, despised, the lowest of men, when you read that he was mute like a lamb at the shearing, are you not reading that he was in some small way diminished? Since not a one of these things which are said of Christ is a mark against his unspeakable majesty, which has always demanded the wonder of men and angels alike, there was no reason why anyone who worships his eminence should be offended by a reminder of his lowliness. For as St Hilary says, 'The majesty of his power is not lost when the lowliness of his flesh is worshipped, because the most divergent things are true of him on account of his different natures.'[184] The fact that he was truly lord of all things[185] did not preclude his being rightly called a servant. If an inferior is one who carries out a humble task, then Christ, in washing the feet of the disciples, was in some sense their inferior, but their Lord all the same.[186]

As to your criticism of my conclusion as being based upon faulty reasoning, I fail to see what you are aiming at. You say, 'The fact that there is no analogy between human nature and God does not allow for Christ to be called a worm, otherwise the Cherubim would have to be called worms as well, since there is no analogy between God and them either.'[187] I ask you, do I anywhere argue in this fashion? To the contrary, in order to show that Christ was made lower than the lowest of men I call upon the testimony of the Prophet. What point was there in proving by argument what Christ says himself through the Prophet? Further, when I add, 'There is no analogy between a human creature and God,' this pertains to what had gone

* * * * *

184 This citation is not based upon a specific text but recalls the passage for which
    n143 above gives the reference.
185 Rom 10:12
186 John 13:1–20
187 *Disputatio* ASD IX-3 213:237–40

before, namely, 'Christ was made not a little lower than God,' a statement which you were not willing to accept. It is just that my method of treating the material involved me in skipping about from one part to another. In the name of friendship,[188] do you really think that your criticism was an example of arguing in friendly fashion with a friend, and not a clear case of cavilling?

However, let us pass over this and return to the question that has been raised. I shall employ the same reasoning to defend the assertion which you attack, namely, 'There is no relation between human and divine nature.' 'But there is a relation,' you respond, 'between Christ and divine nature, and this is one of identity and equality.'[189] Clearly, the very mention of relation has drawn the cavalry onto the field, as they say,[190] and I can see that on this point I shall have no raw recruit in mathematics to contend with.[191] Suppose we grant, then, that there can be a relation which consists in equality, who ever heard of a relation which consists in identity? Or who has ever proposed a relation between infinity and infinity? For Aristotle, just as he denied the existence of any relation between the finite and the infinite, thought, if we are to place any trust in his interpreters, that there exists no relation between two infinites.[192] Further, Paul's remark that Christ is equal with God does not, I think, establish a relation, but simply states that his power is not lesser and is not greater.

However, so that we may put on one side what are more in the nature of clever points than serious contributions to the business between us, employ the term 'relation,' whether it be of identity or equality, as you see fit. Now, do you wish this to be the only relation which applies to Christ, or are you prepared to entertain some other? If this one only, then Christ was not made lower than God, though you would argue the contrary, provided that it be by only a little. For the concept of a relation of identity requires that he not have been made lower to any degree at all. Furthermore, how can what Christ himself says in the Gospel be true, namely, 'My Father is greater than I'?[193] Wherever you hear the words 'lesser' and 'greater,' there must exist some

* * * * *

188 In Greek, this is νὴ τὸν φίλιον [sic].
189 This is a proportional relation (*proportio*).
190 In Greek. *Adagia* I viii 82: *In planiciem equum*
191 Lefèvre had been busy editing mathematical treatises like that of Jordanus Nemorarius, a thirteenth-century author, whose *Elementa arithmetica* Lefèvre published in 1493 in an *editio princeps*.
192 Aristotle *De coelo* 1.6 (274a7) and *Physics* 8.1 (252a)
193 John 14:28. This verse was much discussed during the Arian crisis.

other relation than one of equality. If you are correct in deducing a relation of equality from the passage in the Gospel which says, 'I and the Father are one,'[194] how am I any less correct in deducing a relation of inequality from the passage which reads, 'My Father is greater than I'? If this relation is derived from a comparison between things which are infinitely different one from the other, then either show me from your mathematics what the relation is or admit with me that no such relation exists. Moreover, if in this comparison Christ is said to be less than the Father, he is less either to a finite degree or to an infinite degree. I do not think you would say finite, since you yourself say that there is no relation between a thing created and the creator. But if it is to an infinite degree, how would you defend your view that Christ was made a little less, when you insist that the expression 'a little less' or 'less by a little' must refer not to a length of time but to a level of dignity? Would you not be guilty of referring to something infinite and immense as 'a little'? On this reasoning, am I heretical for having written that Christ was made lower than God not by a little but to a very great extent? I am convinced that here if anywhere you are caught on the horns of a dilemma,[195] though I shall not press down hard upon you or taunt you now that you have been trapped, even if you do seem to deserve it, who heap up abuse against an opponent without any justification.

Meanwhile, to avoid giving the appearance of censuring you instead of simply defending myself, I shall not examine in detail the words which you employ in arguing that there exists a relation of identity between the Son of Man and God. If there is a relation of equality between the Son of Man, in so far as he is the Son of Man, and God, in what manner, tell me, is he less? If to the extent that he is God he is said to be equal with God, what is new in this, and who would deny it? I have no dispute with those who wish to interpret the reference in the Gospel to the Father as greater than the Son in such a way that the Son does not become less than the Father. For me it is sufficient that Augustine was prepared to say, as he did in the third letter to Volusian and in several other places, including On the Trinity, book one, chapters seven and eleven, and book two, chapter nine, that the Son is less than the Father and less than himself.[196]

The same is true of the following argument, namely, that the Word and Son of God is of divine status and of the same nature as God, because

* * * * *

194 John 10:30
195 *Adagia* I iv 96: *Medius teneris*
196 Augustine *De Trinitate* 1.7, 1.11, and 2.1 CCSL 50 pages 45, 60, and 81; Ep 137 CSEL 44 111–12

he is no more a created thing than God.[197] Here again you distinguish the
Son of God from God, and you say that he is no more a created thing than
God, or the Father himself, to bring your words in line with Paul's. My
response is that if the Son of God is not a created thing, and I am speaking
in accordance with accepted idiom, how is he said to be lower than God,
something which even you do not deny? Yet John ventures to say, 'The Word
was made flesh,' and Paul that Christ 'was made from the seed of David,' and
again, 'God has sent his son, made from a woman, made under the law.'[198] Do
you hear the expressions 'made flesh,' 'made from the seed' and still refuse
to acknowledge that Christ is in some sense a created thing? In any event,
this argument entails no risk for me, since I neither claim nor deny that Christ
is a created thing; you have added that of your own accord. But, you say,
Augustine, Hilary, and Ambrose all deny that Christ is a created thing. Yet
what if elsewhere these same persons do call him a created thing? For what
does Augustine mean when he says in one of his sermons for Christmas, 'It is
a remarkable mystery that the creator of the world was willing to be a created
thing,'[199] and again in his exposition of Christ's Sermon on the Mount, as
well as in letter fifty-seven, 'He who is the creator of the world was willing to
be a created thing'?[200] What he is saying, in short, is that as the Word Christ
is the creator, 'for all things were made through him,'[201] while as a man he is
a created thing. St Jerome speaks even more openly in his exposition of the
passage from the second chapter of Paul's Epistle to the Ephesians:

> For we are his work, created in Christ Jesus. Because once we came into the
> name of a created thing, and wisdom in the Proverbs of Solomon says that she
> was created as a beginning of the ways of God: and many, through fear of being
> forced to say that Christ was a created thing, deny the whole mystery of Christ
> and say that wisdom there represents not Christ but the wisdom of the world.
> We freely proclaim that there is no danger in calling Christ a created thing
> when in full confidence and hope we profess that he was a worm, a man, was
> crucified and accursed, especially since in the two preceding verses wisdom

* * * * *

197 *Disputatio* ASD IX-3 216:324–6. *Creatura* does not exist in classical Latin.
198 John 1:14; Rom 1:3; Gal 4:4 respectively
199 This sentence does not appear to be borrowed from the works of Augustine
(*Apologia* ASD IX-3 135:1221n), but it recalls Sedulius' interpretation of Mary's
womb, which contained that which the world cannot contain. When this was
adopted into the Christmas liturgy, the reference to Christ as *creatura* was
nevertheless avoided.
200 Augustine Ep 187 CSEL 57 87:15–88:6
201 Eph 2:10

herself promises that she will declare what will be in the future. But since Christ has brought the future into being and the things which wisdom goes on to say are those which she had promised to declare as things to come, the things which follow must be taken as referring to the mystery of the Incarnation, not to the nature of God.[202]

So Jerome. You hear how Christ, in as much as he was made incarnate, is rightly called a created thing.

Incidentally, you should be advised at the same time that Christ is called a worm by Jerome in the same way as he is called a man, and crucified, that is, not in the estimation of the Jews but in reality, something which you regard as blasphemous and heretical. St John Damascene speaks in like manner: 'Christ is created and uncreated, capable of suffering and incapable of suffering'; and again: 'He is not scandalized at the title "created thing" who calls himself servant, worm, seed, born of a virgin.'[203] Further, what about the fact that the compiler of the *Book of Sentences*, in his treatment of this question in book three, section eleven, does not deny that Christ is rightly called a created thing, but prefers that it not be said unreservedly; that is, he prefers that it be said of Christ as man but not of Christ as God?[204] Moreover, as to the fact that these same writers at other times deny that Christ is a created thing when they are combating the Arians, they are denying that Christ is a created thing only in the way that Arius maintained in teaching that only the Father is the true God and only the Father is truly uncreated. There is also the fact, which you have forgotten, that the very one who you here deny is a created thing you elsewhere make a created thing, when you say, 'There is no distinction between the man who is Christ and God, since he enjoys an approximation and oneness with God which is as close as any could be between a created thing and God.'[205] If Christ is to be in no way called a created thing, what does this statement mean? Unless you admit perhaps that the human form is a created thing, but do not accept that Christ as man is a created thing. But if we are to follow your example and be particular over language, what do you mean when you say, 'Christ has a oneness with God'? By 'Christ' here do you not mean Christ in human form? And may we say, then, 'God became Christ'? If not, how is Christ united with God, since he

* * * * *

202 Jerome *Commentarius in epistolam ad Ephesios* 1.2 PL 26 501. The text to which the citation refers is Prov 8:22–3.
203 John Damascene *De fide orthodoxa* 3.4 PG 94 998D–999A
204 Peter Lombard *Sententiae* book 3 dist 11 c 1
205 *Disputatio* ASD IX-3 218:403–4

is himself God? What grounds did you have for deriding me for appearing to be substituting the name 'Christ' for his other nature? Again and again I ask you, my dear Lefèvre, to see how wide a window you have opened upon yourself[206] in attacking me for the language which I employ.

To move on to another point, what do you mean when you say that the Word and the Son of God is of divine making, when all Christians would deny that Christ was made, at least to the extent that he is the Word and the Son of God?[207] For who has said that the Son of God was made? Not that I am unaware that you have used the word 'making' in the sense of kind or form; but I wished to point out how easy a matter it is, if I were inclined to follow your example, to criticize an opponent on points of language. And here again you distinguish the Son of God from God as though the Son of God were not God, not to mention the fact that when you say, 'For he is no more a created thing than God,'[208] there is an ambiguity which ought to be avoided if ever one should. For you seem to be saying that the Son of God is neither a created thing nor God. If you allow yourself to say this in rhetorical fashion, or rather in your own fashion, of God, why do you attack me so strenuously when I speak with more precision than you? If you demand from me the carefulness which is the mark of modern theologians, why do you display neither the learning of the old school nor the acuteness of the moderns? Were you not failing to realize what a dangerous standard a man sets for himself when he sets himself up as a judge of others?

However, I have neither the inclination nor the time to pursue matters of this kind. I admit that Christ is certain things and is not certain things, since in his divine being he is the same as and equal with the Father, while in his human form he is less than the Father. But as to his being less than the Father, or, if you will allow, less than himself, I ask whether he is less by a finite degree or an infinite degree. Not by a finite degree, you will say. Well then, if it is less by an infinite degree, we will not be guilty of heresy if we say that with respect to the form which he assumed Christ has no relation with divinity. And if I succeed in carrying this point, what grounds do you have for insisting so strongly that he was made lower only than the Father, and this to only a very small degree? Unless perhaps you are going to rely upon sophistical subtleties to argue that just as a man who has five coins also has one coin, so someone who has been made a great deal lower can also

* * * * *

206 *Adagia* I iv 3: *Fenestram aperire*
207 Erasmus is playing on the words *conditio* (condition) and *condere* (to create, to make).
208 *Disputatio* ASD IX-3 216:326–7

be said to have been made a little lower. But if this kind of subtlety were permitted, Christ would be said to have been neither diminished nor exalted. For what degree of majesty could be added to one who is always equal with the Father, or in what way could he have been diminished whose divinity has lost nothing and whose humanity has even been raised up?

However, I have no intention of pursuing these things to the limit,[209] since I would be happy enough for the moment simply to clear myself of the charge of heresy. Moreover, whatever conclusion your endless treatise reaches, it does not much matter whether Christ is said to be lower than the angels or lower than men, that is, whether you think both views heretical, since his very majesty demands equal worship in either case. But with respect to his human form and suffering, Athanasius, Chrysostom, Theophylact, and Augustine have made him, as you yourself admit, lower than the angels, unless you think that to have been diminished is something different from being made lower. Yet these writers, since you did not think they ought to be exposed to criticism, you excuse by saying that they were deceived by the Septuagint translation into thinking that this was the reading in the Hebrew, and so have merely made a mistake.[210] Very well, let us accept that as men whose languages were Greek and Latin they did not know what the Hebrew texts read. But how did it come about that such renowned leaders of the Christian faith did not detect in this interpretation the grave heresy which you claim is present in it? Why am I the only one to be criticized as the author of this view when I was not the first to put it forward, when I do so not to defend it but simply to make note of it, and when, if I am leaning one way or the other, I appear to favour the opposite view? Am I guilty of such a great crime because I have not committed myself totally and unreservedly to your opinion, and because I do not approve one view and attack, assail, and take up stones against the other? For it is nothing if not to 'speak words as hard as stones,' as Plautus puts it,[211] to use such harsh language as 'most unworthy of Christ and God, contrary to the spirit, subverting the meaning of the Prophet,' or 'This is the way the faithful explain it, those who are led not by the letter but by the spirit.'[212] What does this imply? That those who explain it differently are led by the flesh and are unfaithful? Who would not dread these words more than any stones? Yet it is words of this kind and words even harsher that you heap upon your

* * * * *

209 *Adagia* II iv 13: *Ad vivum resecare*
210 See n61 above.
211 Plautus *Captivi* 593 and *Aulularia* 152
212 Lefèvre's expressions; *Disputatio* ASD IX-3 210:134–5, 216:329–30

friend in this well-meaning treatise of yours, a work undertaken in a friendly spirit.

Now, if I had hurled back at your head the stones which you undeservedly hurled at mine, who of our future readers would blame me? Instead, I have been mindful of Christian modesty and been content merely to admonish you, though, as I have said, I do not fully understand your meaning when you say 'most unworthy of Christ and God.' If you mean God the Father, I did not speak of him; if you mean the Son, how do you distinguish God from Christ by joining them together? If you make me out to be stupid, a rock, a brute, a pumpkin, a fool, or anything else you wish, I shall not be perturbed in the least, I shall say not a single word in protest: but forgive me, this is one kind of insult I cannot tolerate. For who would put up with it when you write, 'Moreover, in the light of these taunts, and many others as well, I would admit, even though the truth was otherwise, that Christ the Lord was made worthless and greatly diminished in the eyes of the Jews and has been also in the work of my opponent, who sees no merit at all in my opinion.'[213] In what spirit did you write this? How do you think those who read it are going to interpret it? Me, a friend, you associate with the Jews, who have an ill opinion of Christ, while you in the meantime take your place in the ranks of the pious as a defender of Christ, and say that Christ has been cast down by what I have said, and appear to be sounding a warning to me not to cling to my words. You call me an opponent, when in fact I was taking your side in this matter. Or perhaps you will make me out an opponent of Christ, in order to make it more offensive, and call me Satan.[214]

I would not go over these things, my dear Lefèvre, except to make it clear to everyone that I undertook this *Apologia* unwillingly and my nature shuns nothing more than confrontations of this sort. But there is more: 'Look, Christ calls his own suffering not dejection or disgraceful humiliation, but exaltation.'[215] What is the point here? Believe me, I am barely able to suppress the anger I felt just now. Have I attributed dejection and disgraceful humiliation to Christ, whom I worship as the source of all glory? Has your treatise been sprinkled all over with fair and kindly remarks like this? Who, indeed, in time to come will not applaud the friendly tone which you have brought to your confrontation with a dear friend? What is more, in order to make certain that these compliments should not be lost to view, you worked

* * * * *

213 *Disputatio* ASD IX-3 214:246–50
214 Lefèvre only stated that the vision of the humiliated Christ is that of Christ's enemies. 'Satan' signifies the adversary.
215 *Disputatio* ASD IX-3 214:253–4

them into the middle of your commentaries, and as if this were not enough, you did not think to give me the slightest word of warning in case I should discover my error and cleanse myself in time, or apply an antidote before the poison had had time to spread.[216] For this is the interpretation which future readers of your remarks are likely to put on them.

I shall not belabour here what lack of learning, indeed what impiety is evident in your argument that Christ was not humiliated in his suffering on the cross because his body was raised from the ground, that is, because he was nailed up on the cross, even though Paul calls this a humiliation that glorified the Father, and through the resurrection the Father in turn glorified the Son. His humiliation earned him his glory, while our glory is the cross of Christ,[217] unless, of course, when Paul says, 'wherefore God exalted him and gave him a name above every name,'[218] it means that God raised him up again onto the cross. But to return to our starting-point: if you are prepared to excuse Athanasius, Chrysostom, Augustine, indeed all the learned theologians on the ground that they were following the Septuagint, which was demeaning to Christ, why do you bring a charge of blasphemy against me who follow the authority of orthodox men, or rather merely review their opinions? If it is sacrilege to say that Christ 'was made lower than men' because he has always been owed the worship of men, it will be no less a sacrilege to say that Christ 'was made lower than the angels,' or 'placed beneath the angels' (for it does not matter at this point what words we use to explain the matter), because he has always deserved their worship. Moreover, if it is proper and true to say that Christ was made lower than the angels by reason of the weakness of our flesh and the misfortunes of this life which he took upon himself for our sake, misfortunes to which no angel is subject, then I think it is not at all heretical to say that for a time Christ was made lower than most, in fact all, men, seeing that he took upon himself more afflictions than any man ever suffered or would be able to bear. And what does it matter if you make one out of three and treat Athanasius, Chrysostom, and Theophylact as a single person? Suppose that Athanasius alone said this, would his authority alone be light? However, if the number of votes adds weight, there is nobody who does not adopt this view, with the sole exception of Jerome, though in fact he too follows it when immediately afterwards he quotes this passage according to the Septuagint version.

* * * * *

216 See n30 above.
217 This passage is reminiscent of Gal 6:14. Again Erasmus insinuates that Lefèvre could be accused of emptying Christ's cross of its significance (cf 1 Cor 1:17).
218 Phil 2:9–10

Finally you come to the issue which you ought to have challenged at the outset, when the main point of my treatise was being presented. I repeat, it seems to me that the expression 'a little less,' which in Greek is βραχύ τι, is not to be referred to the degree to which Christ's majesty was diminished, but to the length of time which Christ spent on earth; that is to say, Christ was made lower than the angels for a short while.[219] This was the direction in which the essential part of my treatise was leading, namely, that the Greek words βραχύ τι, which the Septuagint translators rendered 'a little,' are to be taken as referring not to the degree but to the duration of Christ's humiliation. If you could not see that this was my intent, what could be more blind? If you did see, and pretended that you did not, what could be more shameless? For it will be worthwhile going over the arguments which you employed with me earlier. 'The following,' you say,

is a naïve piece of reasoning: 'The Son of Man was made lower than even the most worthless of men; the most worthless of men have been made far lower than the angels; therefore, the Son of Man has been made a much greater degree lower than the angels.' For if he has been made 'much' lower, then he has not been made 'a little' lower (for the two terms are contraries), even though this, according to my opponent's opinion, is what the Prophet means. For according to the Septuagint the Prophet says, 'You have made him a little lower than the angels,' an interpretation of which my opponent approves. Furthermore, if he was made much lower than the angels, then he was made an even further degree lower than God: therefore, the Prophet is undermined whether we read 'than God' or 'than the angels.' Accordingly, my opponent's argument destroys itself and shows itself false in every part.[220]

I have quoted your remarks up to this point, remarks in which, not to mention the absurdity of the language and the phenomenal wordiness, you make me out as lacking not only in logic, an art which you have toiled over all your life,[221] but also in common sense. My argument reads simply as

* * * * *

219 Erasmus now arrives at the exegetical solution which he proposes. The adverb found in the psalm ought to have a temporal nuance.

220 Here is a lengthy passage from Lefèvre (*Disputatio* ASD IX-3 210:140–8) cited to emphasize all the more how much Lefèvre 'missed the point.'

221 Lefèvre published and commented on Aristotelian logic in such works as his *Introductiones logicales* of 1496, very frequently republished, later with the addition of Josse Clichtove's commentaries or even the *Organon* of 1501. Erasmus mischievously returns several times to the subject of Lefèvre's incoherence, which he finds inexplicable in the works of such a great *connaisseur* of Aristotle.

follows: 'that Christ was diminished not a little but for a little while, meaning that he was greatly diminished but for a brief period only; and that this meaning was consistent with either of the two readings, "than God" or "than the angels."' Out of this you create an entirely new syllogism and argue that I have undermined the meaning of the Prophet whichever reading is adopted. Who will not marvel at such subtlety, the likes of which Chrysippus himself could not match?[222] Who could escape this dilemma,[223] its twin horns threatening me, one on this side and one on that? Who would not admit that the effort which you have invested in the study of logic over so many years has paid off handsomely? With such fine argument you show that a friend has spoken with impiety! For that piece of reasoning you called upon God in heaven and you offer eternal thanks to the giver of all light. Again and again, my dear Lefèvre, I appeal to your conscience.[224] When you go over these things in your mind, are you not at all ashamed of yourself? If you were serious in what you wrote, and I will not say that you were, where is your philosophy? Or, since you regard me as a novice in that line, where is your basic human reasoning? If you were joking, tell me, please, is this how you jest with a friend? If you adopt that method of arguing out of conviction, what more ridiculous thing could be invented? If you are making fun of me, where is that deep friendship of ours? What is fitting for a mountebank is not fitting for Lefèvre.[225] Are you so unconcerned over what you write in your books? Do you have so poor an opinion of the intelligence of your contemporaries that you think they will tolerate such nonsense, or fail to perceive it? Who will not admit that your statement 'This argument destroys itself and shows itself false in every part' should with justification be turned against yourself? For my part, I would not wish to exercise my right to do so; I am satisfied to have shown you to yourself in the hope of saving you from fooling in the same fashion again, if fooling is the word for using linguistic deceptions to accuse a friend of impiety and making out that he is undermining prophetic meaning. But what do you intend when you say that 'according to my opponent's view,' that is, my view, when the Prophet says, 'You have made him a little lower than the angels,' he meant that Christ was made a great deal lower than the angels, when I clearly say that he meant that Christ was diminished for a short time, and, further, when it was not under discussion at this point whether he was diminished greatly or a little? Nor

* * * * *

222 Chrysippus of Tarsus (d 209 BC) is the second founder of the Stoic school.
223 The word in Greek signifies an animal with two horns.
224 An appeal to conscience is a Christian humanist's last resort.
225 Seneca *Epistulae morales* 29.7

will I simply grant you what you assume as conceded, namely, that the most worthless of men were made much lower than the angels. For it can be the case that the most worthless man, to accept your use of the superlative, is in some way greater than the angels.

At this point I was minded to bring my refutation to a close,[226] except that you are incapable of halting your attack, and as if you had not talked enough nonsense already, you keep going and add the following: 'For the same reason he contradicts his own assertion when he adds, "He was not even made a little lower than the angels when he was reduced to hunger, thirst, beatings, the cross, and finally death." If Christ was not even made a little lower than the angels, how can the reading in the Prophet be taken to be "You have made him a little lower than the angels"? Are not the expressions "a little lower" and "not a little lower" mutually exclusive, and likewise "a little" and "not a little"?'[227] How delighted, how triumphant, how pleased with yourself you are over this, and how silly you make yourself look in making fun of me! Who denies that 'a little' and 'not a little' are contraries? I am sure you would not have seen it had it not been for the years you spent on Aristotle, though it is as clear as day to a blind man, as they say.[228] But what are in no way contrary are 'a little' and 'for a long time,' and 'for a long time' and 'much.' I do not equate 'Christ was made a little lower' with 'Christ was not made a little lower'; what I say is, 'Christ was made much lower than the angels, but not for a long time,' or 'Christ was made lower than the angels for a little while, but not just a little lower.' You should have refuted this before launching into self-congratulation, so that no one could criticize you for singing the victory ode before the victory, as the Greeks say.[229] Instead, as though you had the battle already won, you begin to sport and jest like ever such a sharp and witty fellow. 'I would concede willingly,' you say, 'that Christ was made not a little lower than the angels, since he was not made lower than the angels at all.' But all the time you fail to realize that while you wish to deny absolutely that Christ was made lower than the angels, you are in fact admitting that he was. If you had said, 'the Son of Man was not made a little lower than the angels,' this could perhaps be consistent with saying, 'He

* * * * *

226 Erasmus has already announced his conclusion on several occasions, but he has hardly crossed the mid-point of his *Apologia*. Shortly, he will announce an epilogue which will summarize his various arguments.
227 *Disputatio* ASD IX-3 210:149–54
228 *Adagia* I viii 93: *Vel caeco appareat*
229 *Adagia* I vii 55: Πρὸ τῆς νίκης τὸ ἐγκώμιον ᾄδεις. *Ante victoriam encomium canis* resembles an expression found in Plato's *Lysis* 205D.

was not made lower at all.' But when you say, 'He was made not a little lower,' you are stating an affirmative proposition, because the negative 'not' does not govern the verb 'made lower,' but the adverb 'a little.' It does not matter in the Latin where the negative is placed, only what it governs. If you claim that it governs both, all the expert Latinists will oppose you. Unless perhaps you think that when I say, 'Peter loves you not a little,' this can be taken to mean that you are loved by Peter neither much nor a little; or if I were to say, 'This man gave you not much,' it can be taken to mean that he gave you nothing. It would be the same as your saying, 'Christ was diminished not even a little'; for you would be saying that he was not diminished in any way at all. You see how careful he must be who contrives to make fun of another, and still more the man who contrives to charge another with impiety.

However, let us pass over these trifles and return to the serious challenge which you commence to launch over my having written that the words βραχύ τι should be given a temporal reference, that is, covering the time which Christ spent on earth up to his resurrection. First of all, my dear Lefèvre, I would have you take note that on this point I am not making an assertion; I am speaking rather in a tentative and exploratory fashion, as much as to say, 'It seems to me.' I repeat, I am amazed that you feel so strongly that this opinion must be challenged, since far from hindering your own it actually supports it; unless, of course, you feel obliged to disagree with me at absolutely every turn. Let us suppose that you have won your point that the correct reading is 'a little lower than God' and not 'a little lower than the angels,' a second difficulty confronts you as you still have the sticky problem of explaining how he who as God came down to human nature and was reduced to suffering its injuries, or its insults, if you prefer St Hilary's term, can be said to have descended only a little.[230] If it is a difficulty which has escaped your notice, then I fail to find in you that sharpness for which you are known. If you are pretending not to notice it, then I miss your frankness. Do you consider it impious of me to be pointing this difficulty out and urging you to address it, a difficulty which has to be removed if your interpretation is to stand? I have explained with the aid of so many witnesses and so many arguments that Christ was diminished not just a little but a great deal. But imagine that I am stripped of all my support troops, that I am facing you with one weapon only, which Paul himself supplies when he says, 'He desolated himself' – where will you turn?[231] What stratagem will you use to escape? Will you interpret 'desolated' to mean that he humiliated himself to a

* * * * *

230 Hilary De Trinitate 2.25 CCSL 62 61
231 Phil 2:7

small extent? Who would not burst into hissing and hooting at that interpretation, and judge it worthy, if anything is, of all the hellebore in Anticyra?[232] It is like someone interpreting the saying 'Pleasure destroys the mind's faculties' to mean that pleasure has a slight weakening effect upon the mind's faculties, or someone announcing the annihilation of the army as the loss of a few soldiers. What the verb *exinanire* means to Latin writers is clear enough: Quintus Curtius used it to mean 'exhaust.'[233] Paul's Greek reads ἐκένωσεν, that is, 'He emptied,' or alternatively, 'He reduced himself to nothing,' so that he could not have found a stronger verb to emphasize the utter humiliation of Christ and to express the extreme degree of his diminution. You push to the opposite extreme in your anxiety to have Christ humiliated to the least degree possible, and twisting this way and that, as the Greeks say,[234] you misrepresent whatever speaks of his remarkable humiliation as merely the low estimation of him on the part of impious men. I, on the other hand, in as much as I wish there to be in Christ an example of humility, maintain that his humiliation was very real. Of course, there was no reason why you should have been caught up in this difficulty had you chosen to accept my interpretation of βραχύ τι instead of criticizing it, since this interpretation of mine, the interpretation of the older Greek writers, virtually solves the problem which was causing you difficulty.

Yet here you are, advancing upon me with an array of Greek and Hebrew examples to back you up. The latter we shall look at in due course. For the present, let us examine the strength of the Greek evidence which you bring against my view. 'I do not believe you,' you say, 'since for the Greek writers and for those who are experts in the Greek language βραχύ τι does not denote a measure of time, but rather a measure of worth and estimation.' You allude to Eustathius commenting on the words 'and ten talents of gold' in Homer's *Iliad* and saying, 'If it refers to Greek talents it is a trifling amount' [βραχύ τι].[235] You think that this is sufficient to prove that for Greek writers βραχύ τι cannot have a temporal reference. Now, in the first place I think it amusing that you should be relying upon the Homeric scholiast Eustathius to

* * * * *

232 'Anticyra': *Adagia* I viii 52: *Naviget Anticyras*. This means 'You make me out to be insane.' Anticyra was famous for producing the hellebore which was supposed to heal madness.
233 Quintus Curtius Rufus *Historiae* 4.13.34
234 In Greek. Plutarch *Marius* 30.5
235 *Disputatio* ASD IX-3 216:332–5. This citation from Eustathius, the twelfth-century bishop of Thessalonica who was particularly known for his commentaries on Homer, was originally written in Greek (*In Homeri Iliadem* 1.122).

demonstrate that βραχύ τι has the meaning 'a trifle,' when this can be shown from any author you wish. I hardly think that you are indulging in display to remind us that you are well versed in Homer's epics. The point is, however, that Eustathius is read as an interpreter of Homer, not as an authority on correct linguistic usage. Likewise, if I wanted to substantiate the correctness in Latin of the expression *fregit navem*, I would not offer an example from the commentaries of Beroaldo or Bade before one from Cicero or Terence.[236] In any event, I cannot see what need there was to prove something of which everyone is aware and which nobody denies. Though let me remark in your defence, even though you are my accuser, that I suspect you did not read it in Eustathius himself, but found it somewhere in someone's notes.

Yet how does it follow that βραχύ τι, or 'a trifle,' granted that it may refer to an estimation, cannot also be used to refer to time, or whatever you wish? For example, if one can properly say 'a trifling amount of money,' can one not also properly say 'a trifling amount of time'? Or if we say in Latin 'a short cloak,' is it not possible also to say 'a short day'? For this is how you reason who a little later consign me for treatment at Anticyra because I seem to you to reach a conclusion which is based upon faulty logic, something which I shall speak of in the appropriate place.[237] As for me, I do not intend, either here or anywhere else, to imitate what to me seems foreign to Christian modesty. Yet here I do find lacking that expertise in logic which, if I am not mistaken, you have been either acquiring or imparting now for more than twenty years; and the same is true of your mathematical skill.[238] I beg you, my dearest Lefèvre, recognize how you have been carried away in the heat of the argument. You are behaving like a schoolmaster with a rod giving us our Greek lessons, and prescribing new rules: 'If it is a case of indicating time, it is preferable to say ἐπ' ὀλίγον, for this is how the philosophers generally speak, or μικρόν, which is used with reference to time in the Gospel.'[239] Without objecting to the fact that you make philosophers authorities on correct usage, who denies that μικρόν and ὀλίγον indicate a measure of time if you add or understand the word χρόνον [time]? But the same words will denote a gold coin, a field, or a donkey, if you prefer, if you add or understand any of these nouns. I ask you, what are learned and serious men going to say when they read these things in your books, especially in a place where you are

* * * * *

236 Filippo Beroaldo (d 1505) wrote a commentary on Apuleius; Beroaldo's student, Josse Bade (d 1535), was a friend of Lefèvre.

237 See n232 above.

238 See n191 above.

239 *Disputatio* ASD IX-3 216:338–42

bringing a charge of impiety against a friend? Imagine the scorn, the sneers, the derision on the part of some who are in the habit of criticizing even proper linguistic usage.[240] If you had written anything of this kind to me privately, I would have hidden it away to save you embarrassment; now you have published it in all seriousness as something worth reading and likely to bring you credit.

Not content with these remarks you go on to say, 'If the authors of the Septuagint had wished to signify time they would have said ἠλάττωσας ταχὺ, because the word ταχύ indicates a small lapse of time.'[241] What am I hearing? Would someone who meant that a man lived for a short time say in Greek ταχὺ ἔζωσεν, that is, 'He lived soon,' or would he not rather say, 'He died soon'? By your reasoning you arrive at the translation 'You soon made him lower than the angels.' So help me, my dear Lefèvre, I feel shame at these things on your account, and I wish that you had either not stepped so readily into an arena which, as I have said, is not properly yours, or were not so intent upon staying there, since you would be better off dealing with more general topics.[242] Suppose that Eustathius did teach, which he did not, that the word βραχύ does not refer to time, do you think that Athanasius and Chrysostom were less expert in Greek than Eustathius, individuals who had phenomenal reputations for eloquence in Greek? I would not hesitate for a moment to put up either one of these against even three Eustathiuses. Come now, what if I produce for you a passage from Luke himself where βραχύ τι clearly refers to time, will you still persist in evasion? Look, here is Luke himself speaking in chapter 5 of the Acts of the Apostles: 'ἐκέλευσεν ἔξω βραχύ τι τοὺς ἀποστόλους ποιῆσαι.'[243] Will you think that we are to translate here as follows: 'He ordered the apostles to do something outside a little less'? It is absolutely impossible to pretend that βραχύ τι here does not refer to a measure of time;[244] it is the meaning which the original translator handed down, and we translate 'He ordered the apostles to spend a little time outside.' The sense itself does not allow for any distortion; it must refer to time. Tell us that the writers of the Septuagint, that Athanasius, Chrysostom, Theophylact, and Augustine did not employ βραχύ τι in this sense; tell us that Jerome himself, for he is with me on this point, was incorrect in using the expression in a

* * * * *

240 On the Latin expressions to which Erasmus refers, see *Adagia* I vi 81: *Odorari*.
241 *Disputatio* ASD IX-3 216:342–9
242 This is a perfidious reproach, because a humanist, in the primary sense of the word, was first and foremost a philologist, especially of Greek.
243 Acts 5:34
244 For βραχύ τι, the *Vetus Latina* uses *paulisper* where the Vulgate uses *breve*.

temporal sense. You see how much wiser it is sometimes, my good Lefèvre, to hold back cautiously than to make bold assertions, in which respect you sometimes appear to me to be rather too forceful and to take your aversion to the Sceptics too far. And we might add that the same Luke, whom everyone accepts as the author of Acts, has been credited by some as being also the translator of the letter we are discussing.[245]

To take another point, what about the fact that in this very passage Paul makes it quite clear that he was thinking of an interval of time when he adds, 'Nevertheless, this Jesus, who was for a while made lower than the angels through his suffering and death, we shall see crowned in glory and honour'?[246] As to the fact that he began to be a man, he never ceased to be a man, but quickly ceased to be a mortal. Does he seem to you to be diminished only a little who is reduced even to suffering the punishment of death? Since I do not believe that even you would claim that, to what are you going to refer the words $\beta\rho\alpha\chi\acute{\upsilon}$ $\tau\iota$ if not to time, as so many eminent Greek writers have done? Nor will it serve your purpose very much to do as you have done in your translation, namely, to transfer the words 'through his suffering and death' from their proper place to another to prevent them being taken according to their true reference. For you write as follows, 'Nevertheless, we shall see Jesus, who was made a little less than God, crowned with glory and honour through his suffering and death.'[247] There is no shift you are not prepared to make, no stone left unturned in your effort to defend that newborn child,[248] that brand-new view of yours. But take care that your offspring does not charm you too much.

Again, heaven help me, what am I to say of your behaving like some Aristarchus prescribing a linguistic rule for us?[249] For this is what you give us: 'When "much" and "little" and the like are joined to words which denote increase or decrease, they never signify time; and here *paulo minus* is joined to the verb "you have diminished," which denotes a decrease; it would be

* * * * *

245 An allusion to the Epistle to the Hebrews, which will be taken up again later. From the next sentence onwards, however, Paul is considered the author of this Epistle. For more on this discussion, see 79–81 below. In fact, Erasmus' position is merely to maintain that there is a certain doubt concerning the identity of the author.
246 Heb 2:9
247 In his Pauline commentaries, Lefèvre indeed changed the traditional order of the words in Heb 2:9.
248 *Adagia* I iv 30: *Omnem movere lapidem*
249 Aristarchus (d 114 BC) was a famous grammarian in Alexandria. Cf *Adagia* I v 57: *Stellis signare.*

different if the expression were joined to an adverb denoting time.'[250] Do I detect an enthymeme here,[251] implying that it will be a solecism if I say, 'You have extolled me for a little while with your praises'? All the same, I readily admit that in Latin certain words refer exclusively to time, *paulisper*, for example, and *aliquantisper*, while it is not the case with others, such as *multum* and *parvum*, unless you add a temporal reference. However, the same distinction does not hold for Greek, and while in Latin a temporal word must be added, in Greek one is frequently added, but frequently also simply understood, a practice which we too sometimes adopt, when we say, for instance, 'I shall come in a little,' meaning 'I shall come in a little while.' Not that I think that this has been done in the present case, that is, in the expression ἠλάττωσας αὐτὸν βραχύ τι; I think rather that a neuter adjective has been substituted for an adverb in the same manner as we demonstrated earlier from the words of Paul himself.

Let us briefly examine next the evidence which you adduce from Hebrew texts. You cite several passages where the word *Meat* refers not to a measure of time but to something else. I readily admit that in this language I cannot be a judge, nor do I think that you have advanced to a point where you would ask us to defer to your authority in this matter.[252] Moreover, no matter which Hebrew writer you place before me, his authority does not carry such weight with me that it would be a crime to disagree with him. Furthermore, after producing so many passages, you yourself demonstrate only that *Meat* sometimes refers to something other than time; you do not demonstrate that it cannot refer to time. It would not be surprising or novel for a word which has different meanings sometimes to denote things other than just one particular thing. What if someone were to produce for you a passage where it clearly refers to time, what would you do with your new rule? Take Psalm 36 [Vulg]: 'In just a little while there will be no transgressor.'[253] In the Hebrew text we have *Meat*, and it can be taken only of shortness of time. Again, Psalm 108 [Vulg]: 'May his days be few,'[254] where the Hebrew for 'few' is *Meatim*. Will you deny that here *Meat* refers to the shortness of time? Again

* * * * *

250 *Disputatio* ASD IX-3 216:308–11
251 *enthymema*: a figure of logic which is a syllogism reduced to two propositions
252 For further information on Erasmus' knowledge of Hebrew, see Ep 181:36–45. As for Lefèvre, he made no special claim to having mastered this language. He says at the end of his commentary on Ps 114 (Vulg), eg, that he leaves the discussion to those more competent in Hebrew than he (*Quincuplex psalterium* 1513 ed fol 167v).
253 Ps 37:10
254 Ps 109:8

in Psalm 2, 'for his anger will soon flare up,'[255] is the Hebrew not *Bimeat*? I have no doubt that one could find thirty passages if one had the time to look for them, since these turned up in the book of Psalms alone, this being the book written in Hebrew which happened to be at hand, even though a single passage would be sufficient to discredit your rule.

Now if you thought it appropriate to argue over words with such exactitude, you ought to have examined what the words *paulo minus* might signify in Latin writers. You would have found that it is nothing other than 'almost' or 'all but.' Suetonius, for example, employs the words in this sense in his *Life of Nero*: 'After the world had put up with such a ruler for almost fourteen years, it at last cast him off.' Again, in his *Life of Tiberius*: 'and seeming likely soon to die, which all but came about'; and in the same work: 'Once freed from fear he played at first a very modest role, more modest almost than that of a private person.'[256] You see how to so respectable a writer *paulo minus* is no different from 'almost,' and in similar fashion Apuleius used the superlative form *minimo minus* in the sense of 'very nearly,'[257] just as Greek writers use the expression μικροῦ δεῖν when they wish to indicate that something is but a little way from taking place. I am surprised, since you are such an Aristarchus[258] when it comes to the Greek and Hebrew languages, that you dictate rules of usage to the world, and since you are so sensitive to little words that you say those we are discussing have the effect of diminishing Christ; I am surprised, I say, that in your translation you did not change their meaning, even though it would invert the entire sense which the Prophet intended. Unless you think that 'to be almost diminished' and 'to be diminished a little' mean the same thing, when with the latter he is understood to be diminished to a small degree and with the former not to have been diminished at all, even if he came close to being so. Just as the prophet Balaam, as Augustine says, was not astonished at his ass breaking into speech because he had become used to strange happenings, will you likewise show no reaction at all to these kinds of linguistic monstrosities?[259] I deliberately omit many examples lest I be doubly tiresome to my reader through making things which are in themselves offensive and distasteful even more so by stringing them out. For example, when I point out that Aquinas was of one mind with Chrysostom because he reminds us that *paulo*

* * * * *

255 Ps 2:13
256 *Nero* 4.1 and *Tiberius* 39 and 26 respectively
257 Apuleius *Metamorphoses* 1.4.4
258 See n249 above.
259 Augustine *Quaestiones in Heptateuchum* 4 CSEL 28 part 2 355–6 on Num 22:28–30

minus can be taken in two ways, referring either to quantity or to length of time, you excuse him as though I were bringing this forward to his discredit. Were it not for the honesty which I have had occasion to remark in you, there might lurk the grave suspicion that some Thomist was in league with you when you were writing these things, since you treat him with somewhat more politeness than you do Athanasius or Chrysostom.[260]

Let me respond, however, to the remaining points in your *Apologia*, or rather your indictment. You say that I wrote, 'There are those who think that Luke was the translator of the Epistle [to the Hebrews], and if this view is accepted, this translation cannot be challenged.'[261] What offends you here, my dear Lefèvre? Is it that I have stated that certain persons are of this opinion? But does not the preface to this Epistle contained in our manuscripts clearly support it? Granted that this preface is not the work of Jerome, whether it is by Bede or Isidore or someone else it is certainly not the work of any completely unlearned person, and it is approved for the public use of Christians.[262] I need not bring forward arguments from others when what is read in this argument is reported by Eusebius in book six, chapter fourteen of his *Ecclesiastical History* on the authority of Clement of Alexandria,[263] and when Jerome in his *De viris illustribus* does not demur.[264] But though the identity of the translator may not be absolutely clear, upon what authority are you relying when you pronounce with such superiority against Luke? Is it because the translator followed the Septuagint text? Why would it be surprising if Luke as translator should do so when Paul often does the same when he is his own translator? Still, I have given you a free choice of accepting this view or rejecting it. If you do not accept it, then you have no quarrel with me. If it is a correct view, then it is certainly the case that the translation is not to be called into question, unless you think that Luke should be put on the stand. Nevertheless, you add, 'But here truth

* * * * *

260 See n8 above. On St Thomas, see n59 above. The passage under discussion is found in the *Disputatio* ASD IX-3 220:457–76. For Chrysostom, see *Enarrationes in epistolam ad Hebraeos* hom 4 PG 63 38. Athanasius is taken for Theophylact (cf H. de Jonge ASD IX-2 131 n437).

261 See n245 above; *Disputatio* ASD IX-3 220:476–83.

262 On previous prefaces to the different books of the Bible, see Samuel Berger *Les préfaces jointes aux livres de la Bible dans les manuscrits de la Vulgate* (Paris 1902); Maurice E. Schild *Abendländische Bibelvorreden bis zur Lutherbibel* (Gutersloh 1970); and *Apologia* ASD IX-3 151:1625n. The Venerable Bede (d 735) and Isidore of Seville (d 636) used the Vulgate.

263 Eusebius *Ecclesiastical History* 6.14.2

264 Jerome *De viris illustribus* 5 PL 23 650A

should prevail, not the authority of the writer, whoever he happened to be.'
Are you being serious, Lefèvre, or is this said in jest? Whoever the author or
translator of this Epistle was, will his authority carry no weight, even if the
author was Paul himself, or the translator Luke himself? What you mean here
only you will know; what you have expressed in words can certainly not be
mistaken by anyone. However, I shall not press you on your words, since I
am fairly certain that what you meant was that it did not greatly matter who
the translator was since you are convinced it was not Luke.[265]

Next you take exception to my indicating from the notes of teachers of
Hebrew literature that they take the word *Eloim* to be singular or plural and
to be a word with more than one meaning.[266] Yet this did not disturb you
when you were writing on this psalm. Indeed, you apply its plural number to
the three Persons, Father, Son, and Holy Ghost.[267] As for this new rule, which
is owed to some Hebrew scholar,[268] I neither endorse nor reject it. What is
a fact is that none of the Hebrew writers denies that *El* is proper for God,
or that *Eloim* is sometimes substituted for God when his function is added,
as when, in creating the world, he said, 'Let us make a man,'[269] sometimes
for angels, sometimes for leaders and judges, sometimes for gods. The only
distinction they wish to preserve between *Eloim* and *Malachim* is that angels
are called *Malachim* whenever they are being sent to perform a function, but
Eloim whenever their dignity or eminence is pronounced. You claim that the
authors of the Septuagint, whenever *Eloim* is used without any mark that it is
plural, consistently translated it as 'God.' If this were true, they would have
translated it as 'God' in this instance too, since no mark is present, as you say.
I identify my authority for this, and it is someone to whom you attribute a
great deal, if I am not mistaken. And he teaches the same in volume three
of his recently published work, complete with several citations from Holy

* * * * *

265 Lefèvre cannot accept the possibility that Luke the Evangelist might have
translated the Epistle to the Hebrews because that would cast doubt upon his
own concept of inspiration.

266 The Greek term is πολύσημον.

267 This is Lefèvre's pious interpretation in the *Quincuplex psalterium*. He believes
that the Holy Spirit, as the author of Scripture, implied the mystery of the
Trinity through the plural word *Eloim*. That was also the position of certain
Fathers of the church concerning the 'we's of the creation narratives in Genesis,
to which Erasmus refers a little further on.

268 The expression seems to designate a Jew, but it was François Vatable, Lefèvre's
collaborator and companion, who rendered his services to Lefèvre as a Christian
scholar of Hebrew.

269 Gen 1:26. See n267 above.

Scripture.[270] Recognize, then, how what you say contradicts itself. You claim that the Septuagint writers followed the same principle throughout, yet here you admit they translated differently. It is like saying that the whole of a swan is white while admitting that the same swan has a black beak. It would not be surprising for someone who is a dullard like me in subtleties of this kind to make a slip; it is extraordinary that a superb logician like yourself should be wandering astray in this fashion, especially since you are such a demanding critic when it comes to little errors of this kind in the writings of a friend. To me it seems probable that the Septuagint translators recognized that here too *Eloim* could be taken as plural in reference, that they were reluctant to say 'God,' and 'Gods' did not seem right, so they translated it as 'angels.'

I do not believe I have omitted anything which I have not been able to demolish with clear proofs and on which I have been unable to satisfy you. But since your whole treatise lacked order, because you were tearing away at individual parts of my treatise as they came, and in my reply I was forced to follow your sequence, the reader may find my own presentation rather unfocused and for this reason less than clear. Accordingly, by way of an epilogue, it may not be out of place to draw the main threads of the argument together into a summary. First of all, I have shown that as far as the central issue is concerned there is no argument between us; indeed, in fighting against me you are fighting against yourself. I rehearse the question of the alternative readings, both of which enjoy the support of such great authorities that, in my view, neither deserves to be rejected out of hand, and each is in its own way acceptable, provided that the word *Eloim* in Hebrew can be singular or plural, and sometimes mean God, sometimes gods, sometimes judges, sometimes angels, as has been noted by those who teach Hebrew literature, but chiefly, in case his authority carries more weight with you, by the Master of the Sentences, as his title is, in section three of his first volume.[271] As to your being so astonished that anyone should be so bold as to take *Eloim* as plural when out of 275 instances it is singular in all but

* * * * *

270 Johann Reuchlin, who defended the importance of studies in Hebrew, was attacked by the theologians and defended by the humanists. Cf Guy Bedouelle and Franco Giacone 'Une lettre inédite de Gilles de Viterbe (1469–1532) à Jacques Lefèvre d'Etaples (c 1460–1536) au sujet de l'affaire Reuchlin' *Bibliothèque d'humanisme et Renaissance* 36 (1974) 335–45. According to Steenbeek (*Apologia* ASD IX-3 151:1659n), the book to which Erasmus refers is *De rudimentis Hebraicis*.

271 Peter Lombard *Sententiae* book 1 dist 2 c 4

one, I in turn am astonished at your boldness in giving your observations the status of rules. For what is to prevent the word being used as a plural, even if it has been used as a singular two thousand times? Unless you think that because the word 'boy' has been used more than six hundred times in the Scriptures to denote the person's age, it is wrong to use the same word to mean 'servant.' Equally nonsensical is your assertion regarding the particle *Col*, namely, that unless it is added the word *Eloim* cannot be taken as plural, an assertion which you base upon the fact that it is added in several instances. Yet take that passage from the Psalms which Christ himself cites in the Gospel according to John: 'I have said, "You are gods"'; even Jerome translates into the plural, despite the fact that the particle *Col* is certainly not present. Again, 'God stood in the synagogue of gods,' and 'Mighty gods of the earth have been powerfully raised up,' and 'Cast out foreign gods.'[272] But why do I point to these? There are so many instances in the Old Testament of the word 'gods' where there is no sign of your particle *Col*, which you would like to establish as so consistent a mark of the plural that anyone who translates *Eloim* other than as 'God' where it is absent deserves to be brought to trial. It is very clear, therefore, that the instances which you cite, following someone who is not the best authority, whoever he is, do not prevent us from taking *Eloim* in this instance as plural and as signifying something other than God.

Second, there is the fact that whichever of the two readings is adopted, the adverbial expression *paulo minus*, or *paululum*, causes a problem, though it is one which is more acute if we choose the reading which you regard as the only possible one,[273] because while we grant that there is only a moderate distance separating the nature of angels and mortal flesh, the distinction between the divine nature which assumed and the human nature which was assumed must be acknowledged as immense, and it is only on the basis of a comparison between these two natures that Christ can be said to be less than the Father. This problem I alleviate by taking *paulo minus* in the sense of 'for a short time,' so that Christ is understood to have been diminished to a great degree, but for a short while, or to a very considerable degree if we measure his diminution or humiliation, as Ambrose does and which I approve, in terms of the afflictions which he suffered in this human life of ours which

* * * * *

272 Pss 82:6, 82:1, 47:10; and Gen 35:2 respectively. In John 10:34, Christ cites Ps 82:6.

273 Here, Erasmus has clearly perceived the weakness of Lefèvre's hermeneutics, which reduces the meaning of Holy Scripture to the Christological component alone. Cf Bedouelle *Quincuplex psalterium* 147–51.

he assumed.[274] Furthermore, I demonstrated that the Greek words βραχύ τι can have a temporal meaning, even though this was clear in itself to those who know the Greek language, and I based my demonstration upon Luke himself, upon Paul himself, and even upon this very Epistle of Paul,[275] just in case you found the authority of Chrysostom and the other Greek writers insufficiently weighty.[276]

Up to this juncture the debate between us centres around the main point at issue. As for the remaining matters, either you have added them of your own accord or you have seized upon them from remarks which I made casually in the course of my argument, either by way of expansion or by way of supporting my position. Chief among these is my remark that 'Christ was made lower than the most worthless of men.' So far from there being anything in this which is unworthy of Christ, it greatly promotes his glory, if we remember that Paul said that Christ desolated himself, and that the words of the prophets refer to him as 'a worm and not a man.'[277] Moreover, if we bear in mind our own salvation, it was advantageous to us that an example of humility that was in the highest degree remarkable and genuine should be displayed through him who is truth itself, especially since emphasizing his humiliation in this fashion in no way detracts from his sublimity, because just as he could be called both mortal and immortal, most afflicted and most blessed, so could he be called in different senses highest and lowest, on account, that is, of his opposite natures united in the same substance, and above all on account of the extreme tortures which he took upon himself beyond all mortals; for I prefer to follow St Ambrose[278] in associating the things which are said of Christ's desolation with these afflictions rather than with the nature which he assumed, for the reason that if they are associated simply with the flesh which he took on, he could on this reasoning be said to have been made lower than God to an immense degree on the very day when he became man. Accordingly, no one can fail to see that the insults which you direct towards me when you say that this statement also (by which you imply, of course, that there are others of the same stripe) is most unworthy of Christ and God, on the ground that it clings to the letter which destroys while opposing the spirit which gives life, undermines the meaning of the Prophet, casts down Christ as do the unholy Jews, and other things of this

* * * * *

274 See n139 above. It is a question here of Ambrosiaster.
275 The Epistle to the Hebrews
276 Cf 63.
277 Ps 22:7
278 See n139 above.

kind, are such as do not deserve to be levelled by you or against me, and are a far cry from that most gentle spirit of Christ which does not destroy life, but gives it,[279] and which does not abuse the mistakes of men, but amends them, especially the mistakes of one who speaks with reverence and in accordance with the opinion of the orthodox Fathers of the church.

Next, with respect to those passages from the prophetic writings which speak clearly of the extraordinary diminution of Christ, some you distort by interpreting them as the appraisal of unholy persons, others you lay at my door. However, I have demonstrated by means of fitting arguments and with the help of the weightiest authorities that these statements refer to Christ in a true and literal sense. Moreover, I have pointed out that there is nothing in your lengthy treatment of Christ's dignity which stands in the way of his utmost humiliation. Christ's inferiority to the angels is in no way affected by the fact that they are ordained to worship him, just as his superiority over his parents is in no way affected by the statement in Luke that he was placed under them.[280] If Christ can in no way be called lower than the angels for the reason that none of these raised up the dead, healed the sick, to say nothing of the miracles which Christ performed through their agency, then it follows that Christ was inferior to his own disciples, since they, as he himself declared they would, did greater things than these.[281] Furthermore, with respect to what you say about Christ's authority, Christ yields the authority for his own words to the Father: 'I do the works of my Father; as my Father has commissioned me, so do I do; the word which you hear is not my word but that of my Father who sent me; my teaching is not mine.'[282] As to your denying that Christ is called 'a created thing,' I have made it clear that he has been so called by the highest authorities, even if not by me. Likewise, with respect to your assertion that Christ enjoys a relationship of equality with God and for this reason cannot be called a 'worm,' I have proved my point that he enjoys also another relationship on the basis of which he has been called a 'worm,' not by me but by the Prophet. Furthermore, with respect to your statement, which you offer as a reductio ad absurdum, that 'the Cherubim too can be called "worms" when compared with God,' I would personally not object to this, especially if the prophetic books attributed this title to them.

You make a large number of statements of this kind which in the course of my treatise I decided to ignore; for example, the following: 'Bodily

* * * * *

279 Cf 2 Cor 3:6; John 6:63; 1 Tim 6:13.
280 Heb 1:6; Luke 2:51
281 John 14:12
282 Cf John 14:31; followed by exact citations from John 14:24 and 7:16

torments can be so great that greater torments cannot be devised.'[283] But however much you emphasize torments to the body, they may certainly be rendered more excruciating if they are compounded with equal torments to the spirit. Further, with respect to your strenuous objections against words for 'substance'[284] being taken as referring to one only of Christ's two natures, I have pointed out in the first place that I have nowhere done this, and in the second that had I done so I would have had earlier orthodox writers as precedents; unless you think, perhaps, that when St Augustine writes, as he does in *On the Trinity*, book two, chapter six, 'because the creature was not so assumed, in which the Holy Spirit should appear, as the Son of Man was assumed,' he does not take 'Son of Man' as referring to the one of Christ's two natures.[285] I also remarked in passing that it is safer to take words for substance as referring to one of Christ's two natures than to do as you prefer, which is to take them as referring to both his natures together, that is, his divine and human natures combined, even though they signify two natures. I also demonstrated, though it was superfluous to do so, that what can be stated of Christ using a word for substance can be stated not only of his two natures separately but also at different times of any of the three substances or things in Christ.[286] I think I have said enough to make it evident that though you think you have been convincing with syllogisms in which there is an abundance of errors and a complete absence of effectual arguments, you have in fact failed to convince. But let us proceed to what is left.

In what follows you attack and hound me to such a degree that I must confess I ought to have written with greater care and attention if I was going to encounter such harsh critics. My first concern, however, was the rather humble one of composing annotations, and in this type of exercise the older writers always assumed a certain licence.[287] I was not expecting to run up against someone who was intent upon examining every detail and finding fault unfairly. I thought my readers would be people like myself. But while I am willing to acknowledge your charge of naïvety, I reject your assertion that I am stupid. For in the first place I am of the opinion that those commentaries

* * * * *

283 This sentence does not appear in any of Lefèvre's works; it is a summary of Lefèvre's argument made by Erasmus.
284 *hypostasis*
285 Augustine *De Trinitate* 2.6 CCSL 50 93
286 Erasmus calls *caro*, *anima*, and *divinitas* three *substantiae* (cf *Apologia* ASD IX-3 110:636–9), thus following the terminology of Augustine *De Trinitate* 2.11.20 CCSL 50 107. See also n103 above.
287 *libertas*. See also nn20, 23 above.

which you cite are not the work of St Jerome and were not collected together by him.[288] Why, then, do you cite them under his name? You ought to have given them some title, and then we could have dispensed with arguing over their authorship. And you know that Jerome[289] attributes to Paul a certain artfulness, if I may use the word, of this kind on the grounds that he twists certain things to his own purpose and on occasion says things which are at variance with Holy Scripture, even though they are perfectly appropriate in their original context, as when in the Epistle to Titus he puts the profane saying of Epimenides the Cretan prophet to work for Christ.[290] Similarly in Acts, what Aratus said of Jupiter, Paul applies to God, and by changing some of the words twists the profane and impious inscription on the altar into an argument for the faith.[291] For though the inscription read TO THE GODS OF ASIA AND AFRICA AND EUROPE AND TO UNKNOWN AND FOREIGN GODS, he distorts it by reporting that he has seen an altar on which was written TO THE UNKNOWN GOD, as we are told by Jerome in his commentary on Paul's Epistle to Titus.[292]

You are well aware also, I think, that almost all the old writers indulge in allegorical interpretations, especially Ambrose, Origen, and Jerome, and they deny that there is any danger in this provided that the allegories are made to conform to devout principles.[293] Yet despite all this, see how anyone who knows Latin will recognize how egregiously you twist my meaning even when I have explained it. For I did not say that these things 'do not apply to Christ,' but that 'Jerome does not appear to prove adequately that they are meant strictly of Christ.' You, so it seems, think that 'strictly' here has the same force as if I had said 'truly.'[294] What I do mean is that those things are attributed 'strictly' to Christ which are attributed to him in such a way that they apply to no one else. Thus the First Psalm, in the way in which the holy teachers interpret it of Christ, does not apply to just any devout person you wish. If you grant me this liberty here, then it will be true that

* * * * *

288 See n93 above.
289 Jerome *Commentarius in epistolam ad Titum* 1 PL 26 606–9. For the same idea, see Erasmus *Annotationes* LB VI 501E.
290 Titus 1:12. *Annotationes ad Titum* LB VI 968D; Reeve III 696
291 Acts 17:28. Aratus was a poet from Sicily who lived in the third century BC. Paul's citation is taken from the *Phenomena* of Aratus.
292 Acts 17:23; Jerome *Commentarius in epistolam ad Titum* 1 PL 26 607B
293 These are authors whom Erasmus edited – Jerome in 1516; Origen, a posthumous edition of whose works appeared in 1536 but had been begun in 1527, the same year as Erasmus' first edition of Ambrose.
294 *proprie et non vere*

those things which may apply in a figurative sense to the rest of men also should not be applied 'strictly' to Christ. And there is nothing in the psalm we are discussing which cannot be made to apply without fear of heresy to all devout men.[295] For if you grasp the essential meaning of the Prophet, he seems to be marvelling at God's singular beneficence towards us, who though he is higher than the heavens, nevertheless shows concern for men who dwell on earth, and considers them worthy of such great honour that he has set man over all creatures, recalling almost to the letter what was said in Genesis, namely, 'Fill the earth and subdue it, and rule over the fishes of the sea and over the birds of the air and over all the creatures which move upon the earth,'[296] and has made man almost equal with the divine by granting him his special gifts of the mind. For when the Prophet says, 'What is man?'[297] he seems to acknowledge the humbleness of the human condition. When he adds, 'You have made him a little lower than the angels,'[298] he shows how he has been raised up from below by the gift of God. For what we take to refer to the diminution of man appears to have been said there in the opposite sense: 'You have made him a little lower than the angels,' that is, you have made him almost equal with the angels. You are dreaming, you will say.[299] No indeed, it was Arnobius, not the worst of writers, who was dreaming long ago, when he referred this entire psalm not to Christ but to the members of Christ.[300] Certainly, what follows, namely, 'You have put all things under his feet, all sheep and oxen, and also the beasts of the field, the birds ...,'[301] this clearly does not apply to Christ, but to us. For of what moment is it if Christ has been set over the beasts and fishes and birds? And you see that the translator of the Epistle to the Hebrews took the testimony of the psalm in this way when he wrote, 'You have put all things under his feet,'[302] omitting those items which did not accord equally well with what Christ then did, and made absolute what seemed to him to be restricted by the list which follows in the psalm, namely, sheep, oxen, and so forth.

Besides, if the Prophet had in mind the power by which Christ rules over every creature on the earth and in the sky, how was it appropriate for him to

* * * * *

295 Ps 8
296 Gen 1:28
297 Ps 8:5
298 Ps 8:6
299 *Adagia* II i 62: *Somnium*
300 Arnobius *Commentarii in psalmos* 8 CCSL 25 10
301 Ps 8:8
302 Heb 2:8

name only those things which represent the lowliest aspect of this power? I am aware, of course, that translators take these things allegorically,[303] and I certainly do not reject that approach, though in this case I do think the allegory is a little too forced. Since at the time I was pondering something of this kind, and my objective was to put all possibilities to the test, probing them as it were like so many sacrificial victims, and to place before the reader a variety of material for him to consider, which is the legitimate role of an annotator, it seemed only proper to indicate this politely; for there are certain things which are there to be pointed out rather than explained; it is something which we see the earliest theologians doing, and even contemporary theologians do not say altogether the same things in their school lectures as they do in the private company of scholars, or if they say the same things, they do not say them in the same way. But to attack me with the kind of language that you employ, and to make an exhibition of me before an uneducated and uncharitable public, is to my mind lacking in civility and still less the mark of a friend. If you care to take note of the kind of language I employ, it will be clear in an instant that it is the language of someone who is not being categorical, but simply exploring the issue.[304] 'He seems not to have fully proved,' I say. In fact, his arguments seem convincing when they are nothing of the kind, even though they give a certain impression of truth. Yet this too I tone down by adding the word 'fully,' that is, not in every particular. But, you will say, give me an instance of that impression which creates the illusion that his statement is true. Well, in the first place, he names his authority[305] in such a way as to place the weight of proof on him. Second, of what importance is it that Paul takes this passage as referring to Christ when Jerome himself takes the entire psalm as referring to Christ? I warned the reader of this briefly and with reluctance so that he might reject whatever deserved to be rejected. Indeed, it is not at all a case of doubting whether this psalm applies to Christ, but whether it applies to him exclusively, that is, to Christ alone in such a way that it cannot be made to apply to the rest of mankind, despite the fact that common sense clearly dictates that the entire psalm refers to the human race, under which God has placed all the products and creatures which the earth brings forth, reserving for his own divine mind meanwhile to attend to the things above the earth. St Augustine, it is true, explains the psalm as referring to Christ, but in such a way as to accommodate it to us as well, having been reborn

* * * * *

303 Augustine *Enarratio in psalmum 8* CCSL 38 52–3
304 Ep 1581:864–7 to Béda 25 June 1515
305 The author of the Epistle to the Hebrews

in Christ.[306] A great crime indeed that I wished to give the reader a tiny word of caution!

Let me now mention in passing the following verse, interspersing my comments with your interpretation of it: 'What is man that you are mindful of him, or the Son of Man that you visitest him?' You write as follows:

> Of the rest of mankind there is only a certain mindfulness of God, and at the same time a certain absence, if I may use the term, as is indicated by the words 'What is man that you are mindful of him?' For mindfulness is of things absent. But of the Son of Man, that is, Christ, there is already a visitation and presence on the part of God consisting in Christ's union with him, a union so close that it is one of substance and closer than any other could be, something which is indicated in the words 'or the Son of Man that you visitest him'; and visitation, union, or presence of this kind on the part of God does not diminish man, but raises him up above all things in such a way that he is made only a little lower than God; and to be made a little lower than God is to be exalted above all other things and is for all things to be subjected to him. The apostle Paul says, 'In that he has placed all things under him, he has made nothing that is not subject to him, except the one who has placed all things below him.' And concerning that visitation, union, or embracing on the part of the Divinity, Paul adds towards the end of the chapter: 'For nowhere does he embrace the angels, but the seed of Abraham he does embrace,' and 'seed of Abraham' he elsewhere interprets as Christ.[307]

I have given your exact words up to this point. Now first, what do you mean when you say, 'Of the rest of mankind there is only a certain mindfulness of God'?[308] Do you mean that men are mindful of God or that God is mindful of men? Second, do you mean that men are absent or that God is absent? But even more perilous than this ambiguity is the one you were guilty of earlier when you said: 'The Word and Son of God is of divine making and of the same nature as God. For he is no more a created thing than God.' For this may be taken in one of two ways, either that God the Father is

* * * * *

306 Augustine *Enarratio in psalmum 8* CCSL 38 50
307 Erasmus cites a long passage in which Lefèvre refers to Heb 2:8, 1 Cor 15:27, and Heb 2:16 (*Disputatio* ASD IX-3 218:386–401), in order to refute it step by step by demonstrating that if one analyses each sentence, one ends up enmeshed in difficulties concerning 'unspeakable' matters over which one must not quibble.
308 *Memoria* is a central theme in Augustinian thought which Lefèvre associates, like that of visitation, with Ps 8:5.

not a created thing, or that the Son of God is not God. Now when you say, 'of the Son of Man, that is, Christ, there is a visitation,' do you mean that Christ visited man, or that he was visited by God? If you call a visitation the taking on of human form, in what way do you say that Christ was visited? Or, as we rightly say 'God assumed man,' will we properly say 'God assumed Christ'? You see, here is the very sort of language for which you chastised me a little earlier, not because I spoke in this way, but because you thought I did. Again, when you say 'does not diminish man,' are you taking the word 'man,' which is a word of substance,[309] to mean human form, something which you earlier said could not be done? Further, when you speak of that visitation, union, and embracing by God, I am amazed that when it comes to my language you seek a knot in a bulrush,[310] as the saying goes, while you allow yourself to talk such nonsense as this about matters unspeakable. For who has ever used the expression 'embracing by God,' not to mention your intolerable and pervasive repetitiveness?[311] Furthermore, when you go on to say that 'by this union Christ was made a little lower than God, but in such a way that he was exalted above all things,' if this was to be exalted, namely, to be visited by God, and if he is visited who is united in the assumption, then as soon as the Word became incarnate, Christ was exalted above all things. Where in this is the fact that Paul says Jesus was 'made a little lower than God and then crowned with glory and honour on account of his suffering'? And again, 'On account of this God exalted him and gave him a name . . .,' indicating that he was exalted not on account of his birth, but on account of his suffering on the cross? Moreover, when you say that God 'embraced the seed of Abraham, who is Christ,' do you not see that you are saying that Christ was embraced? For I think that what you mean here by being embraced is nothing other than being assumed. Likewise, in what follows, namely, 'But he did not embrace any other man,' you understand, I think, 'than Christ.' You perceive, I am sure, how much material for criticism there is, if someone wished to cavil as you do. Though Augustine, from whom you have taken the cue for your interpretation, does not say that Christ was visited by God, but speaks of two men, as it were, the former a sinner, of whom God was none the less mindful, extending his kindness even as far as him, and the new man, reborn into holiness.[312] In all of this I consciously and deliberately shut my eyes to a great deal for fear of giving the impression that I am enjoying what I am simply forced to do.

* * * * *

309 *hypostasis*
310 *Adagia* II iv 76: *Nodum in scyrpo*
311 *Adagia* II i 92: *Battologia*
312 Augustine *Enarratio in psalmum 8* CCSL 38 53–4

From this point on things go from bad to worse in Mandraboulos' fashion, as the Greek proverb has it.[313] One charge leads to another, each more serious than the one before. Take the heavy charge you bring against the end of my annotation, where I added the following: 'There has been so much doubt concerning the authorship of this letter that it is only of recent date that it has been accepted by the Roman church: indeed, of all the letters this is the only one on which Ambrose wrote no commentary, and Jerome says that "it has not been accepted by some because there are a few things in it which are not found in the Hebrew text." '[314] Here you bring a triple charge against me. First, you accuse me of slow-wittedness for having added these comments when they have no bearing upon the issue. Second, you charge me with deception for saying that the letter was accepted only at a late date when it has always been accepted. Third, you charge me with ignorance, or madness, as you say, and such a degree of madness as to stand in need of all the hellebore in Anticyra,[315] because in an ill-tempered argument I concluded wrongly that it was accepted at a late date by the Roman church because it is the only one on which Ambrose does not comment. Let me respond briefly to each of the points in turn. If my additional comment was in no way relevant to what was under discussion, why did you wish to imitate my slow-wittedness by examining things which have no bearing upon your case? You had determined to defend your opinion and you had completed your task. What point was there in drawing the matter out further? Unless, perhaps, you were determined to scrutinize every single one of my annotations. Suppose I had suddenly forgotten myself and become oblivious to all that had preceded, had suddenly tumbled from my donkey and found myself in another world, as they say, what had that to do with your case?[316] After you had made the points you wanted to, politeness required that you control and hide this madness of your petty little mind and put an end to attacking me in savage language and mocking me in published volumes.[317] There is hardly a person who does not at some time experience what I did. Nor was there any want of reasons why you should have shown this degree of politeness quite apart from our friendship. Alone, I was carrying out a double assignment, the correction of Jerome and of the New Testament,

* * * * *

313 In Greek. *Adagia* I ii 58: *Mandrabuli*; Ep 785:11
314 See n245 above.
315 See n232 above.
316 *Adagia* I vii 31A: *Ab asino delapsus*; *Adagia* I ii 97: *In alio mundo*
317 The plea and the attack become more personal. Erasmus often mentioned the speed with which he had had to prepare his edition of the *Novum instrumentum*.

each on its own a very difficult task. You know the state of my health, and I was under pressure from several publishers. They were amazed that I had been able to write as much as I had, an amount it would have been difficult enough even to read; I was amazed on my part that they were able to publish anything from pages which had been scribbled out rather than properly prepared. And you see that in the work itself I promised a revision of my hasty edition. These writings, then, were surely deserving of a more sympathetic critic, especially since you are a friend, if at any point I had gone off the track. Yet, lest you think that I have gone totally astray, let me say that I thought my comment was to some degree relevant to the issue. For since there was a problem facing both readings, I was looking for a possible way out, and I thought I was pointing out an opening[318] by demonstrating that the words βραχύ τι referred to time. However, in case my arguments should prove unconvincing, and not wishing to leave anything unexplored, I decided to offer a reminder that there had long been some dispute as to the author of this letter, especially among the Latin Fathers. Given this uncertainty, and a justified uncertainty at that, his authority ought to have less influence over us, and we should feel a greater liberty in challenging his interpretation; moreover, it would not be necessary to place entire blame on the poor translator. I realize, of course, that I shall seem to have cleared myself of the charge of slow-wittedness only to run into a charge of impiety through appearing eager to diminish the status of a letter whose authority is held sacrosanct by all orthodox believers. My dear Lefèvre, what is expressed in the letter is quite excellent. Indeed, I would pay a large price for the church of Christ to have some more letters of this sort from whatever author. If it were perfectly clear to me what the position of the church is, I would happily accede to its judgment; or let me say, rather, that for all that I am at the moment less than sure with what enthusiasm the church has accepted the letter, one thing is most sure, and that is that I am prepared to follow wholeheartedly whatever it has decreed, and, even if my own opinion should differ, always to defer to its judgment, provided that you do not interpret as a decision of the church whatever has appealed to just any theologian, or perhaps to no theologian at all. If the church has rightly determined that this letter was written by Paul and orders me to accept this, then I believe and proclaim that Paul is its author. But if it has accepted the letter as something worthy for Christians to read, whoever the author may be, I concentrate upon the contents and make no argument concerning the author.

* * * * *

318 *Adagia* III ii 75: *Reperire rimam*

If the church wishes it to have the same authority as the rest of Paul's letters, I raise no objection, but follow willingly wherever ecclesiastical authority has summoned me.[319]

But it is impious, you say, to dispute over these things when the letter has been readily received in all quarters as Paul's. If it is impious to challenge what the church through public use has approved, what is more generally accepted as more familiar than that reading which you attack as being false, namely, 'You have made him a little lower than the angels'? Are you to be allowed to call an error what the church has for so many centuries adopted and followed, to which the authority of almost all orthodox believers gives enthusiastic support, while I shall not be allowed to question politely in what spirit the church has accepted this letter, especially since this acceptance has been hesitant and late in coming? You face me with the authority of the synod. Bring forward the synod which has named Paul as the author.[320] If you do, then I shall turn your own weapon against you and face you in turn with the fact that the synod has approved the very passage which you reject as being heretical and unworthy of Christ.[321] Your taking refuge behind the Hebrew text means nothing. Granted that the letter was written in Hebrew, certainly no one has ventured to claim that he has seen this Hebrew version, which, as several scholars estimate, had been lost already in Luke's time. Whichever synod approved this version at the same time approved this reading which you claim to be false and heretical, unless you are going to say that the text which had the reading 'a little lower than God' was emended by the synod, and that all the subsequent Greek and Latin copies were from that point on corrupted. Even if you were to bring yourself to say this without blushing, I cannot imagine anyone being so stupid as to believe it.

The only point I make is that there is uncertainty as to the author. It could be that the letter is not by Paul and yet is even better than the Pauline letters. And I add that it was accepted with hesitation by the Roman church. You strongly reject this and deny that its authorship has been questioned. It is only fair, my dear Lefèvre, to forgive me for following the authority of

* * * * *

319 Erasmus avows his obedience to the church while distinguishing, as usual, the levels of adherence to the several kinds of propositions which are required of the believer.

320 In its decree of 1442 on the Jacobites, the Council of Florence had enumerated the fourteen Epistles of the apostle Paul, with the Epistle to the Hebrews listed last. This text was to be taken up again in 1546 during the Council of Trent.

321 Erasmus' argument must be that the Council of Florence approved the translation of Ps 8 which Lefèvre condemns when it accepted the Latin Vulgate.

St Jerome and St Augustine in this matter. There is frequent mention of the letter in Jerome, who several times draws upon it in such a way as to leave it open whether he is prepared to accept it as genuine or not. But I have at hand, meanwhile, one or two places which will suffice to absolve me from the charge of falsehood. For in his exposition of the thirty-first chapter of Jeremiah, Jerome says, 'The apostle Paul, or whoever else wrote the Epistle to the Hebrews, used this testimony';[322] and Jerome is here being quite orthodox. If there was agreement that Paul was the author, it was ridiculous for him to add 'or whoever else wrote the Epistle.' Likewise, in his Letter to Dardanus, he says:

> I must say this, that this letter, which is inscribed 'to the Hebrews,' is taken not only by the eastern churches but also by all in the past who wrote in Greek to be the work of the apostle Paul, though a number of people think it the work of Barnabas or Clement; in fact, it does not matter who the author was, since it is the work of a man of the church and is sanctioned every day by being read in the churches. If there is no consensus among the Latin Fathers to give it a place among canonical writings, neither do the Greek churches feel bound to accept the Apocalypse of John. I accept both, following by no means the current practice, but the authority of the old writers, who commonly accept the testimony of both, just as they are sometimes in the habit of doing with apocryphal writings; indeed they frequently use examples from pagan literature as though they were canonical and ecclesiastical.[323]

So much for my quotation from Jerome. Now everyone knows how forceful Jerome is when he is on the attack. Yet here, where he is employing every means possible to establish the greatest degree of authority for this letter, he admits that in his own generation it has not been accepted as canonical by the Latin Fathers, with the result that they have doubts not only about its authorship but also about its teaching. On the strength of your remark that no one has had doubts about it except the Ebionites, the Marcionites, and heretics like them, almost all the Latin Fathers were heretics, indeed heretics of the worst kind.[324] Furthermore, as to Jerome's statement that he accepts both the works mentioned, as though he were neither a Latin nor a Greek,

* * * * *

322 Jerome *In Hieremiam* 31 CCSL 74 319
323 Jerome Ep 129.3 CSEL 56 169
324 This is Lefèvre's argument (*Disputatio* ASD IX-3 223:557–224:564). The Ebionites seem to have rejected the Pauline corpus completely, whereas the Marcionites accepted only ten of these Epistles along with the Gospel according to Luke.

he is speaking not from the authority of a synod but in the manner of writers whose custom it is to appropriate for their own use whatever happens to please, regardless of the source. Indeed, in setting up arguments even apocryphal and pagan material is valid. Again, when he says 'as though they were canonical,' he is clearly admitting that they were not really canonical.

Jerome again writes in his commentary on the twenty-sixth chapter of Matthew: 'For Paul too, in the letter which is inscribed "to the Hebrews," though many of the Latin Fathers have doubts about it . . .'[325] He did not say 'many of the heretics,' but 'many of the Latin Fathers.' Similarly, in his exposition of the fiftieth chapter of Isaiah, he says: 'It is said in the letter which purports to be to the Hebrews.'[326] Origen, in his *Homily on Matthew*, chapter twenty-six,[327] adduces the testimony of this letter, but in such a way that he does not require his discursant to accept Paul as the author, and virtually concedes that it may belong to that part of the Apocrypha which is entitled the *Secret Sayings of Isaiah*.[328] If you regard Origen as a heretic, certainly he was not condemned by Jerome on the ground that he rejected canonical writings. In fact, the church approves of Origen in those areas where he was not condemned by Jerome.[329] Augustine, in book sixteen, chapter twenty-two of the *City of God*, prefaces his citation of this letter as follows: '. . . in the letter which is entitled "To the Hebrews," which many claim to be by the apostle Paul, but which some deny is his, . . .';[330] he did not say that the orthodox claim Paul as the author while the heretics deny it, but 'many claim . . . some deny,' distinguishing between the parties in terms of their numbers, not their faith. Augustine again, while he was accustomed in other places to acknowledge quotations from Paul by citing his name, when it comes to this letter simply records, 'It has been written in the letter to the Hebrews,' 'It has been understood in this way in the letter to the Hebrews,' and 'concerning that one reads in the Letter which is entitled "To the Hebrews."'[331] It is clear, therefore, that Augustine was far from certain of its authorship.

* * * * *

325 Jerome *Commentarii in Matheum* 4 CCSL 77 247 (on Matt 26:8–9)
326 Jerome *In Esaiam* 50.11 CCSL 73A 557:15
327 Origen on Matt 23:37–9, *Die griechischen christlichen Schriftsteller der ersten drei Jahrhunderte* XI (Berlin 1976) 50
328 Erasmus is undoubtedly referring to the *Ascension of Isaiah* from the second century. Origen mentioned the prophet's martyrdom in his description of Heb 11:37 in his commentary on Matthew (Matt 10:18, PG 13 881–2).
329 Origen was condemned posthumously for certain propositions and rejected by Jerome, who, nevertheless, had read much of his writing.
330 Augustine *De civitate Dei* 16.22 CCSL 48 524
331 Augustine *De civitate Dei* 16.28, 16.32 CCSL 48 533, 536

You are convinced that the letter was written by the apostle Paul and that it was composed in Hebrew; you are unsure only of the translator, and the general tendency to hold him totally responsible you would think legitimate. Yet whoever it was who added the argument to this letter said, 'The Apostle is said to have sent this letter, written in Hebrew to the Hebrews, whose meaning and form were retained by Luke when he put it into Greek.'[332] How hesitatingly he speaks, how cautiously he steps! Why, when he makes two statements and gives them equal weight, do you accept one and reject the other? And let me add this in passing: if the Hebrew version was extant, why does he add 'whose meaning and form were retained by Luke'? If the Hebrew version was already lost, it is surprising that such an important letter dealing with such important matters was lost so early, since the church at Jerusalem was populous. You see, then, that there have been those who have had doubts about the authorship of the letter and who have not been altogether convinced that it was written in Hebrew. That you have no doubts at all does not surprise me. After all, you are the person who is so credulous as to believe that some pettifogger's remarkedly tasteless letter, which decreed that the words 'Glory be to the Father . . .' be sung at the end of each of the Psalms, is the work of Jerome, simply because it bears Jerome's name; you are the person who believes that letters inscribed 'from Paul to Seneca' are really by Paul; and you are the person who added to the rest of Paul's letters as genuine and authentic that feeble forgery entitled 'Letter to the Laodiceans.'[333] It is dangerous to trust those who trust so easily. I would rather be selective and discriminating in what I believe than believe everything. But St Jerome, you say, cites this letter under Paul's name and argues elsewhere that Paul is the author.[334] He cites it under Paul's name because most people read it as Paul's; there was no call for drawing swords over the authorship on every occasion. It is true that elsewhere Jerome does argue for Paul's authorship, but this is not the only issue on which Jerome is cunning and capable of pretence. I can well believe that he thought highly of the letter for its learning

* * * * *

332 See n262 above.
333 Erasmus finds in Lefèvre's biblical work what seems to him to be a lack of critical spirit, overcharged with credulity. To prove this point, he notes Lefèvre's acceptance of an interpolation into Jerome's prologue to the Roman Psalter – see *Quincuplex psalterium* 1513 ed sig Aiv recto, and Berger *Les préfaces jointes aux livres de la Bible* 42 n81 (see n262 above); the inclusion in his Pauline commentaries of the apocryphal correspondence between St Paul and Seneca – see Ep 1620:25–7; and the attribution of the 'Epistle to the Laodiceans,' an apocryphal text which undoubtedly stems from the fifth century, to the Apostle.
334 Eg Jerome *Commentarii in Matheum* 3 CCSL 77 197

and its piety, and being not ill disposed to Plato's and Origen's view that the crowd must sometimes be deceived,[335] provided that the deception is for its benefit, he was prepared to have Paul regarded as the author so that the letter might be read with greater profit. But what his own opinion was is uncertain, though not that uncertain if one cares to read through all his works carefully. Origen, according to book six of the *Ecclesiastical History*, admits that many have claimed that the letter was not by Paul even though he does not count himself among them.[336] Furthermore, many have been of the opinion that the letter owes its elegance of expression to Clement, disciple of the apostles and bishop of Rome; others have made the same claim for Luke. Jerome, in his *Catalogus scriptorum*, carefully notes that there is a good deal of correspondence between the letter which Clement wrote to the Corinthians and this letter which is said to be from Paul to the Hebrews. Indeed, in his *Gaius* he writes as follows, 'Enumerating thirteen letters of Paul, Gaius says that a fourteenth, which is called "To the Hebrews," is not by Paul.' In virtual agreement with this judgment, Jerome adds, 'But among the Latin Fathers even today the letter is not regarded as Paul's.' So Jerome.[337]

As for myself, I make no pronouncement concerning the author; I am satisfied that doubt about the authorship arose early on, if I am not mistaken, and doubt on the part of a number of orthodox believers, certain of whom have gone so far as to deny that it was written by Paul, as we have just now seen from the testimony of so many authors, including Augustine and Jerome, despite your claim that no believers have gone this far, only Ebionites, Marcionites, and the worst heretics of this sort; for this is how you speak, as though the label heretic was not enough without adding 'worst.' Incidentally, I shall not cavil over the linguistic error by which, when you mean to indicate a different brand of heretic, you have spoken of the very same brand by saying 'heretics of this sort,' even if there is added the none too fitting adjective 'worst.' I was deserving of the same leniency when I said that the letter was only lately accepted by the Latin Fathers, since I was taking Jerome as my authority for this, who, as you are aware, writes elsewhere that the Epistle to the Hebrews is not accepted as genuine by the Latin Fathers in the same way that the Greek Fathers reject the Apocalypse.[338] Now if the letter was not accepted in Jerome's time, then it was accepted only at a late date, in fact only after almost five hundred years.

* * * * *

335 Plato *Republic* 3.389B–C; Origen *Contra Celsum* eg 4.9 PG 11 1038D–1039A
336 Eusebius *Ecclesiastical History* 6.25. In this passage, Origen comments on the scriptural canon.
337 Jerome *De viris illustribus* 15 and 59 PL 23 663, 706
338 See n323 above.

You insist that it has always been accepted by the orthodox and rejected only by heretics. You would have some justification for taking this stand if Jerome alone, speaking for the Latin Fathers, believed that only heretics rejected it. No one rejects the letter simply because he does not accept it, for the person who has not yet expressed his opinion has not accepted it. Heretics reject this letter on the ground that it is lacking in piety, and I admit that their arguments are in part those which Jerome indicates. You add this, namely, that no Christian should subscribe to their view, even if the letter was for some time rejected even by some orthodox believers on account of a few passages which they suspected on first reading as seeming to lean towards certain heretical views. Now if you are firmly convinced that the letter is by Paul and that its authorship has been confirmed by the Holy Synod, why are you the first and only one of mortals to dare to challenge even an iota in it? I attack the translator, you respond, not the author. As though the synod saw a different version from the one which the church uses. If the synod read and approved the letter as we have it, it would be strange if it did not also approve this reading, which you demand be changed on the ground that it is false and heretical.[339]

Your final charge, that of ignorance, I hardly took seriously. In fact, it afforded me some pleasure and amusement. Take my argument that since Ambrose made no comment on it at all, the letter was not accepted by the Roman church, or not until a late date. You come out with a variety of witty ripostes to make sport of this. 'By the same rule,' you say, 'I could argue that the letter of James, two letters of Peter, and others were accepted only late by the Roman church since Ambrose made no comment on them, and for my pains I will be hooted off, laughed to scorn, and show myself in need of all the hellebore in Anticyra.'[340] Attack all the annotations in which I take a different stand from you, and I do so with every justification, and see whether I shall ever mock you with clever remarks of this kind. In one place only, where you had made an egregious error and one which would be truly embarrassing were it not such a common one for men to make, I remark merely, 'I am surprised that such a deep slumber crept upon this fine man.'[341] This is the most openly critical remark I make. Could I have found a more reasonable way of referring to a glaring error than to ascribe it to a sudden drowsiness, not to mention the fact that I tried to soften even this by adding as a compliment 'this fine man'?

* * * * *

339 See n321 above. It is still a question of the Council of Florence.
340 *Disputatio* ASD IX-3 222:542–7. See n232 above.
341 Lefèvre's error in translation concerns Titus 1:3. Cf Reeve III 694.

Now I make no claim for my powers in dialectic, even though I have studied it since a boy. But even if I had never read my Aristotle or my Boethius, both of whom I certainly have read, and others besides, just the *Topics* of Cicero or Quintilian's *Institutio oratoria* could have taught me that it does not necessarily follow that because Ambrose did not comment on this letter the Roman church did not accept it. I do not reason as stupidly as you suggest, a suggestion which reveals the truth of Terence's remark that 'nothing is so straightforward that it cannot be distorted by being wrongly reported.'[342] What I wrote was, 'There was so much doubt concerning the author of this letter that it was accepted by the Roman church only at a late date, since it is the only one on which Ambrose made no comment.' I do not argue, as you think, that it was not accepted because Ambrose did not comment on it; rather, I fasten one indication onto another, joining one thread to the next, as the saying goes, to make a firm connection.[343] For where matters depend upon indications and compelling evidence is lacking, I have the right, I think, to argue from the weight of probable proofs, especially when I am not making an assertion. Jerome testifies, as I have pointed out, that the letter was accepted only at a late date, that is, by the Romans. And I mean the Roman church here, the Romans themselves, as Cyprian calls them, not the Catholic church, as we now term it.[344] So it is clear that there has been doubt concerning the author, and I indicated a little earlier that there are in the letter certain passages which some had found objectionable; and I add to the stock, as it were, of other indications the fact that the Latin Father Ambrose, though he wrote on all the other letters, omitted to comment on this one only. This is not the same as saying that because Ambrose did not comment on the letters of Peter they were accepted as genuine only at a later date. Since Ambrose wrote on all the Pauline letters with the single exception of this one, which is the longest and the most learned, it is likely that he too had doubts about the authorship of it, something which can be concluded from other arguments as well. A closer analogy would have been the case of Dionysius, who numbers and lists by name the sacraments of the church and omits only matrimony, from which it is reasonable to infer either that matrimony was at that time not yet numbered among the sacraments, or that Dionysius was unaware of the seventh sacrament, or whatever else might

* * * * *

342 Terence *Phormio* 696–7
343 Erasmus uses the Greek word.
344 The church in Rome and not the universal church (Cyprian Ep 60 CSEL 3 part 2 692)

seem legitimate.[345] At least let this stand for the sake of illustration. Or, if a king were to reward all of his officers with a gift with the exception of just one officer, it would be reasonable to conclude that the king was not as pleased with him as with the others.

Admittedly, this form of argument does not lead to a necessary conclusion. Nevertheless, where a matter rests upon indications I do not think this kind of reasoning deserves to be hooted at as needing all the hellebore in Anticyra,[346] especially when there are a number of considerations which give one another mutual support. For this is how you mock a friend. You really are a jolly fellow,[347] a very model of wit and eloquence. Otherwise, who would tolerate that celebrated deduction which Boethius recounts, as well as the rhetoricians, namely, 'How could he not have loved her if he carried her off?' or 'If she is the mother, she loves her son'?[348] Or how will you defend the argument which you employ in this very context, namely, 'This version existed before Jerome; therefore, it was accepted by the Romans before Jerome'? As though there is no distinction between being published and being accepted. Or this argument, which appears in the same context a little further on, namely, 'Jerome draws upon this letter in replying to a heretic; therefore, it was accepted by the Romans'? By this method I could reach the following conclusions: 'He uses the evidence of the Nazarene Gospel[349] against the heretics; therefore, this Gospel was accepted by the church.' Or, 'Paul uses the evidence of Epimenides and Aratus; therefore, their works were accepted by the church.'[350] Or, 'Theologians constantly employ the works of Aristotle against the heretics; therefore, Aristotle was accepted by the church.'

The conjectures which I brought forward from time to time, if they could not be used as the basis for affirming anything, were appropriate enough to serve as a warning to the reader that there was something he might

* * * * *

345 For further discussions of marriage as a sacrament, see the other texts in this volume. There is perhaps also an allusion here to Lefèvre's naïvety, in so far as he does not doubt the identity of Pseudo-Dionysius, whose works he edited in 1498.

346 See n232 above.

347 *Festivitas* is one of the characteristics attributed by Erasmus to his friend Thomas More.

348 Erasmus lists some examples of false reasoning. In 1496, Lefèvre edited an abridgement of Boethius' mathematical books, which was often reprinted.

349 This refers to an apocryphal Gospel which is sometimes called the Gospel according to the Hebrews.

350 St Paul cites Epimenides in Titus 1:12 (see n422 below) and Aratus in Acts 17:28 (see n291 above).

examine further. At the same time, I frankly admit that had I been advised by you at the time, or had I had more time to give the issue closer attention, I would either have omitted mention of the matter in this context or have brought it forward more carefully. But mistakes of this kind, which are the result of carelessness, or are ones which human nature fails to anticipate, I shall be only too pleased to correct at some other time, and I shall take the greatest care not to give a handle to the critics, since I see that you, who are so frank and civil in other matters, are violently upset over these points, and this when they have no bearing, as you admit, upon your case.[351] You wish, of course, to appear to have been drawn into this controversy against your will, though the crux of the whole matter lies in this, namely, your assertion that we should read 'than God,' not 'than the angels.' Since I do not reject your position on this, what additional reason could there be for you to write against me? Even if I had rejected your view out of hand and were less deserving than I am of your usual politeness, your own nature should have kept you from using abusive language, if only to prevent others from thinking the worse of your character and of my teaching. I wish I had been permitted to escape this task of replying to you and been allowed to devote my energy to pleasanter things.[352] As it is, you attack me so many times in the harshest language, and this in the middle of a published work, so that it can only be deliberate, that silence on my part could be construed as an admission of guilt. I have done my best to refrain from anger, and I have defended my innocence in a polite and open manner, determined to keep my pen free from abuse, and determined to do so for as long as you allow me. If my reply offends you in any way, you ought to place the blame not on me, but on those who have taken advantage of your naïvety by encouraging you to take on this piece in the hope that by setting us at odds they might be able to use our discomfort as a source of their own amusement.[353]

You know Aristotle's sound observation that 'wickedness needs only an excuse,'[354] and you are aware how 'the wicked outnumber the upright,' as the Greek sage puts it.[355] Several people are by their very nature disposed to

* * * * *

351 The question of the Pauline authenticity of the Epistle to the Hebrews is related to the question under discussion in this controversy.
352 In order to compose the *Apologia*, Erasmus must have interrupted his translation of Theodorus Gaza's *De linguae Grecae institutione* for a week (Ep 771:6–8).
353 See n8 above. The enemies are the conservative theologians.
354 *Adagia* II i 68: *Occasione*; Aristotle *Rhetoric* 1.12.23
355 Bias of Priene (sixth century BC), one of the seven sages of Greece according to the testimony of Diogenes Laertius *Lives of the Philosophers*.

rejoice freely in others' discomforts and to believe that others' pains are their own good fortune. To some people all writing is distasteful; to a great number good writing is; and there is hardly anyone whom novelty does not offend. All these people, my dear Lefèvre, are just awaiting their chance. All the more reason, then, for us to take care not to give it to them and to make sure that the tail does not wag the dog, as they say.[356] For since we have both taken on a loathsome duty in the interest of the general good, it would be better for us to be playing our role in harmony, or in concert, as they say.[357] If our critics were to sense that we are in conflict and disagreement with one another, we would not only double our unpopularity but be robbed as well of all profit from the energy which we have devoted to our work. Those who are now howling in criticism because in the Lord's Prayer I have had the temerity to change 'forgive us our debts' to 'remit our debts,'[358] how do you imagine they are going to react if they see us stabbing at each other with blow upon blow like gladiators in the arena, and playing the buffoon like Horace's Balatro and Nomentanus, who trade witty sayings for the merriment of the banqueteers?[359] Look at our distinguished correctors, they will say, on whose authority the edition which has been approved for so many centuries is to be revised. How are we to trust them if they do not agree between themselves? We shall turn out to be the talk of the world, and all around the meeting places, the market squares, the drinking shops, the courtyards, the barber shops, the parade grounds, and the dockyards you will hear the names of Erasmus and Lefèvre.[360] For all the toil which we have endured, this is the prize we shall end up taking away. My dearest Lefèvre, I beg you in the name of our friendship, which I for my part have always tried to foster in sincerity and openness, in the name of that love of study which draws us both along wherever it may lead, though the greater success has been yours, I beg you, return to your natural self, return to your true ways. To this point I have caused you no harm, not even when I have been provoked. Allow me to stay true to myself. All you need to do is to be prepared to change your attitude in the present instance and display that former Lefèvre, the Lefèvre you have always been, both in our meetings and in all our correspondence. What has happened cannot be wished

* * * * *

356 *Adagia* I ii 77: *Ex ipso bove*
357 *Adagia* II iv 41: *Capere provinciam*
358 The controversy set Erasmus and Thomas More, on the one side, against John Batmanson, on the other (Rummel *Catholic Critics* I 118–19).
359 Horace *Satires* 1.8, and 2. Perhaps one should read Pantolabus the buffoon in place of Balatro.
360 Erasmus thus thinks that the whole world is interested in his doings.

away. The book has been published. But apology is possible and I shall be only too pleased to accept whatever excuse you wish to offer: it is an isolated thing which came about through thoughtlessness; it is the result of over-enthusiasm; these are human failings; I was pushed into it through bad advice; others took advantage of my naïvety. If none of these excuses appeals to you, then let us do what Homer's Agamemnon does and fall back upon some madness as the cause of this unfortunate occurrence.[361] When the course has started badly it is better to run back to the start than to keep on to the end.

In heaven's name, I bitterly regret my fate, or rather my misfortune, in being forced to descend to this kind of writing. I had more than enough to keep me occupied, and it is the last thing I would wish to spend my hours upon. If you had expressed your anger to me in a private letter, I would have either ignored the business altogether or apologized to you privately. If you had questioned my intelligence, I would have overlooked the insult. As it is, when in published works you make me out to be an opponent, when in fact I am on your side, and present as the ground for our dispute the fact that you are upholding Christ's dignity while I am detracting from it; that your book is pious and devout, while mine is quite unworthy of God and Christ; that yours belongs to Christians and those who are led by the spirit, while mine belongs to Jews and infidels and those who stick to the letter which destroys, and when you are not content with having said things once, but attack and abuse over and over again throughout your whole treatise, I ask you, what could be done?[362] Ought I to have ignored your criticisms in silence, especially when I not only had entertained no such thoughts in my mind but had made not even a verbal slip? If you think that I have pleaded my case too freely, bear in mind that there is nothing more free than innocence. If certain of my remarks betray my hurt, think in how many particulars I have not allowed my hurt to show. I think that I have displayed enough moderation by answering your brand of abuse and criticism with arguments instead of insults. So far my pen has been stained with nobody's blood. Allow me to enjoy this distinction for ever. So far I have controlled my outrage, even though it has been justified. But I am a man and I cannot predict what I might be able to tolerate in future. 'Patience abused turns often into anger.'[363]

* * * * *

361 Homer *Iliad* 19.88–91. On Ate, see n435 below.
362 Erasmus repeatedly rehashes those sentences of Lefèvre which have wounded him.
363 *Adagia* I v 67: *Funem abrumpere.* Publianus' or Publilius Syrus' expression is *Furor fit laesa saepius patientia* (ASD II-1 543:573–4).

If you must attack me, attack me with charges of such a kind that my forbearance in ignoring or excusing them is taken to my credit. As it is, if I am to clear myself, I am compelled to harm a friend; if I remain silent, I am forced into an acknowledgment of a crime which it would be worth fighting to the death to deny. If it is an inescapable and necessary condition of scholarship to be compelled to undermine the reputations of others by attacking their books, or to be fighting with one critic after another to clear one's own name, then I would rather bid it farewell. Either I sleep in silence, or I look out for myself and my studies.[364] For what has been so carefully written that one cannot find something in it to criticize? And what has been so faultily written that it cannot be defended on one pretext or another? But if it has been determined that all the writings of the older generations of commentators are to be defended equally, while those of the moderns are to be subjected to your kind of abuse, then it is now time to put my pen away. How much more proper it is to revere the older writers without absolving them from reasonable criticism, and to challenge the moderns, but with a proper degree of impartiality. Since we are human beings reading the works of other human beings we ought to overlook many things and be prepared in certain instances to interpret things to the author's advantage.

Besides, of what importance is it to find in my humble notes, who am nobody, something which an ungenerous critic might distort, when there are more things in the writings of Jerome, Ambrose, Cyprian, Augustine, and Gregory which no amount of ingenuity could defend if they were given an unfair hearing? For, not to leave you without an example, how in all conscience will you defend what Ambrose wrote in defence of Peter's denial: 'For one who said, "I do not know the man," it was reasonable, when asked whether he was one of the man's disciples, to say, "I am not." So he did not deny that he was a disciple of Christ, he denied that he was a disciple of a man. Thus, both Peter and Paul denied that the one whom they confessed as the Son of God was a man'?[365] I ask you, if you would condemn a writer out of his own mouth, what more heretical statement could be made than that Christ was not a man, with Peter and Paul brought in as support? Compare what Augustine says on the Eighth Psalm: 'Why "a worm"? Because he was mortal, because he was born of the flesh, because he was born without intercourse. Why "not a man"? Because in the beginning was the Word, and the Word was with God, and the Word was God.'[366] Who would tolerate

* * * * *

364 See Ep 785:9–10 to Thomas More.
365 Ambrose *Expositio evangelii Lucae* 10.84 CSEL 32 part 4 487
366 Augustine *Enarratio* II *in psalmum 21* CCSL 38 125

Christ being said to be not a man because he is God? Again, consider what Augustine writes in *On the Trinity*, namely, that when Christ was about to ascend into heaven the apostles 'believed only what they saw.'[367] Do you not consider it a blasphemy against the apostles to suggest that they did not believe he was God, when Peter admitted long before that the Son of God lived, and Thomas had openly confessed him as his own Lord and God?[368] If we believe that these things and many others like them were devoutly written, and if we are prepared to put a generous interpretation on them in such renowned writers, why are we so niggling and uncharitable when it comes to the work of more recent commentators? Even the most eloquent babble as best they can about divine matters. Moreover, is our own writing letter-perfect? But, you will say, we do not apply the same standard to Erasmus as to Augustine. Certainly, to the extent that he is the greater, my authority is no doubt less than his; yet I deserved the greater indulgence. Though I do think it is unworthy of learned men to measure authority in terms of age rather than substance.

However, enough of this digression. When the sincerity of a writer's belief is not in question, it is churlish to raise a storm over his language.[369] Moreover, it is not only quite alien to human feeling but also contrary to Christian charity to be on the prowl against other men's writings while excepting your own, and to play the Momus, or denunciator,[370] all the time failing to realize that the practice which you are endorsing may work unfairly against you as well. Unless you imagine that your own writings are so precise in every detail that they leave no room at all for criticism, even though in this one small treatise alone there are so many things to offend even the generous reader. Perhaps you think it a fine show when Jerome battles with Rufinus with volume after volume, or with Augustine, even if afterwards he renews his friendship with him, though not before their argument was concluded.[371] There is no one who yields to genius willingly, as Martial has it.[372] Or perhaps you do not consider it a grand crime that I have overthrown, or shaken rather, Pico's ten conclusions and diverted so happy a talent from promoting the

* * * * *

367 Augustine *De Trinitate* 1.9 CCSL 50 53–4
368 Matt 16:16; John 20:28
369 See n18 above.
370 *Adagia* I v 74: *Momo satisfacere*; *Adagia* II iii 81: *Sycophanta*
371 Jerome is famous for his theological quarrels with Rufinus of Aquileia, against whom he wrote an *Apologia*, whose title Erasmus has chosen for his work against Lefèvre. Augustine set himself in opposition to Jerome over certain biblical translations.
372 Martial *Epigrams* 8.18.10

Holy Scriptures.[373] And perhaps you approve of that unceasing and ill-tempered barrage which so many schools of theology and the whole tribe of preachers have kept up for several years against some obscure book of Reuchlin.[374] Because of our friendship I found it painfully disturbing to see you too being assailed by those hornets. For I read at Basel the letter in which the cardinal of Sinigallia pleaded your case against those who were denouncing you over an annotation on the Thirteenth Psalm based upon the view of Cardinal Nicholas of Cusa to the effect that the soul of Christ suffered torments in hell, and he was satisfied if his defence could so much as clear you from a charge of heresy.[375] More than that, I heard personally some learned and distinguished men damning your commentaries, and certain of them went so far as to mark some passages in them with a pen. If you approve of that kind of peevish and spiteful attention to detail, then tell me, I beg you, what purpose it serves and what benefit it gives. There will always be something to criticize for the person who picks up a book with the express purpose of finding it. If there is not a single one of the old writers who does not at some point need to be read with indulgence, then to scrutinize so unfairly the modern writers is not attention to detail, but envy.

We turn a blind eye to the fact that Jerome not only defends but argues vehemently for the view that it is permissible for someone who has been married before baptism to be a priest on the ground that having been baptized and having concluded his former contract he has entered into a new one, and calls the view of those who uphold what both the pontifical laws and the schools of theology now teach the heresy of Cain.[376] And this is to take just one example from many. It does no damage to St Ambrose's reputation that in commenting on the seventh chapter of the first letter to the Corinthians he maintains that it is legal for a man who has divorced his wife for adultery to marry a second time, while denying the same right to the wife. I shall quote his exact words: 'It is permissible for a man to take a second wife if he has divorced a wife who has sinned, because he is not constrained by the law as a woman is; for the man has authority over the woman.'[377] It is ridiculous and

* * * * *

373 In 1486, Pico defended thirteen theses, out of nine hundred which had been declared suspect, in an *Apologia*.
374 Lefèvre sided with Reuchlin just as Erasmus did. See n270 above.
375 On this episode, see Bedouelle *Quincuplex psalterium* 154–61. The cardinal of Sinigallia was Marco Vigerio (d 1516), who wrote an *Apologia* in defence of Lefèvre. The term *apologia* thus frequently reappears in this passage.
376 Jerome Ep 69 CSEL 54 679–80
377 Ambrosiaster *In epistulas ad Corinthios* CSEL 81 part 2 75. The assertion that Ambrose is the author of this passage is too insistent. See n139 above.

clearly a mark of desperation for the compiler of the *Book of Sentences* to excuse Ambrose by claiming that these words are an interpolation when the total of Ambrose's books is agreed upon and there is no inconsistency in style.[378] Our reverent regard for Cyprian is not diminished because he thought that those who had been baptized by someone who had been suspected of heresy should be baptized again. Yet this one issue caused the Donatists and the Rogatiani to be regarded as heretics even though they were orthodox in other respects, as even Augustine admits.[379] Nobody challenges Augustine for writing that on the night when her son was taken and then suffered, the mother of Jesus wavered greatly in her faith, though less than did the rest of the apostles. Should anyone desire it, the reference is question seventy-three in his *Questions on the Old and New Testament*. For those who do not have it at hand I shall quote his exact words: 'Now in adding, "Sorrow will pass through your own heart so that the thoughts of many might be revealed," Simeon indicated that even Mary, through whom the mystery of the incarnation of the Saviour was brought about, would waver at the death of the Lord only to be strengthened through the resurrection.'[380] Likewise, nobody is about to bring an action against him for attributing to the chief of the apostles, Peter, even after receiving the Holy Ghost, a wicked pretence and an evil zeal for oppressing the gentiles. For in commenting on the Epistle to the Galatians he writes as follows: 'When Peter had come to Antioch he was scolded by Paul, not because he kept the custom of the Jews in which he was born and raised, though he did not do so when he was with gentiles, but because he wished to impose it upon the gentiles.'[381] Again, in *Concerning the Christian Battle*, chapter thirty, he terms this conduct on Peter's part 'superstitious pretence,' and adds it to the list of his other shortcomings – his lack of faith, and his resistance to and denial of Christ. Moreover, a little later in the same chapter he speaks more strongly still in attributing cowardly pretence to Peter, saying, 'The Catholic church accepts these into its motherly bosom, such as Peter, despite his weeping when warned of his denial by the crowing of the cock, and despite his cowardly pretence when

* * * * *

378 Peter Lombard *Sententiae* book 4 dist 35 c 3
379 This is the subject of a controversy between Cyprian and Stephen, the bishop of Rome, in the year 256. The Donatists were opposed to the administration of the sacraments by those who had betrayed the Christian faith during the persecution, or their successors. The Rogatiani constituted a moderate branch of the Donatists, directed by Rogatus of Cartenna in Mauretania (Augustine Ep 93 PL 33 321ff).
380 *Pseudo-Augustini Quaestiones Veteris et Novi Testamenti* 77.2 CSEL 50 131
381 Augustine *Ad Galatas* 1.15 PL 35 2113 (on Gal 2:11–16)

corrected by the voice of Paul.'[382] And far from retracting these statements,[383] Augustine went on to challenge Jerome, who had been unwilling to attribute wickedness to Peter, to change his mind – a wickedness, we might add, which we cannot believe was in him even before he came to know the teaching of Christ. For whatever sins Peter committed were due not to any intended wickedness, but either to a zealous but mistaken passion or to some sudden panic or human weakness. And I believe that the same holds true for Paul.

Nobody calls Chrysostom to court because he attributed to the Virgin Mary the kind of passion which characterizes the general run of mothers, who are domineering with their children and eager to secure praise and reputation through them. For in his commentary on the twelfth chapter of Matthew he includes the following: 'Some measure of maternal forwardness naturally besets every mother. Consider the forwardness, therefore, as much his mother's as his brothers'. For when they ought to have gone inside and listened to Jesus along with the crowds, or at least waited outside until he had finished speaking and only then gone in, they were driven by a certain vanity and ostentation to summon him outside in the presence of all.'[384] And the rest of what he goes on to say is in the same vein. Chrysostom again says the same things when commenting on chapter 11 of the Gospel according to John, but more clearly and emphatically, in speaking of Mary in the following manner: 'For she desired to procure the good opinion of men and to become more famous herself through her son's reputation, and was perhaps beset by a human forwardness. Just as his brothers too, when they said, "Show yourself to the world," were desirous of securing fame for themselves through his miraculous deeds.' And a little later he says, 'Indeed, up to that point they did not have the opinion of him that he deserved, and Mary, as mothers do, thought it proper for her to direct her son in all things, even though she must revere and honour him as Lord.'[385] Why need I go on to mention something which is frequent in all the older writers, namely, the view that Christ alone is free from the sin of his birth? This is a serious charge against them and as reproachful to the Virgin Mary as the tribes of Scotists wish it to appear.[386]

* * * * *

382 Augustine *De agone christiano* 30.32 CSEL 41 135
383 Literally, 'to sing a palinode.' *Adagia* I ix 59: *Palinodiam canere*
384 Chrysostom *Commentarius in Matthaeum* hom 44–5 PG 57 464–5 (different text from that of Erasmus)
385 Chrysostom *Commentarius in Iohannem* PG 59 129–30 (different text)
386 The Scotists defended the theology of the Immaculate Conception of the Virgin Mary and thus would not suffer anyone to speak of her weaknesses.

Now we mention these examples not for the purpose of publicly mocking the mistakes of the older generation of commentators, but in order to make it clear how unfair it is to allow nothing in the writings of more recent commentators to escape scrutiny, and to distort and criticize statements which are made sincerely and devoutly: 'This smacks of heresy,' 'This has a bad sound to it,' 'This could be a stumbling block,' 'This has a suspicious ring,' 'This displays too little reverence for our teachers.'[387] Rather, let us agree to apply to all writers the principle which St Augustine wishes to be adopted in the case of all his writings, and which he enunciates in *On the Trinity*, book one, chapter three: 'Whoever reads these writings, wherever he is equally as certain as I am, let him go along with me; wherever he is equally doubtful, let him investigate with me; wherever he recognizes an error as his own, let him come back to me; wherever he detects an error which is mine, let him call me back: in this way let us proceed side by side along the path of charity, making our way together in search of him of whom it has been spoken, "Seek always his face." This is the sacred and secure agreement I seek in the presence of our Lord with all who read what I write, in all my works and most especially in this one, where we are inquiring into the unity of the Trinity.'[388] How much more sensible is this approach, my dear Lefèvre, than for us to destroy our work and others' by engaging in mutual criticism, or, as St Paul puts it, by biting and being bitten in return.[389] I really do not think that even Christ would be pleased to have his dignity defended if it means that we ruin our reputations as Christians. He is the author of peace; he is best pleased by harmony among his own. Whatever you allow to be done to a brother, whether it be a kindness or an abuse, when it is done it rebounds upon itself. Discord arises from ever so faint a spark, and once aflame spreads fire all around. Then they rush forward on this side and that, partisans and allies, the hateful and the malicious, some to pour cold water, as they say,[390] others oil, upon the blaze,[391] and suddenly what was an argument between two becomes a full-scale war, and there is no stopping before the whole thing ends in mayhem. Meanwhile, we lose what I regard as our dearest possession, and that is friendship. Your supporters are angry at me,[392] and some of mine, I suspect, are indignant at you. How much more

* * * * *

387 Comments attributed to the theologians
388 Augustine *De Trinitate* 1.3 CCSL 50 32
389 Gal 5:15
390 *Adagia* I x 51: *Frigidam aquam*
391 *Adagia* I ii 9: *Oleum*
392 See nn43, 55 above.

acceptable it would be for us to share as friends and reap a double harvest. If there is some chance that we can contest on the field of the Scriptures, as Jerome puts it,[393] without causing ourselves pain, then let us join in competition with each other and either teach or learn something. But if anyone who disagrees with you in any way at all is your enemy to be assailed by such rocks as you hurl, then I quit the field and reject the terms of combat; that kind of battle belongs to gladiators, not to theologians.

Error is human and so is Christian reproof. I corrected your mistakes with the hope of receiving your thanks, as anyone who corrected mine would receive thanks from me. I would not hesitate to correct Jerome himself in the same way if he were alive. And I have no doubt that he would take it in good part. If I cannot ignore your errors it is because I hold you in too high regard. Yet you have preferred to retaliate rather than accept my advice and correct your mistakes. I merely mentioned in a restrained manner and without any exaggeration that you had slipped up in certain particulars. You, on the other hand, charge me with impiety even where I have committed no error. This is how you calculate the repayment which charity is owed. St Augustine does not consider himself above criticism when he has made a slip,[394] while you, not yet a bishop, nor elected yet, I think, to the senate of theologians,[395] thought it would be a disgrace to change anything in your second edition. Did you think it more desirable for many to err with you than for you to acknowledge your own mistakes? I have not yet drawn up a list of all the instances, but I have come across some places where frankly, my dear Lefèvre, I completely fail to understand your intention. With reference to chapter 2 of the Epistle to the Colossians, I noted that you had made a mistake over the word καταβραβευέτω; and when I had proved my point using the testimony of Jerome, the Greek scholiasts,[396] and finally Ambrose, I added, 'These authorities make it quite clear how far from correct in this passage is the opinion of Jacques Lefèvre, a man who is otherwise most learned.' See whether there is anything insulting here, whether there is anything which resembles your style, whether I refute you in a hostile fashion by suggesting that you are unworthy of God and Christ. To the contrary, of my own accord I excuse your slip by adding, 'But he has been led into this by

* * * * *

393 Jerome Ep 115 CSEL 55 397
394 Augustine wrote his *Retractationes* at the end of his life. See n115 above.
395 Here, Erasmus picks up again the prejudice of the theologians against Lefèvre, who was first and foremost a philosopher.
396 Pseudo-Oecumenius PG 119 38–9 and ASD IX-2 195 n539; *Apologia* ASD IX-3 185:2412n

Valla, who thinks that the verb καταβραβεύειν means "to call before a judge" or "to threaten with a judge." '[397] Yet despite my advice you did not think you needed to make a change, and even now your translation reads, 'Let no one willingly call you before a judge.' Right up to the present you cling tenaciously[398] to this most unnatural interpretation, which differs from that of all the older commentators, adding in your explanation only the following: 'Let no one deprive you of the prize, or else, let no one call you before a judge. For there are those who think that the word καταβραβευέτω in this position means the latter, and it is upon their assumption that I have based my interpretation.'[399] Now, first of all, there is no difference, is there, whether you say 'deprive you of the prize' or 'turn aside the judge'? Second, does Valla's authority stand so great with you that you prefer to follow him alone against all the theologians of the past, including Jerome,[400] especially when Valla points to nobody's authority to confirm what he says? Recognize, I beg you, that when you were treating these matters, when you wished to alter the meaning which the world accepted, it was unworthy of you to dismiss the reading which Ambrose had preferred,[401] the notation which Jerome had made, a man who is exceedingly scrupulous in these matters, and the interpretation which the Greek commentators had handed down. Or did you think that you could deal with so serious an issue in such an offhand and cavalier fashion?[402] I did not say what I did in order to condemn you, my dear Lefèvre, but in order to make you pay more attention in the future, the kind of attention, indeed, I wish you had paid to previous commentators, of whom there are very many, when you published your *Commentaries on the Psalms*.[403]

Again, with reference to chapter 4 of the Epistle to the Ephesians, where in an embarrassing slip you mistook κυβείαν for some word κυκείαν, since you could not find a way to evade your mistake you did in your translation substitute 'treachery' for 'disturbance'; but in your exposition you have

* * * * *

397 On Col 2:18, see Reeve III 640. Erasmus himself was the first to publish Valla's annotations.
398 *Adagia* I iv 22: *Mordicus tenere (pertinacia)*
399 Lefèvre *Commentaries* on Col 2:18
400 In the Vulgate
401 Ambrosiaster *In epistulam ad Colosenses* CSEL 81 part 3 189. Jerome did not write any commentary on the Epistle to the Colossians.
402 *Adagia* I iv 27: *Molli brachio*
403 The *Quincuplex psalterium* certainly contained some patristic references, but Lefèvre remained very independent of them (Bedouelle *Quincuplex psalterium* 81–92). It is also true that his preface honoured the Fathers of the church who had commented upon the Psalter.

retained 'disturbance' and do not change your ridiculous and strained interpretation. In your examination, meanwhile, you have retained your original
note, but without explaining what κυβεία means, as though 'treachery' expresses the Greek word literally.[404] If no annotation was required here, why
did you make an annotation in your earlier edition? If an annotation was required, why do you omit one? If what I had proposed offended you, why
did you not offer something better? I do not demand that you acknowledge a
person who corrects you, but in teaching I do require frankness, and what is
more, there was more reason for you to name me here than there, where my
remarks have no bearing upon you. I ask you, what is this pride, I do not want
to call it arrogance? Is it so strong that you think it a disgrace to recant?[405]

To come to another point, with respect to chapter 2 of the Epistle to
the Philippians, where you have translated παραβουλευσάμενος as 'ready to
offer his life after deliberation,' even though I have pointed out the force
of the participle you still cling tenaciously to your 'ready to offer after
deliberation.' In the first place, who ever said 'after deliberation' when he
meant 'voluntarily'? Second, since the participle is aorist, how can it mean
'ready to offer'? The preferred translation would have been 'having handed
over' or 'exposed his life to danger.' Third, who ever has said 'offer' when
he meant 'expose to danger'? For when Christ says, 'I offer my life,' he uses
'offer' in the sense of 'offer up.'[406]

Now just as in my annotations I deliberately overlooked a number of
points in the hope that by commenting on just a few I would encourage you
to be more careful, though I was ready to offer more if by chance you should
have asked me to do so in your letters, so I have no mind to go into every
particular here. All the same, since you were publishing a second edition
of your work, credibility demanded that you remove certain things which
scholars could not read without either laughter or disgust. For example, the
passage in chapter 6 of the Epistle to the Ephesians, namely, 'against the
spiritual hosts of wickedness in the heavenly world,' where, even though the
Greek says 'in the heavenly world,' you assert that it is possible to read it as
'towards those in heaven,' meaning 'against those in heaven,' as if in Greek
the preposition ἐν could in any way mean 'against' in the same way that the

* * * * *

404 On Eph 4:14, see Lefèvre 1512 ed fol 38r. After Erasmus' remark (Reeve III 606),
     Lefèvre changed the text, but removed his note without mentioning Erasmus.
405 In Greek. See n383 above.
406 On Phil 2:30. Erasmus does not name Lefèvre at this point in his *Annotationes*
     (Reeve III 626). Erasmus' most significant reproach to Lefèvre is thus that he
     has been stubborn and maintained his errors throughout his editions.

preposition εἰς can.[407] When you write these things, my dear Lefèvre, what else are you doing except presenting yourself as a laughing-stock even to children? In the same category is your translation of κατ᾽ ὀφθαλμοδουλείαν as 'subjection to the eye,' when the translator had given the linguistically more proper 'eye-service.' Likewise, in chapter 7 of the First Epistle to the Corinthians, the words παράγει γὰρ τὸ σχῆμα τοῦ κόσμου you translate and annotate as 'the shape of this world deceives,' not recognizing that the word παράγει is intransitive, something which you could have gathered from other instances, especially since so many times in the Gospel you read ὕπαγε ὀπίσω, 'get behind me.'[408] Ought you not to have changed this, especially since you are the only one to have proposed it and all writers stand opposed to your view? Yet notice how in my annotations I do not attack you on this matter, even though I would have been entirely justified in doing so.

Again, in chapter 5 of the same Epistle, with reference to the word συναχθέντων you go against all the Greek and Latin Fathers, and against Greek grammar itself, in translating, and defending it in an annotation, 'when you are grieving together' instead of 'when you are gathered together.' What mistake could be more hideous than this? Yet notice the respect and deference with which I express my disagreement with you on this point. You could wish for nothing more from one who is more devoted to you, save only that, not agreeing with you, he make mention of your name, since in other respects my conduct could not have been more charitable and respectful. As it is, the matter itself left me no option, as any perceptive reader who compares your words closely with mine will clearly see. In fact, since not everyone has access to all the volumes, I will quote what I wrote: 'My friend Jacques Lefèvre has emended this passage, claiming that συναχθέντων is formed from the verb συνάχθομαι; but I do not subscribe to his judgment on this point, even though in other things I willingly agree with him as a man who is as learned as he is precise.' This is my annotation.[409] Your mistake cannot be excused, and you yourself have made sure that it not be covered over or disguised.[410] Now although any mistake in books which treat divine matters

* * * * *

407 On Eph 6:6, see Lefèvre 1512 ed fol 39v. Lefèvre could have read Erasmus' *Annotationes*, and even if he was not mentioned explicitly in relation to this point, he could have profited by it.

408 1 Cor 7:31; Reeve II 465. The gospel citation is found in Matt 16:23 and Mark 8:33.

409 1 Cor 5:4; Reeve II 452–3

410 In fact, Lefèvre had for once taken account of Erasmus' criticism, and he even mentioned it in his second edition of 1515, fols 107v–108r.

is significant, the change in this one word, apart from the fact that it gives a weak and pale sense, removes something which weighty and respected interpreters have regarded as noteworthy, namely, that Paul, even though he was appointed an apostle by Christ himself,[411] does not take upon himself the authority to declare his opinion solely in his own name, but prefers that it be grounded in the accepted view of the church,[412] acting differently in this regard than certain bishops today, who wield an absolute tyranny over those under them and in everything act according to their own wishes, without regard for public debate. In addition, this passage serves notice that if anyone shall have committed an act which deserves to be criticized, this criticism should be made openly, not secretly and in private, partly in order that one example might deter the rest from sinning, and partly to protect against someone suffering disrepute as a result of a false accusation and an unjust verdict. Your translation, 'grieving together,' removed this healthy warning. Accordingly, given that it was worthwhile my pointing out your mistake, and the public good almost required me to do so,[413] how could anyone have done it in a more charitable, respectful, and sincere fashion than I did? Come now, compare your gracious treatise, if you please, with my critical attack, if attack is the word it deserves. In my work there is a complete absence of sourness, malice, anger, and display, and I correct a friend's mistake only to give him support. You, on the other hand, in the course of one small[414] treatise virtually drown in spite a friend who has committed no mistake and who is on your side. Moreover, the weight of your authority was not so great that anyone could interpret this politeness of mine as fear, nor was your generosity so marked that I could appear to be flattering you in the hope of a reward. My restraint was the result of charitableness, not agreement or apprehension.

But to continue. With respect to chapter 6 of the Second Epistle to the Corinthians, who, I ask you, is ready to accept these words, 'in good fortune and in bad fortune,' which signify absolutely nothing? Yet you ignored my advice and refused to change them.[415] Again, in chapter 10 of the same Epistle, where out of a single adverbial, or if you prefer, prepositional,

* * * * *

411 See Gal 1:12.
412 A significant remark for revealing Erasmus' ecclesiology, which is based here upon the *consensus ecclesiae*.
413 See n21 above. The responsibility of any commentator on the Bible is also pastoral.
414 This refers to Lefèvre's *Disputatio*.
415 2 Cor 6:7; Reeve II 540

word, ὑπερέκεινα, you have made two words, ὑπὲρ ἐκεῖνα (and ὑπερέκεινα, incidentally, is no different from ἐπέκεινα, since ἐπί often has the same force as ὑπέρ), and you have translated 'which are above those of yours'? In your examination you do not change your translation, except that what you earlier preferred, namely, 'which are beyond yours,' you transform into 'which are beyond you'; and in your second edition you have omitted your rule for the use of ὑπέρ in Greek, presumably because someone advised you that it was completely wrong, since the Greeks, when they say 'over the head,' use the expression ὑπὲρ τῆς κεφαλῆς, not ὑπεράνω τῆς κεφαλῆς.[416] I congratulate you for omitting what you have, but I do not approve of what you fight tooth and nail to retain,[417] since it is clearly ridiculous to anyone who knows Greek.

Again, in chapter 5 of the Epistle to the Ephesians, when you alone of writers of Greek and Latin get 'unhealthiness' out of the Greek word for 'profligacy,' are you not guilty of making the Apostle a doctor? You ignored my advice and decided not to change it. But suppose the word ἀσωτία here is in fact derived from σῶτος, even though the etymologists maintain that it is from σέσωται, ἄσωτος will not necessarily mean 'unhealthy,' but 'wasted,' and even in Terence we have characters who are described as 'wasted by profligacy.' You seem to take 'profligate' to mean 'libidinous' or 'lustful.'[418] Then you turn to jesting, leaving the linguistic argument to the grammarians, as though you were not yourself taking the part of a grammarian in inquiring into these matters, and you add the following fine witticism: 'Grammarians search for the origins of words more diligently than philosophers search for the source of the Nile' – implying, I suppose, that you are excluding yourself from the grammarians' camp and enlisting in the ranks of the philosophers.[419] Whether the grammarians would have you in their number I do not know; and whether the philosophers torture themselves over the source of the Nile you will find out. One thing I do know, that it is more to the point than the source of the Nile whether in this passage Paul understood 'profligacy' as the opposite of temperance and continence, or 'unhealthiness' as the concern of doctors.

Again, in the Epistle to Titus, with respect to your translation of the words ἐν κηρύγματι ὃ ἐπιστεύθην ἐγὼ as 'in preaching, to which I am bound, or committed,' you not only refuse to correct so embarrassing an error, despite being advised to do so, but even compound the mistake in your

* * * * *

416 2 Cor 10:16
417 *Adagia* I iv 23: *Toto corpore*
418 Eph 5:18. The allusion to Terence is to *Adelphi* 760.
419 The headwaters of the Nile were unknown. Cf Horace *Odes* 4.14.45.

second edition by declaring that you have retained your original translation, and adding that there is no difference between 'which has been entrusted to me' and 'to which I am bound.'[420] Here, my dear Lefèvre, I appeal to your conscience.[421] When you were writing this, were you not aware of the amusement you would be giving to learned readers? In Greek, of course, ὃ ἐπιστεύθην and ᾧ ἐπιστεύθην have the same force. You yourself read ὃ ἐπιστεύθην, though even if someone were to adopt the reading ᾧ ἐπιστεύθην I could demonstrate that the meaning is the same, but only in Greek. But does it make no difference in Latin whether you say 'Peter is committed to me' or 'I am committed to Peter'? For this is what you are saying. The fact that you have made so egregious an error I have put down to a sudden case of drowsiness. But as to the fact that you do not correct these things, despite my friendly admonishment, I ask you, what name can I give to that? Now as to that refrain in the same passage, namely, 'Cretans are always liars, evil beasts, slow bellies,' I am amazed indeed that you take such obstinate pleasure in it.[422] Further, in chapter 13 of the First Epistle to the Corinthians, what need was there to note that the words καὶ οὓς μὲν ἔθετο ὁ θεὸς ἐν τῇ ἐκκλησίᾳ can be translated 'and God has set his own in the church,' when it is clear that οὓς there is an alternate form not of ἑούς (his own), but of τούς (some), an alternative which ought not to have appeared strange to you since it occurs more than ten times in the New Testament?[423]

Since there were very many instances of this sort in your *Commentaries*, and I had pointed to certain of them, it was left to your vigilance to weigh the remainder carefully in your second edition, and to deprive sarcastic critics of the opportunity for laughter. Yet anyone who points out your mistakes, and does so in a friendly manner, you regard as an enemy and deserving of the kind of gratitude which you have paid me in your treatise. Would that you had avoided entirely the field of translation and annotation, a field which, as I have said, is not really your forte. There are more important matters you could have engaged in. This field, humble as it is, demands skill in both Greek and Latin, and your expertise in these needs no comment, since your own writings bear clear witness. For example, with respect to the words οἱ μὲν ἐξ ἐριθείας, οἱ δὲ ἐξ ἀγάπης in chapter 1 of the Epistle to the Philippians, you maintain that 'who' would be a better translation than

* * * * *

420 Titus 1:3; Reeve III 694. Lefèvre had maintained his position in his edition of 1515, fol 212r–v.
421 See n224 above.
422 Titus 1:12. This is a citation from Epimenides (Reeve III 696).
423 1 Cor 12:28; Reeve II 497

'some': what you fail to notice is that what we have here is the definite article used distributively, not the relative pronoun which carries an accent, that is, οἵ; not to mention the fact that no sense at all emerges if you read 'who.'[424] Another thing which is constant in your examinations is that whatever your Greek manuscript had in it, you ascribe unhesitatingly to Paul, as though Greek manuscripts do not sometimes vary, or are never corrupt, when I myself discovered in a particularly fine manuscript copy the following words written in the Second Epistle to the Corinthians: δεόμενοι ἡμῶν τὴν Χάριν καὶ τὴν κοινωνίαν τῆς διακονίας τῆς εἰς τοὺς ἁγίους δέξασθαι ἡμᾶς· ἐν πολλοῖς τῶν ἀντιγράφων οὕτως εὕρηται, καὶ οὐ καθὼς ἠλπίσαμεν.[425] What we have here, of course, is a case of several words being transferred by an illiterate scribe from the margin to the body of the text. In order to make this clearer to those who do not know Greek, I shall translate as follows: 'Asking that we receive the gift and the fellowship of the ministering to the saints; in many manuscript copies appears the following: "and not as we hoped."' It is clear that the words 'in many manuscript copies appears the following' represent someone's marginal annotation. It is risky, therefore, to place immediate trust in your manuscript and to make pronouncements before examining all the manuscripts.

My dear Lefèvre, if in your second edition you had taken care to correct these instances and countless others like them, you would have been paying due regard to your good name and to me as well, since friends have all things in common,[426] and when we are working in a similar field an egregious error on your part diminishes my credibility as well among those with less experience. As it is, you were so little inclined to worry over any of these things that your sole motive in hurrying your second edition along might seem to have been a desire to attack a friend. Indeed, I can well see that certain people are likely to come to such a conclusion. For why would they not put this interpretation on your wordy and elaborate criticism[427] when they put a sinister interpretation even on the praises which at the end of your treatise you heap upon me, or which you use rather to stroke my head?[428]

* * * * *

424 Phil 1:16–17. There is no mention of Lefèvre in the *Annotationes*.
425 2 Cor 8:4–5. For further information on the Greek manuscripts which Erasmus used, see *Apologia* ASD IX-3 193:2567n. According to Steenbeek, this interpolated manuscript is MS Greek suppl 2 of the National Library in Vienna, loaned to Erasmus by the monastery of Corsendonck, near Turnhout (193:2569n).
426 *Adagia* I i 1: *Amicorum communia*
427 Erasmus wrote a much more voluminous work than Lefèvre's.
428 *Adagia* III i 37: *Demulcere caput*

Look, they say, he credits Erasmus with a keen eye for detail, he credits him with eloquence, linguistic skill, attention to those who have a passion for learning, but nowhere does he go so far as to call him a fine person; in short, he grants him only industry and talent, when the most important aspect of praise is praise of the person's life and principles.[429] Finally, you do not call me a theologian, but a would-be theologian.[430] What else is a would-be theologian, they say, than one who merely claims and appropriates the profession for himself? In fact, there is nothing I would claim for myself less than the profession of theologian, even though at the insistence of certain of my friends I long ago took that rank. Where in my writings do I boast of being a theologian? Who has ever heard me at any time congratulate myself on that title, even in casual conversation?

Now, take my praises of you. Do you not see how I pour them forth with an open hand, as they say,[431] how unsparing and genuine I am? Perhaps you were afraid that you yourself would be forced to exhibit whatever qualities you attributed to me, in accordance with the old saying, Give a pledge and evil is nigh at hand.[432] But I have no complaint on this score. The qualities which you grant me are more than enough. It is a nuisance only that a handle has been given to those who would snarl at us over this kind of thing. It is not my practice to boast about any praise I might receive; but I do take pride in the friendship we share and in all the learning and discovering we do together. It is clear that someone begrudges me this feeling and that it was at his instigation that you composed your friendly treatise.[433] Look, they say, you enjoy your Lefèvre, you regard him as your friend, and you think that you have done too little to acknowledge his sincerity, his modesty, and his piety. So many of your annotations he has dismissed in a single note, and fully enough at that, he has said.

But let the complaints and recriminations come to an end now. What has been done cannot be made undone in this fashion. The only thing left is for both of us to join together in repairing the damage. If my response causes you pain, I am the more pained for having been forced to reply. I would have preferred to devote my energy to praising a friend, even with false

* * * * *

429 See n40 above.
430 These are Lefèvre's words (*Disputatio* ASD IX-3 224:576–7), but he did not say them maliciously. Erasmus wants to be known as a theologian. See, for example, his *Praise of Folly* (*Moriae encomium*) ASD IV-3 68.
431 *Adagia* II i 16: *Plena manu*
432 *Adagia* I vi 97: *Sponde, noxa praesto est*
433 See n8 above.

praises, than to refuting him, however correct my arguments might be.[434]
I have simply been vindicating myself, not attacking your views; as far as
that is concerned, my dear Lefèvre, I would not want you to discover what
I might be capable of. If in the future I see that you are the kind of person
I have always thought you are, the kind I have always credited you with
being, I shall attribute this isolated and regrettable episode to the Fates, or to
the goddess Strife, or to Homer's Madness,[435] to any god or human you wish.
But if you persist in attacking a friend in unfriendly fashion, I shall be forced
to change my opinion of you. But let us end on a positive note. I am confident
that you will do what I most dearly hope will be better for both of us and
more pleasing in the end to Christ.[436] If so, you will find me gracious and
supportive in every way. If not, then I do not know how I will be. Farewell,
my most learned and, if you will allow me, my most dear Lefèvre.

Louvain. 5 August 1517

* * * * *

434 Ep 627:19–20 to Ludwig Baer 23 August 1517. Erasmus takes up the same
expression.
435 Ate (or Discord) is an infernal divinity who was banished from heaven by
Jupiter (*Iliad* 19.88–91). Erinys is one of the Furies.
436 Lefèvre did not want to excuse himself and answered this whole polemic only
with silence.

AN APPENDIX
ON THE WRITINGS OF JOSSE CLICHTOVE

REFUTATION OF THE ACCUSATIONS
OF JOSSE CLICHTOVE AGAINST THE *SUASORIA*
OF DESIDERIUS ERASMUS OF ROTTERDAM
IN PRAISE OF MARRIAGE

Appendix de scriptis Clithovei

Dilutio eorum quae Iodocus Clithoveus scripsit
adversus declamationem suasoriam matrimonii

translated and annotated by CHARLES FANTAZZI

The *Appendix on the Writings of Josse Clichtove* was appended to the *Supputatio calumniarum Natalis Bedae*, published in August 1526, together with another appendix in answer to Pierre Cousturier's *Antapologia*, apology to an apology. They are prefaced by a letter to the faculty of the University of Paris (Allen Ep 1664) dated 6 February 1526. It is evident that the *Appendix* was meant only as a temporary reply to the accusations made by Clichtove in his *Propugnaculum ecclesiae adversus Lutheranos*, and it is rather subdued in tone.[1]

In 1531, after a long sustained barrage, the University of Paris un-leashed its definitive condemnation of numerous opinions of Erasmus, the *Determinatio facultatis theologiae in schola Parisiensi super quam plurimis asser-tionibus D. Erasmi Roterodami.*[2] Erasmus was beside himself with rage, ex-claiming in a letter (Allen Ep 2575:13) that 'they are not satisfied with killing Erasmus, but wish to annihilate him altogether, robbing him even of his rep-utation.' It was not only his ill fame in Paris that worried him; he and others with him were concerned that the condemnation might spread to the Nether-lands.[3] With his usual assiduity he set about to answer the criticisms and by the end of the year his defence was ready. The voluminous *Declarationes ad censuras Lutetiae vulgatas* was published by the beginning of February 1532 and was followed by a revised and enlarged edition[4] in September of the same year. He prefaced his answer with a letter to the faculty couched in a reserved and respectful style. He then proceeded to list each of the cen-sures, one by one, to which he appended his respective responses. Among the charges levelled at him is that Erasmus wrote disparagingly of the virtue of ecclesiastical chastity (*titulus xx*, with Erasmus' brief reply, LB IX 902D–903A).

While he was engaged in his head-on conflict with the Parisian doctors, Béda in particular, Erasmus decided to lay to rest also the old complaints of Clichtove, using the same oil, as he puts it in a later letter: 'De eodem, quod aiunt, oleo respondi et Clitovei veteribus naeniis.'[5] Together with this lengthy apology there appeared a revised text of the *Epistola de esu carnium* with an ap-pendix of scholia explaining no fewer than fifty-seven points of the treatise in

*****

1 A manuscript of the text of the *Appendix* is extant in the Marburg Library, and a copy of it was procured by Professor Clemens Bruehl. The form of the document, with a salutation (obscured in Bruehl's apograph) and a *vale* at the end, seems to indicate that the *Appendix* originated as a letter.
2 Contained in C. du Plessis d'Argentré *Collectio iudiciorum de novis erroribus* (Paris 1728–36; repr Brussels 1966) II part 1 47–77, with a preface by Erasmus
3 Cf Allen Epp 2573:1–7 and 2566:41–50 from Maarten Lips; 2588:66–9 from Gaspar Schets; and 2573 from Conradus Goclenius.
4 It is this version that is printed in LB IX 813–954.
5 Allen Ep 2604:40

answer to objections made by Clichtove in the third book of his *Propugnaculum ecclesiae*. The *Dilutio*[6] responded in more detail to chapters 30 to 34 of the second book. A third text was joined to these two defences, *In elenchum Alberti Pii brevissima scholia*, a list of 122 citations from the index of Pio's exhaustive attack on Erasmus' doctrine with an accompanying refutation.[7] The sale of all these works, considered as one book, was promptly forbidden by the Sorbonne.[8]

The *Dilutio* was omitted by Beatus Rhenanus from the Basel *Opera omnia* probably through an oversight, as Augustijn suggests, rather than intentionally, as Telle maintains,[9] nor does it appear in the Leiden edition. It remained for Emile V. Telle to produce a modern edition of the work, *Erasmus Roterodamus. Dilutio eorum quae Iodocus Clithoveus scripsit adversus Declamationem Des. Erasmi Roterodami suasoriam matrimonii* (Geneva 1968), based on an exemplar of the Froben edition held by Harvard University. With the exception of a number of banal misprints this has served as the basis for the present translation.

C F

* * * * *

6 Telle is of the opinion that the work had already been written in 1526 immediately after the publication of the *Propugnaculum*, as he affirmed first in his *Erasme* 344, and more vehemently in his edition of the *Dilutio*, where he accuses Erasmus of withholding publication because of fear of repercussions from the proceedings against Louis de Berquin, translator of the *Encomium* into French. Telle says of Erasmus, in rather unbridled language, 'Le fait qu'il édita la *Dilutio*, et si tard, révèle sa vanité, sa recidive, son goût de la singerie, ses inquiétudes pour sa sûreté à lui et non son honnêteté intellectuelle' (Telle *Dilutio* 47–8). Augustijn argues to the contrary that certain statements from the *Appendix de scriptis Clithovei* and from Epp 1780:41–3 and 2604:40 indicate quite clearly that the apology was written in 1531 (ASD IX-1 59 n53).

7 Pio's last attack on Erasmus, *In locos lucubrationum variarum D. Erasmi XXIII libri*, was published by Ascensius Badius (Josse Bade) in March 1531, two months after his death. Erasmus' counterblast, one of his most fierce writings, appeared in June 1531 and again on 5 January 1532 with the title *Apologia brevis ad viginti quattuor libros Alberti Pii quondam Carporum comitis*. Brief it was not, filling seventy-three columns in Leclerc (LB IX 1123–96). The scholia published with the *Dilutio* are more brief, occupying fifteen pages of the Harvard exemplar used by Telle in his edition. Other copies are listed in *Bibliotheca Belgica* (Brussels 1964) II 776ff and IV 663.

8 L. Delisle *Notice sur un registre des procès verbaux de la faculté de théologie de Paris pendant les années 1505–1533* (Paris 1899) 338, 396. Telle asserts that this measure was responsible for the disappearance of the treatise, 'Elle décida de la faire disparaître et y réussit presque' (Telle *Dilutio* 48), but Augustijn points out that in the Rotterdam union catalogue thirty-one exemplars are cited (ASD IX-1 62 n72).

9 Augustijn ASD IX-1 63; Telle *Dilutio* 59

AN APPENDIX
ON THE WRITINGS OF JOSSE CLICHTOVE

I regret that I have not yet had the time to read the books of Josse Clichtove to which he gave the title *Bulwark of the Faith*.[1] I merely examined them to see if there was anything of direct relevance to me. His harangues on continence, abstinence, and the regular life agree very much with my own views, and would that he had as well such persuasiveness of speech that he could inflame all monks and priests to a love of these virtues. But as for his inserting in the index to the volume[2] that I attempt to give advice against the observance of the law on priestly continence, if he wished to debate the question with me, he should have represented my opinion more accurately in the following manner: 'In view of the present status of those who profess celibacy, Erasmus wonders whether it would be a lesser evil for the church to permit wives for those who after making every effort still do not lead continent lives, or to leave things as they are.' And furthermore in those passages of the *Encomium of Marriage* to which he refers I cannot help but take notice of his lack of candour. As one formerly not ill-versed in the study of letters he knows what a declamation is, namely, a fictitious topic of discussion with arguments presented on both sides for the sake of practice in elocution. Who ever heard that the examples of grammarians or dialecticians, who transmit the teaching of this art, had to conform to the opinions of theologians? If they have so

* * * * *

1 *Propugnaculum fidei.* Erasmus purposely, it seems, misquotes the title of the work, *Propugnaculum ecclesiae.*
2 *Propugnaculum* 169r, in the edition published by de Colines, Paris 1526. The *index alphabeticus* enumerates these censures of Erasmus: the *Encomium matrimonii* composed by Erasmus is not to be approved in all respects; Erasmus attempts to give advice against the practice of the law concerning priestly celibacy; Erasmus entertains erroneous opinions concerning fast and abstinence as defined by the church. Erasmus' essay on the prohibition of eating meat (*Epistola de esu carnium*) is refuted in the third book of this work.

much leisure time, why don't they weigh Donatus[3] and Poggio's *Facetiae*[4] in the same balance? Those who put forward before theologians tenets of Aristotle that are diametrically opposed to the teaching of Christ have only to say: 'I speak as a philosopher.' But if it is the role of the orator in actual judicial proceedings not to speak the truth at all times but only to give the appearance of truth, as long as it contributes to the victory, then it is much more unreasonable to submit particular passages in a fictitious theme to the rigours of a theological examination.

Whoever professes to write a declamation deliberately exempts himself from credibility and puts only his skill in oratory at risk, as in the example of one who before pronouncing a eulogy of justice must first praise injustice.[5] Josse quotes my writings as if acting as a theologian I had seriously recommended those arguments to the faithful. On the contrary one must imagine the true circumstances of the composition, namely, that a schoolboy engaged in the study of rhetoric is delivering a speech in a school of declamation, and is giving proof of his ability to use different approaches in treating the same argument. I had included this example among the rhetorical rules of suasion in my book *On the Writing of Letters*.[6] Lest you should think I am inventing this, there are people in England[7] who have the original copy, written in my hand almost thirty years ago. And I have an exemplar copied by a clerk[8] twenty years ago, in which there is also a preliminary sketch of another section.[9] If in the first part there was no argument to be refuted, what would the speaker representing the opposite side have to say? Well, suppose I were to put forward a statement from St Thomas[10] which says that in the sacrament

* * * * *

3 The two works on grammar, the *Ars minor* and the *Ars major*, of Aelius Donatus (fourth century AD) were favourite school-books in the Middle Ages.
4 A collection of mostly scurrilous tales written by the Florentine humanist Poggio Bracciolini
5 As does Glaucon in Plato's *Republic*. Cf *Dilutio* 127 n64.
6 Probably referring to the two sample letters, one of persuasion and one of dissuasion, on the subject of marriage, CWE 25 129–48
7 Erasmus gave a copy of the first draft of the treatise to Robert Fisher in 1498 to bring with him to England. It already contained the text of the encomium in the form of a letter of persuasion. He also sent a revised version to William Blount, fourth Baron Mountjoy in November 1499. Cf Epp 71 and 117.
8 In Ep 80:26 addressed to Jacob Batt, Erasmus mentions that his copyist Caminadus had the only copy of the work.
9 The brief instructions on how to dissuade a friend from marrying that were inserted as a counterpart to the long letter counselling marriage. Cf CWE 25 145–8.
10 *Summa theologiae* III q 74 art 1 obj 1

of the Eucharist the body of the Lord, that was slain for us, would have been better represented by the flesh of animals than by the species of bread and wine because they were more perfect representations of what they signify. If I were to impute the charge of blasphemy to him, would not Clichtove immediately object that I was not acting fairly since I was constructing a false accusation from arguments that precede the refutation? That is the way they talk. If this method is valid in theological disputation, it is much more valid in a fictitious subject, in which the speaker is compelled to give his support to neither side.

Moreover, this declamation is concerned not with the general question of whether marriage is better than celibacy, but with a question limited to specific circumstances, namely, whether marriage is more profitable than celibacy for the particular person whom I imagine. And although I am dealing with a fictitious topic, I still did not yield to the freedom of the declamation to the extent charged by Clichtove. He claims that I recommend that it would be in the better interests of mankind if priestly and monastic continence, consecrated to God, be done away with, obliterated, violated, and changed to the conjugal state.[11] The verb 'recommend' is not in my declamation, and I do not speak in my own name. The one whom I represent as speaking says, 'It seems to me.' He does not condemn the continence of priests and monks, and indeed the declamation commends the virtue of continence even in marriage,[12] which he wishes to be very similar to virginity, that is, that there be as little gratification of lust as possible, the principal goal being the generation of offspring.

In the next place I compare virginity to the angels while I attribute marriage to men. Naturally, to those who by the gift of God can live continently I attribute qualities beyond those of mere mortals. The declaimer of the speech does not refer to chaste priests and monks, but to those who lead impure lives, of whom alas! there is a great multitude everywhere even if we pretend not to notice secret depravities. If there is no other remedy for these hapless creatures, the speaker thinks it would be expedient for the church to permit them to marry, as a kind of second plank to save them from shipwreck.[13] And he adds, 'If the circumstances required it';[14] that is, if it seems

*****

11 *Propugnaculum* 121v. Cf *Dilutio* 130 n69.
12 CWE 25 137–8
13 Jerome Ep 84 PL 22 748. In this context the 'second plank' refers to the sacrament of penance.
14 CWE 25 137. Erasmus uses here a slightly different Latin phrase from the one used in *De conscribendis epistolis*.

proper and fitting to the leaders of the church. But if someone should answer that the church cannot release one from a solemn vow, let him then explain precisely how it can release one from a simple vow, even though it is something done publicly and generally known. I also think that the church can do what the Roman pontiff,[15] highest pastor of the church, does in official documents, when for grave reasons he makes a monk into a non-monk. Although I am not here formally advocating this, since my declamation talks not about the initiated but about those who have yet to be initiated, surely the church can decide that from now on those who become priests or monks need not be bound by the obligation of the vow of chastity if after trying every means they are overcome by the weakness of the flesh. This is what that speaker meant, a far cry from Clichtove's vehement utterances. Nothing of the sort was ever my intention, nor is it to be found in any of my writings, even the most frivolous of them. Nevertheless, that speaker by right of the licence granted to orators twists certain arguments to the advantage of his case. What a spectacle it would be if in the classroom of the declamatory school one who had dissuaded Alexander the Great from attacking Tyre[16] should be answered by some theologian with the grave dogmas of the schools. Yet Clichtove's response is no more relevant than that. There is no time at the moment to respond to his other charges. His book was delivered to me late when the book fair was already close at hand, and I could hardly finish what I was engaged in. I made some reply[17] several years ago to Jan Briart, then wrote something in response to Béda's criticisms,[18] not yet aware that Clichtove had touched on this subject. I also had a special defence against the detractors of this declamation, which for limitations of time I have not had occasion to publish. In this I shall declare that my views on the chastity of those who profess celibacy and on marriage are no different from those of the Catholic church. To his other criticisms concerning the eating of meat and fasting we have partly responded[19] and partly will respond in such a way as to satisfy at least the impartial reader. It would be preferable to devote our energies to resolving our differences rather than to providing seed-ground for new disagreements through biased inquiries.

* * * * *

15 Papal dispensation from vows. Cf *Dilutio* 131 n75.
16 A favourite topic in the schools of declamation was Alexander's deliberation whether or not to besiege the island fortress of Tyre in 332 BC.
17 The *Apologia de laude matrimonii*, 1519
18 *Prologus in supputationem calumniarum Bedae* (August 1526) LB IX 488F–489A
19 As part of the *Divinationes ad notata Bedae* LB IX 484D–489A

REFUTATION OF THE ACCUSATIONS OF JOSSE CLICHTOVE AGAINST THE *SUASORIA* OF DESIDERIUS ERASMUS OF ROTTERDAM IN PRAISE OF MARRIAGE

I have finally read through Josse Clichtove's attack in the second book of his *Propugnaculum*[1] against my *Declamation in Praise of Marriage*. But his earnest attempt to do battle with a fictitious theme, using the testimony of the Scriptures and the Fathers and decrees of the church, almost provoked me to laughter. It was as if I had before my eyes a veteran soldier in full battle array exerting all his strength to fight with shadows, regaling his audience with an amusing spectacle of shadow-boxing. Nevertheless I admired his spirit, inflamed, as it appears, with an extraordinary love of chastity.[2] I am convinced that none of this is feigned, for I consider him to be a good man totally without pretence. And on this account I once regarded him with affection,[3] that is, before I incited this hostility in him. But Satan with his many wiles knows how to deceive even the simplest spirits with the blandishments of piety. Otherwise, if he had recalled the integrity that befits a Christian priest, the circumspection proper to a theologian (especially one from Paris), the moderation expected of one who finds fault, and the piety proper to a defender of the church, he would not have made false accusations or magnified things beyond all proportion in such offensive language. Such example would have been more useful to this most celebrated of all Faculties and would have brought more honour to the name of theologian.

For the moment, however, I shall not present a true apology, for fear that after having given a foolish account of myself as a young man in treating this subject, I should now as an old man appear even more foolish in taking seriously what is meant as playful. I shall simply call attention to certain

* * * * *

1 Quotations are taken from the edition of the *Propugnaculum* published by de Colines, Paris 1526.
2 Erasmus is making fun of Clichtove's zeal for chastity manifested at his advanced age.
3 Cf Ep 1620:78–9 to Noël Béda 2 October 1525: 'I always liked Josse Clichtove . . .'

passages in which I am forced to note the lack of moderation and sincerity I might have expected of him. First of all, he disallows me in this dispute the evidence I adduce in an apology[4] I wrote against the charges of Jan Briart, namely, that I had written on this subject as a young man not for myself but for a distinguished gentleman, William Mountjoy.[5] At that time I was instructing him in the art of rhetoric, and I wished in this exercise to set before the eyes of the young man an example of what I had taught him in the exposition of the theory. Clichtove says, 'Since you were an old man more trained in sacred learning when you published what you had written as a young man, you should have given preference to virginity over marriage.'[6] I was not so unversed in the Scriptures, my dear Josse, as not to know that virginity entered into voluntarily through love of a holy life is to be preferred to matrimony; but that was not what was in question there. If I had wished to revise this treatise according to the precepts of the Scriptures and theological reasoning I would have needed a sponge, not a pen. I thought I had made allowances for any scandal that I might cause to the weak when in the prefatory title[7] I stated that it was a topic of declamation devised to develop skill in speaking and not to instil the dogmas of the Christian religion.

He cites the example of Enea Silvio,[8] who, when he was an old man and sovereign pontiff, ordered the book on the love affair of Euryalus and Lucretia[9] that he had written as a youth to be condemned. But I am not yet

* * * * *

4 *Apologia de laude matrimonii*, Louvain, 7 March 1519
5 William Blount, fourth Baron Mountjoy, student of Erasmus in Paris and lifelong friend, to whom he addressed what appears to be a dedicatory preface of a revised version of *De conscribendis epistolis*, Ep 117
6 *Propugnaculum* 127r. Erasmus does not cite Clichtove's objections exactly. His opponent says that in publishing his youthful work as an older man Erasmus should have removed certain statements that were not in harmony with the church's teaching or could give bad example. Clichtove does not say specifically that he should have given preference to virginity over marriage.
7 *Declamatio in genere suasorio de laude matrimonii*
8 Pope Pius II. Clichtove gives an excerpt from a letter of retraction (*epistola poenitudinis*) that Enea Silvio as pope prefixed to the rather unedifying tale he had written as a youth. In it he asks his readers to put their faith in an old man rather than a young man, to reject Aeneas and accept Pius, explaining that the gentile name was bestowed upon him at birth by his parents, but that he took the Christian name on his accession to the papacy: 'Aeneam reicite, Pium suscipite. Illud gentile nomen parentes indidere nascenti, hoc christianum in apostolatu suscepimus'; *Aeneae Sylvii Piccolominei Senensis opera quae extant omnia* (Basel 1571) 870 Ep 395.
9 The *Historia de Euryalo et Lucretia* written by Enea Silvio in 1444 is a melancholy tale of a young Sienese bride, married to an old Menelaus, who falls in love with a handsome French knight in the retinue of Duke Sigmund of Tyrol.

pope, nor did I write, as he did, prurient tales of how a wife deceived her husband in defiance of conjugal fidelity and took herself a lover. I invented a speaker in a declamatory speech who recommends a chaste marriage, closely resembling virginity, to a young man on whom depended the propagation of an excellent family. If I had proclaimed after the example of Enea, 'Reject the young Erasmus and accept the old,' I would have been guilty of an utter falsehood, as if I had taught that marriage was to be preferred to virginity without qualification.[10] Did I not condemn this insignificant treatise sufficiently when I proclaimed more than once that it was a declamation and was concerned with proficiency in public speaking and not with faith and morals?

Homer did not correct his *Battle of the Frogs and Mice*,[11] but wrote the *Iliad* in its place. And Virgil did not correct the *Gnat*,[12] but went on to write the *Bucolics*. Besides, what would I have accomplished by correcting some statements in this exercise? Now I have done more by removing credibility from the whole declamation. In scholastic disputations, even if something is said that is contradictory to the Catholic faith, it is sufficient to say, 'I speak now as a philosopher.' But it did me no good to shout at the top of my voice, 'I am speaking as a rhetorician; I am not fashioning morals, but I am teaching language.' Who could have restrained his laughter if someone had examined the letters and declamations of Carolus Virulus[13] according to theological canons? Now suppose that I would have been willing to correct that short oratorical exercise according to the severe norms of theology, who would not have cried out in protest: 'You fool, what are you doing? Why decorate a cooking-pot?'[14] Epictetus would have added, 'Let a pot remain a pot.'[15]

But Clichtove does not even allow the title to be used in my defence, the fact that I called it a declamation. Still, he showed a little more sense than the theologian[16] who thought that the Latin word for declamation was equivalent in meaning to a sermon, and as a result of this error publicly excoriated me in very vehement language in a crowded university lecture-

*****

10 Erasmus uses here and elsewhere in this apology the term *simpliciter* taken from scholastic argumentation.
11 A parody of Homer probably written in the fourth century BC. Erasmus mentions these examples in the prefatory letter to the *Praise of Folly* (*Moriae encomium*), written to Thomas More, Ep 222.
12 A mock-heroic poem long attributed to Virgil
13 Charles Menniken of Ghent (c 1413–93), author of a treatise on letter-writing which Erasmus ridicules in *De conscribendis epistolis* CWE 25 50
14 Said of useless toil; *Adagia* I iv 66. Quoted in Greek
15 Arrian *Discourses of Epictetus* 4.10.34
16 Jan Briart of Ath. Cf CWE 71 86–7.

hall. I learned of his error afterwards in a private conversation with him. Such is the risk we run when certain individuals have not learned Latin. Clichtove admits that a declamation concerns itself with a fictitious subject, but this is so especially in forensic debate,[17] in which both sides argue with a certain degree of probability. To persuade us of this he produces several arguments from the declamations of Quintilian.[18] Then he calls on me to answer whether it is a fictitious argument or not, and whether the question 'Should celibacy be preferred to marriage or vice versa?' is one to be debated[19] before a magistrate's tribunal. In the first place, who taught Josse that a declamation is concerned particularly with law cases that are conducted before a judge when Seneca,[20] whom I think he has read, lists so many declamations as suasoriae?[21] But even if we concede that declamations usually deal with forensic cases, does it immediately follow that declamations do not belong to the suasorial or encomiastic genre? And what name shall we assign to one who exercises himself in the encomiastic genre, praising a man or a city or a nation? Moreover, suppose one were to treat a trivial subject,[22] for example, if one were to write a eulogy of Busiris, as Isocrates did,[23] or of Phalaris,[24] as Lucian did, or of quartan fever,[25] as did Favorinus, or of baldness, as did

* * * * *

17 *Propugnaculum* 127v
18 A group of nineteen model pieces illustrating popular themes of the schools of declamation, attributed to Quintilian in the Middle Ages and in Erasmus' time, but definitely not written by him. Clichtove *Propugnaculum* 128r proposes the fifth and thirteenth of these speeches, which treat of the usual fanciful subjects debated in such exercises.
19 Clichtove's argument is that the subject is not debatable, since it has been proved both by Scripture and by the writings of the Fathers of the church that celibacy is preferred to marriage. Hence it would be false to call the treatise a declamation.
20 The elder Seneca, regularly confused in Erasmus' time with his son, Seneca the philosopher. One book of his *suasoriae*, speeches of exhortation to historical or semi-historical characters on their future conduct, is extant.
21 See the preceding note.
22 Erasmus uses the Greek term ἄδοξον, literally, an unexpected or improbable topic. Cf Aulus Gellius *Noctes Atticae* 17.12.
23 Actually, Isocrates wrote a rejoinder to a mock encomium of Busiris written by Polycrates, an Athenian sophist of the fourth century BC. Busiris was a legendary Egyptian king who slaughtered all foreigners entering Egypt.
24 In this exercise Lucian has the tyrant defend his cruel conduct before the people of Delphi. Cf *Lucian* trans A.M. Harmon I (Cambridge, Mass 1959) 3–21.
25 Favorinus, a Gallic rhetor of the second century, wrote an encomium on this subject. Plato in the *Timaeus* (86A) argues that quartan fever may be a blessing, for when one gets well, he will enjoy surer health. Guillaume de l'Isle, a disciple of Erasmus, also wrote an *Encomium febris quartanae* (Basel 1542).

Synesius,[26] or the happiness of brute animals, on which Plutarch[27] wrote –
would these be excluded from the category of declamations because the topic
cannot be argued with probability on both sides? On the contrary, learned
men think that topics of this kind are particularly effective in producing
quickness of intellect. This type of exercise is not unlike the scholastic dispute
that goes by the name *obligatoria*,[28] in which, notwithstanding, examples are
sometimes taken from sacred writings. Many false things are said, some
of them even blasphemous, if they were not excused by the nature of the
exercise. But where did he ever get the idea that the subject of my treatise
was whether celibacy should be preferred to matrimony or vice versa? I
never even dreamed of such a thing. It is not an inquiry before a judge as
to whether the state of an unmarried man is preferable to that of a married
man. Yet Quintilian[29] reminds us that the question of whether a philosopher
should take a wife is often debated in deliberative speeches. I treat a question
that pertains to *suasoriae* and it is limited to specific circumstances. So then he
corrects the title[30] and calls it a commendation of marriage or an exhortation
to marriage. Even I occasionally call it an encomium of marriage, but what's
the difference? Do not exhortations or eulogies fall into the category of
rhetorical exercises? I don't think he is so ignorant of the art of rhetoric that
he does not know that the encomiastic genre is also appropriate for judicial
cases, especially the suasorial type. The name of the exercise is taken from
the main argument.

In this case, therefore, marriage is praised so that a young man will
be induced to take a wife. Now this topic belongs expressly to the suasorial
genre. If the title deceived him, he could at least have perceived from the
argument that the topic was a *suasoria* and not to be taken seriously. Finally,
my apology,[31] which he claims to have read, demonstrates clearly the nature
of the subject.

* * * * *

26 Bishop of Cyrene, fifth century AD, wrote a mock encomium of baldness in
answer to a praise of long hair written by the orator Dio Chrysostom, PG 66
1167–1206. A Latin translation was done by John Free, an English humanist,
who taught rhetoric at the school of Guarino in Ferrara in 1456. It was published
together with the *Folly*, Basel 1515.

27 Plutarch's *Bruta animalia* (*Moralia* 985D–992) is a dialogue between Ulysses and
one of his men, who has been transformed into a swine by Circe and finds
himself happier in his new existence.

28 Disputation held in summer at the University of Paris for the reception of the
licentiate in theology in January

29 Quintilian *Institutio oratoria* 3.5.13

30 *Propugnaculum* 128r

31 The *Apologia de laude matrimonii* CWE 71 81–95

But perhaps Clichtove had already written against my rhetorical exercise before he had learned from my apology what the word declamation meant in Latin, and that the argument was treated from both sides. In that case he should also have changed his method of argument, but he preferred to leave room for calumny through pointless evasions. Therefore Josse goes astray right at the beginning, going aground[32] in the harbour, as they say. He declares, 'Those who exhort invite to what is better; Erasmus does the opposite.'[33] But they are not writing a declamation. Elsewhere I too proclaim the praises of virginity, namely, in my little book on the comparison of a virgin and a martyr,[34] and again in my essay on the solitary life;[35] and in a thousand other places I admit that in absolute terms continence is superior to marriage. But if the main object of his attack is to draw discredit upon the form of the declamation as such, why is only the first part singled out for condemnation although I treated both sides of the question, arguing for marriage in the first part and against it in the second? That is no more fitting than if one were to combat the arguments of Thomas or of Scotus in which they impugn vows or defend fornication,[36] while neglecting to mention the rebuttal that follows. If he was eager to make false accusations, he could just as well have condemned each section equally. For those who censure matrimony and those who censure virginity unfairly are equally in error. One should not be criticized, however, for thinking that it would be more feasible for this or that person to marry rather than to live a life of celibacy, even if he were not composing a declamation but pleading a real case.

Moreover, since this is only one letter among many proposed as examples, why is it alone submitted to rigid scrutiny? In his whole argumentation he deals with me as if I treated only this side of the question, and as if I were not writing a declamation, but sincerely wished to make this recommendation to a particular friend. Whereas, after proposing various rules, I say, 'The following will serve as an example of this brief set of rules' [CWE 25 129]. Why did that much-quoted dictum of Aristotle not occur to him: 'We set forth examples, not because that is the way things are, but in order that

*****

32 *Adagia* I v 76
33 *Propugnaculum* 128r
34 *Virginis et martyris comparatio* (1524) LB v 589–600. Virginity is here depicted as a daily martyrdom hardly attainable by an ordinary mortal.
35 *De contemptu mundi* CWE 66 135–75
36 Erasmus refers to the scholastic format, in which first the objections were stated and then the rebuttal. In Thomas vows are discussed in the *Summa theologiae* II-II q 189 art 2–4; immorality (*stuprum*) at II-II q 154 art 2–4 and in the *Quaestio disputata de malo* 180. Scotus discusses simple and solemn vows in the *Commentaria Oxoniensia ad* IV *libros Magistri sententiarum* 4 d 38.

the learners may understand through them.' For example, when Aristotle[37] borrows examples from mathematics, he is not obliged to be answerable for the truth of the borrowed material.

I could have been more justifiably criticized for transferring an argument pertaining to good morals to the school of declamation. Plato[38] forbids those who are chosen to watch over the republic to be instructed in dialectic until an advanced age, lest having been trained to approve or reject anything whatsoever, they waver in decisions concerning virtue and vice, in which there should be great firmness. I too should not recommend that young boys have too much training in topics of this kind, but the same danger is inherent in scholastic disputations, since they debate subjects about which it is wrong to entertain any doubt.

Since the foundation of Clichtove's entire argument is insubstantial, it is inevitable that what he built on it must crumble. He is wrong in his assumption that I do not propose[39] a subject restricted to certain circumstances, but throughout the discussion make use of general, common, and universal arguments. In the first place, there are many particular circumstances in the narration right from the start. It does not adduce arguments itself, but it contains the seeds of argumentation. Then in the division part of the speech, 'But I shall show by the clearest of proofs that this alternative would be far more honourable, profitable, and pleasant for you' [CWE 25 130], when I say 'for you' I indicate a specific person, not a universal truth. Likewise when I say, 'Besides, if virginity were to merit special praise in all others, in your case it cannot escape censure' [CWE 25 138], and since I refer to him again and again, am I not presenting arguments from the particular circumstances of a specific person? Frequently I make reference to outstanding individuals or to the corrupt morals of these times, as when I show that there is a great diversity between the characteristic behaviour of the time of the apostles and that of our own age [CWE 25 137]. Again when I say, 'I speak now as one man to another, as one commoner to another, as one weak mortal to another' [CWE 25 138]. Again when I say, 'You must remember that the survival of your race rests with you alone' [CWE 25 144, not exact]. Again when I turn to the opposite effect, the example he cites of his sister's dedicating herself to God [CWE 25 144]. Next when I say, 'You who are the elder must remember that you are a man' [CWE 25 144]. Then the whole concluding part of the argument consists of particular circumstances. Yet my friend Clichtove proclaims and

* * * * *

37 Aristotle *Rhetoric* 1.2.8 (1356b), 18.3 (916d)
38 Plato *Republic* 538A
39 *Propugnaculum* 128v

insists with much verbiage that through the whole course of the oration I do not touch on any specific circumstances, obviously so that there will be opportunity for false accusation. And yet it would have been more becoming to a theologian's moral integrity and more profitable to young boys, about whose chastity he seems to be preoccupied, to make it clear that this whole argument was a rhetorical declamation and was totally lacking in any credibility. Moreover, the reader was instructed to await the presentation of the other side of the argument, of which we gave only an outline indicating the principal sources of the arguments. We have explained why we did not complete this part of the work in the *Apology*,[40] which Josse dismissed. As to the fact that I use many common arguments, I had every right to do so. Cicero does the same, and so does Jerome[41] when he advises against marriage and assembles all the usual material about the marriage bond. Can it be that he thinks that commonplaces are not to be used in persuasion? As if one were to advise the Emperor against war with the Turks, but were not allowed to support his case by citing the usual disadvantages of war.

On top of this, he does not allow me[42] to say in my defence that I prefer marriage to celibacy, not to continence, since in Latin celibate means free from marriage even if one has two hundred concubines. Just as a childless person is contrasted to a parent, so a celibate person is contrasted to a husband. Horace[43] calls himself celibate although he was far from continent. Josse claims[44] that the word *caelebs* was used in that sense by profane writers but that sacred writers never used the word except to designate one who lived a pure and chaste life. He says further that there is no more distinction between celibate and continent than there is between justice and equity.[45] I won't mention that for those who have knowledge of Latin a just judge and an equitable judge are not at all the same thing, nor are the justice of laws and the equity of law. But whence can he prove to us that in the sacred writers the word 'celibate' is used solely and exclusively to mean 'continent'? As far as I

* * * * *

40 The *Apologia de laude matrimonii* CWE 71 91
41 Jerome *Adversus Iovinianum* 1.48 PL 23 291B. Jerome refers to a story concerning Cicero's repudiation of his wife, Terentia, who then proceeded to marry Sallust, Cicero's enemy. In his misogamist argument Jerome emphasizes that this could happen even with a *good* wife, who had imbibed some of the wisdom of her husband. Clichtove cites this passage at *Propugnaculum* 116r.
42 *Propugnaculum* 128v
43 Horace *Epistles* 1.1.87–9
44 *Propugnaculum* 128v
45 For the distinction between justice and equity cf Aristotle *Nicomachean Ethics* 5.10.3–7, and the *Rhetoric* 1.13.17–19.

know, this was never the case, at least in those writers who knew Latin. I am
not speaking of those who think that there is no difference between lust and
promiscuity. It is not surprising if at times they call one who is celibate chaste,
since nothing prevents a celibate person from being continent. But Joseph
and Mary, although they were most chaste, were not celibate. Again, there
are many monks who are celibate by profession but do not live a continent
life. Likewise if I were to call an Italian learned it does not follow that there
is no difference between a learned man and an Italian. Among Christians,
since all sexual intercourse outside of marriage is illicit, all those who are
celibate should also be continent. Finally, I share the opinion of those who
think that by their vow[46] monks and priests do not renounce incontinence,
which is forbidden to everyone, but marriage.

    In his second book against Jovinian, Jerome[47] introduces a new etymol-
ogy: *caelebs* means worthy of heaven [*caelum*], because the celibate abstain
from sexual intercourse. But it is not unusual for him to seize upon any
weapon in the fight in order to gain the victory, and he declares in more than
one passage that it is his right to do so. What wonder is it if he harnesses for
his purpose an all but arbitrary etymology of one word, when in that same
place he forces several citations from Sacred Scripture to support his argument, twisting their neck,[48] as the saying goes? But let us grant him his use of
the word. Is that to say that all those who refrain from sexual intercourse are
worthy of heaven, while those who legitimately engage in sexual intercourse
are unworthy of heaven? And yet in that same passage he does not use the
word *caelebs* wholly and entirely in that sense, but in place of the word 'widower.' This is what he says: 'A marvellous word, and one which the spouse
of Christ would hear among virgins and widows and celibates.'[49] The word
virgin is applied to both sexes, but since it seemed to sound jarring to say
widows and widowers, he calls men who were free from marriage through
the death of their wives celibates. And yet the word celibate is also used of

        * * * * *

46 Many theologians, including Gerson *De consiliis evangelicis* in *Oeuvres complètes*
   ed P. Glorieux 10 vols (Paris 1960–75) III 19–20, considered that acts of incontinence were transgressions of the commandment of God, but not violations
   of the vow of chastity, since a vow must concern supererogatory works, not
   matters forbidden *de praecepto*. Luther defended this opinion in his *De votis
   monasticis*. Clichtove, citing St Thomas *Summa theologiae* II-II q 186 art 10, argues against this view in some unpublished writings, Bibliothèque Mazarine
   MS 1068 fol 280r–v.
47 Jerome *Adversus Iovinianum* 2.37 PL 23 351
48 *Adagia* IV ix 50
49 Jerome *Adversus Iovinianum* 2.37 PL 23 351

one who never had a wife, and continent is used of one who in any state of life whatever lives a chaste life. Deficiency of vocabulary forced them to misuse words. If every widow is continent, and if there is no difference between a widow and a continent woman, then celibate and continent can mean the same thing. But if the word celibate includes all those who live continent lives, what need was there for three words? In the second book [actually the first] the same writer uses the word continent for those whom he here calls celibate. He said, 'The sum of money that was promised in marriage was varied and distinct, according to whether they were widows, continent women, or married women.'[50] It is not that these words mean the same thing, but that among Christians those who profess celibacy should abstain from intercourse.

But again, granted that the sacred Doctors used the word consistently in that way, will I not be allowed to speak good Latin[51] in an exercise devised to perfect the language of young students? No doubt he will cite Priscian,[52] who interpreted celibate as celestial, because the celibate person leads a heavenly life, in chastity and purity, although Clichtove[53] added that last phrase of his own. But while etymology may have some importance in other contexts, in this case, at any rate, it was long ago derided by the learned Quintilian.[54] These are Quintilian's words: 'Gaius imagined that he was clever in deriving *caelibes* from *caelites*, because the celibate are free of a heavy burden, and he supported his case with an example from Greek, stating that the word ἠίθεος[55] is used in the same way. Yet Modestus does not yield to him in invention. He says that those who are without a wife are called by this name because Saturn cut the genitals off the sky.' You see that the etymology of the jurisconsults was ridiculed by such a learned man. Other examples of the same kind are

* * * * *

50 Jerome *Adversus Iovinianum* 1.33 PL 23 252
51 In his *Paraphrasis in Elegantias Laurentii Vallae* Erasmus defines the word *caelebs* clearly as 'one who lives outside marriage, whether he be bereft of his wife or never had one, whether continent or incontinent. Therefore celibacy is the opposite of marriage' (ASD I-4 232:673).
52 Priscian *Institutio de arte grammatica* 2.8.10
53 *Propugnaculum* 129r
54 Quintilian *Institutio oratoria* 1.6.36. The modern text of Quintilian reads Gavius, presumably Gavius Bassus, a grammarian of the age of Cicero. Modestus is probably a freedman of C. Julius Hyginus mentioned in Suetonius *De grammaticis* 20. Apparently Erasmus understood them to be the jurists Gaius and Modestinus, who belong to a later era.
55 ἠίθεος: the word signifies a young unmarried man in Greek and is a cognate of the Latin *viduus* and the English 'widower.' It is not connected with the word θεός as the Latin etymologist claims.

oratio from *oris ratio*, and *testamentum* from *testatio mentis*. But let us admit the validity of this derivation. Gaius, who was the first to teach this etymology, thought that *caelibes* was derived from *caelites* not because the celibate lived chastely, but because they lived happily and contentedly, free of the marriage halter and the other troubles that marriage brings with it. On the other hand the gods of Gaius and Modestus are neither celibate nor continent. Jupiter in addition to Juno has a host of nymphs[56] without including his Phrygian cup-bearer.[57] Mars[58] is not satisfied with his legitimate spouse but has secret assignations with Venus, the wife of Vulcan. I won't mention the rest, since with them it is an endless tale of immorality, incest, adultery, and rape. Yet they are called blessed and 'living a life of ease' by the poets because of their happy existence. Terence's Micio[59] says the same: 'For this they deem me fortunate, that I never had a wife.'

Clichtove is even less shamefaced in saying that throughout this declaration I used the word celibate to mean continent, when the truth is I do not do so even once; on the contrary, I distinguish between the two in several places. For example, I say: 'You admire celibacy and respect virginity. But if you take away the practice of wedlock, there will be neither unwedded nor virgins' [CWE 25 143]. Another example: 'Yet why do you inquire so thoroughly, nay, so anxiously, into all the disadvantages of marriage, as if celibacy had no disadvantages?' [CWE 25 142]. Do I not oppose celibacy to marriage when I say, '[Roman marriage laws] prove how detrimental it was to the republic that the state either be reduced in numbers through the desire for the single life or be populated with bastards if celibates do not produce children' [CWE 25 132]? Again: 'One who perseveres in the single state simply in order to have a more independent life' [CWE 25 132]. Do I not oppose celibacy to marriage again in that passage? Then, even more clearly: 'We read that men who are truly chaste and virgins are praised, but celibacy in itself receives no praise' [CWE 25 132]. Do I not distinguish here a celibate person from a continent person and a virgin? Likewise a little before that passage in praise of marriage I borrow the image that Christ took from wedlock to express his ineffable union with the church, adding, 'What do we read like this concerning celibacy anywhere in the sacred writings?' [CWE 25 132]. Since all of this is very clearly stated, how shameful it was for a theologian to declare so emphatically that

* * * * *

56 Virgil *Aeneid* 1.71
57 Ganymede
58 Homer *Odyssey* 8.266–366. Of course, neither Mars nor Ares, his Greek counterpart, had a legitimate spouse.
59 Terence *Adelphi* 43–4

Erasmus throughout his treatise used the word celibate to mean continent![60] But this groundwork had to be laid so that he would have ample opportunity for his nasty incriminations, allowing whatever the declamation says against the celibate to be interpreted as pertaining to those who are continent.

But when he strips me of my weapons by dismissing the arguments of my *Apology*, why does he disregard the similarity of a declamation, which treats both sides of a question, to the disputations of the theologians,[61] which first impugn even articles of faith by every manner of device and then untie the knots they have woven? In the second part[62] I demonstrate how one who is advising against marriage ought to exaggerate the disadvantages of marriage and by contrast exalt the advantages of celibacy. By various methods I exaggerate the servitude of marriage, its troubles and dangers, and I express contempt for animal pleasure. I enhance the dignity and happiness of virginity, and rebut the arguments previously used to commend marriage. If he had not ignored all of this, all those distorted accusations he hurls with incredible vehemence against the condemner of continence would fall flat. On the other hand, if, speaking as a philosopher, I had deduced by rational argument that the world was not created so that I could arouse the wits of learned men to prove by philosophical reasoning that the world was created, no one, I dare say, would convert the philosophical debate into an inquiry into the Catholic faith, but would merely approve or disapprove of the display of ingenuity. Giovanni Antonio Campano[63] condemned beneficence and praised ingratitude, but no one charged him with impiety. In Plato, Glaucon[64] praises injustice in order to incite Socrates to praise it, but no one ever thought less of justice because of it. In our times, too, someone praised drunkenness,[65] but no one used harsh words against him, even though he did not write a corresponding praise of sobriety. Yet the first part of my little declamation has called forth a laborious response from a theologian in a work to which he gave the grandiose title *Bulwark of the Church*, as if it were a matter of

* * * * *

60 In an epistolary exchange in July 1532 with the Dominican theologian Ambrosius Pelargus (Storch), to whom he had submitted his response to the censures of the University of Paris, Erasmus once more defends his use of the word *caelebs* (Allen Ep 2675:1–4).

61 *Propugnaculum* 128r

62 CWE 25 145–8

63 *De ingratitudine fugienda* (Venice 1502) 28r–4or

64 Brother of Plato; he is made to praise injustice in the second book of the *Republic* (358E–362C).

65 Christoph Hegendorff *Encomium ebrietatis* (Leipzig 1519). Philo of Alexandria had also written a *De ebrietate* on the drunkenness of Noah.

great seriousness, and as if there had been no counter-argument. He makes it appear as if I wrote this composition with the intention of convincing the world, contrary to the teaching of the church, that virginity and continence were things to be avoided. Finally, he pretends he is the defender of the church and I its adversary. It is true that I do use some false arguments. That is not surprising, certainly, if we are dealing with a fictitious theme, when theologians do the same in serious discussions. If there were no invalid arguments, what would the other side have to present?

Now consider how even in a fictitious argument I was not totally oblivious of Christian orthodoxy. First I imagine that one layman is persuading another young layman to marry a wife rather than remain single. Thus when Josse pretends so many times that I am really advising a friend against continence, he acts shamelessly on two counts. First, because he substitutes a different person in order to arouse ill will against me; then, because he pretends that I condemn celibacy outright, when all I do is advise a certain person against it; lastly, because he everywhere takes celibacy to mean continence. And yet this last point is not very relevant. No one would deny that this or that person may be advised against a life of virginity or continence. For neither celibacy nor virginity nor continence is praiseworthy in itself unless the purpose is that a man may have more time for piety. The Gospel condemns the foolish virgins,[66] and the decrees of the synods[67] of the church condemn those women who after taking the veil disdain and despise the company of married women. But if we were to speak from a political point of view, it is wrong not to devote oneself to the raising of children. I invent a young man who is not only free, but also weak, for whom the celibate life would not be salutary. He will say, 'Where does that appear?' It is evident from these words: 'But virginity is a divine and angelic prerogative' [CWE 25 137]. To this objection it is answered, 'But wedlock is human; I speak now as one man to another, as one commoner to another, as one weak mortal to another' [CWE 25 137–8]. I use the term 'man' to mean one who is not fitted for virginity, which is proper to those who are in some way superior to man. I use the word 'commoner' to mean a layman who is free to take a wife whenever he likes, and by 'weak' I mean one who would not undertake a life of perpetual continence without risk. I add an exterior constraint, not to omit a part of the suasorial genre, namely, that his line would perish.

* * * * *

66 Matt 25:2–13
67 Council of Gangra in 362, quoted in Gratian's *Decretum* pars 1 D 30 and D 31
     cc 8–9

Clichtove will say that this is not sufficient reason for abandoning continence. But the declamation deals with a free man. Even if it seems absurd to use such arguments in a fictitious theme, we read that the Roman pontiff granted permission to a certain cardinal to join himself in marriage to a noble young woman, because the preservation of his line depended upon him, and after having a male offspring from her he could return, if he wished, to the dignity of cardinal.[68] And this was not a declamation. Again I do not exhort to any marriage whatever, but to a chaste marriage very similar to virginity. Does this smack of Epicureanism? Besides, in many passages I attribute to virginity its proper dignity, stating openly that it has been praised, but in the case of a few, for perfection belongs to the few. When I acknowledge that it is above the condition of mankind and that it partakes of an angelic sublimity, I say, 'Let us who live under the law of nature look up to those things that are above nature, but emulate what is within our capacity' [CWE 25 131]. When you hear the word 'us,' do not imagine that it is Erasmus addressing a second person, but one layman speaking to another, one weak mortal to another. The expression 'within our capacity' reveals his weakness. This passage also refers to particular circumstances, which Josse consistently denied. In another passage I declare that virginity is an image of heavenly life. I say, 'God wished to show men a kind of picture and likeness of that life in heaven where no women marry or are given in marriage' [CWE 25 143]. What more noble statement could be made concerning virginity? I state that it befits apostles and men of apostolic temper as something perfect befitting those who are perfect. He will say, 'Then why do you advise against it?' I advise the addressee against it, not everyone, and not to repeat it so many times, these things are said in a declamation in the person of someone else. I could produce other passages, but I think these are sufficient for my purpose. If Clichtove did not see these passages, why does he say that he examined my declamation? If he did see them and pretends not to have seen them, where is his Christian integrity, his fraternal charity?

Now let us see how he states his case. 'Erasmus,' he says, 'recommends that priests and monks be granted the faculty to have wives, and it will

* * * * *

68 Erasmus may be referring here to the notorious case of Cesare Borgia, who was allowed to resign his cardinalate and become laicized by dispensation of his father, Pope Alexander vi, on 17 August 1498. He then married Charlotte d'Albert on 12 May 1499. Erasmus discusses similar cases in scholia 42 and 119 of the *Brevissima scholia*, also published in 1532, claiming as his source of information Cajetanus' *De dispensatione matrimonii in occidentali ecclesia*, 1505. I am indebted for this information to Professor Nelson Minnich of The Catholic University of America.

be beneficial to the progress of the human race if the continence of priests and monks that is consecrated to God is destroyed, obliterated, violated, and exchanged for the conjugal state.'[69] What was the purpose of this violent statement? The speaker in the declamation, whom I invent, does not speak in that way. He makes no recommendations, but modestly states, 'In my view it would not be ill-advised for the interests and morals of mankind if the right of wedlock were also conceded to priests and monks, if circumstances required it' [CWE 25 137]. What grave offence is it if this opinion is expressed in a declamation by a layman when Pope Pius II said, not in the context of a rhetorical declamation, 'For grave reasons we took wives away from priests, but for graver ones we should give them back to them.'[70] What wrong is there if circumstances require it, if extreme necessity forces it upon us, if it is permitted by divine law, if it is expedient for the church? Not content with this the speaker added, 'especially in view of the fact that there is such a great throng of priests everywhere, so few of whom live a chaste life'[71] [CWE 25 137].

Clichtove says, 'What has once been consecrated to God cannot be turned to profane use.'[72] I shall not discuss such things as chalices and patens, which certain persons have distributed for the uses of the poor not without praise for their piety. Are we to say that a legitimate marriage and an undefiled marriage-bed belong to Satan, although it is a sacrament of the church? And how is it that the holy patriarchs were so pleasing to God in the state of matrimony? How is it that the priests of the Old Law were consecrated to the sacred ministries and yet were not prohibited from marrying? I shall pass over these older precedents, but in the early days of the church,[73] when piety was in its greatest flowering, was marriage not permitted to priests and deacons? But, it will be objected, the indissoluble vow is an obstacle. The speaker in the declamation would not wish the vow to be dissolved except

* * * * *

69 *Propugnaculum* 121v

70 This phrase, which was often quoted by the opponents of priestly celibacy in the Renaissance, was attributed to Pius II by Platina. The actual phrase, which is slightly paraphrased by Erasmus, is 'Sacerdotibus magna ratione sublatas nuptias, majori restituendas videri'; Platina *De vitis ac gestis summorum pontificum* (Cologne 1540) 295.

71 This passage is not contained in the *Encomium matrimonii* but was added to *De conscribendis epistolis*.

72 *Propugnaculum* 121v

73 It was not until the Council of Elvira in 300 that those in sacred orders were obliged to observe chastity. This regulation was reinforced by Pope Siricius at the Council of Rome in 386.

by the authority of those charged with such duties. If the Roman pontiff for suitable reasons can make a monk into a non-monk,[74] what prevents him from allowing marriage for grave reasons? I shall not speak here of the great multitude of those professing celibacy who live very impure lives and how this corruption seeps down to men of various conditions. Such facts do not entirely escape the notice of Clichtove, however much he palliates them with fair names.

Moreover, the wording of the speaker in the declamation can be understood to refer not to the initiate but to those to be initiated. But if he refers especially to those that are bound by oath, if the pope or the church[75] cannot absolve anyone from his vow, the speaker in the declamation does not imply that they be granted the right to marry. Similarly he does not teach that it would be more proper to allow marriage, but judges that it would be a lesser evil; rather, he does not judge, but thinks so, and he qualifies his statement by saying, 'In my view,' which is equivalent to saying, 'That is my opinion at least, although it may be erroneous.' In Greek the particle $\gamma\epsilon$ has the same force. But let us suppose the church allowed priests, monks, and nuns to marry, would that mean that the purity of men and women of the church would immediately be destroyed, obliterated, and violated? The declamation does not wish that anyone be forced into marriage, and it is probable that a great number of people will persevere in the unmarried state, even from among those who live incontinently. Therefore, for those who like chastity, let that remain as their mark of honour; for those who cannot be continent, it would be granted that they have wives instead of concubines. I think there never were more chaste priests in the church than when the refuge of marriage was available to them.

It was equally generous of him to attribute impious aims to me, as if I were trying to persuade everyone that continence was pernicious for the human race, forgetting that these things are said in a declamation and not by me, but by a lay person advising against celibacy. Every time Josse repeats in this tract, 'Erasmus recommends, Erasmus teaches, Erasmus attempts,' he is

* * * * *

74 On the *glossa* see Beryl Smalley *The Study of the Bible in the Middle Ages* (Oxford 1952) 55.

75 St Thomas states in the *Summa theologiae* II-II q 88 art 11 that the pope can dispense a secular priest from his vow, because it is not a solemn vow. The question was the subject of several treatises written at this time, such as Nicolas Boussart *De continentia sacerdotum: utrum papa possit cum sacerdote dispensare ut nubat* (Paris 1505) and *Ioannis Maioris theologi in IV sententiarum quaestiones* (Paris 1521) fol cliv.

straying from the truth. For neither does the speaker recommend anything, nor am I the speaker there, nor is everything that is said uttered with true sincerity.

The declaimer twists the argument in his favour, saying that if everyone were to embrace the state of virginity the whole human race would perish. Josse admits[76] that this is true, but says that it will never happen. That is tantamount to uttering prophecies. Nevertheless, an argument from supposition is not to be rejected in a declamation, since it is often valid in serious discussion. For example, Jerome's answer to Jovinian, 'If they were all to become wise, where would the foolish be?'[77] is a verbal quibble, not an answer. Otherwise it would be offensive to honourable marriage. The difference between marriage and virginity is not that between wisdom and stupidity, but rather that between the gold of ducats and that of florins.[78] Certainly in the case of the addressee in the declamation, his race would have been annihilated if he had not taken a wife.

Now let us review some passages in which Clichtove lashes out with stinging words, not that we regard seriously what was not said seriously, but to indicate how unmindful he was of theological seriousness. He makes the observation that in setting forth the argument I call the celibate way of life lacking in humanity and sterile.[79] In the narration of the case I express doubt as to whether the subject of the declamation had decided on celibacy, that is, abstention from marriage, through motives of religion or because he was overcome with grief. If he abstains through religious motivation, it is not a human action, because it is something above the human condition and not befitting the weak person whom I depict. Man is by nature a sociable animal. We have it from divine testimony: 'It is not good for man to be alone.'[80] There is no more apt company for a man than a woman. If he shrinks from marriage because he is overcome with grief, then it is not only inhuman, but stupid. Again, if he rejects marriage for religious reasons, his action is impious, if it implies that living holily in the married state is not permitted. I treat these sides of the argument in my presentation of the case, sometimes speaking as

* * * * *

76 *Propugnaculum* 122v
77 This phrase is interpolated by Erasmus into the context of Jerome's *Adversus Iovinianum* 1.36 PL 23 271.
78 The two coins were of approximately equal value and were considered as comparable in the international trade of Erasmus' time. Cf John H. Munro 'Money and Coinage of the Age of Erasmus' CWE 1 314–16.
79 *Propugnaculum* 122r. Erasmus does indeed make such statements in *De conscribendis epistolis* CWE 25 130, 135.
80 Gen 2:18

one concerned with the government of the state, sometimes as a rhetorician, sometimes as a natural philosopher, always as a participant in a debate. In a theological argument I would speak in another manner.

In another passage[81] I wonder why his quotation is incomplete, unless he intended to leave room for the reproach that these words were more appropriate to Epicurus or a pagan than to a theologian, again imagining that I wrote those things in my own name, in all seriousness, and as a theologian. The passage is as follows: 'What is more ill-advised than in the pursuit of sanctity to shun as unholy what God himself, the source and father of all holiness, wished to be held most holy? What is more inhuman than to shrink from the laws of the human condition? What is more ungrateful than to deny to one's descendants that which you would not be able to deny, etc' [CWE 25 130]. What, I beseech you, is impious or Epicurean here? Is it not sinful to despise matrimony in the name of religion, as if it were something profane, although it is a sacrament of the church? Would not this attitude be ungrateful and inhuman unless it were excused because of the pursuit of a higher good? Is it not right to say that he who follows an angelic life is not a man? As far as political considerations are concerned, he who remains sterile is not a good citizen in this respect because he diminishes the size of the citizen body, just as Socrates[82] said that he who diminished the flock or the herd was not a good shepherd.

But what follows is harsher: 'It seems all the more shameful that dumb herds should obey nature's laws, but men, like the giants, should declare war upon nature' [CWE 25 134]. When you read 'It seems,' you recognize, I presume, a phrase used by one engaged in a debate, not by someone giving utterance to his own thoughts. When you read later on 'It is clear' [CWE 25 135], you know that I am relating an argument, not stating my own opinion. Still this reasoning, although presented in a fictitious discussion, is not altogether absurd. Celibacy in itself is degrading unless it is entered into for the sake of the kingdom of God. Again I do not call one who does not have a wife a stone [CWE 25 135], but one who is not moved by a desire to marry, since nature has implanted not only in animate things but in plants and herbs the desire to propagate their kind.

Furthermore, the declamation imagines that the addressee is unqualifiedly opposed to marriage, not that he wishes to conquer the promptings of nature through love of piety. The command 'Increase and multiply'[83] has not

* * * * *

81 *Propugnaculum* 122r
82 Plato *Republic* 345D
83 Gen 1:22

been rescinded, but it yields to a more perfect calling. Celibacy that shuns marriage through love of pleasure and ease is shameful and inhuman. More shameful is that which despises and abhors marriage. Almost all the young men depicted in comedies shrink from marriage, but they are not praised for it. It is praiseworthy for a Christian to oppose nature for the sake of the kingdom of heaven, which, according to the words of the Lord, 'suffers violence.'[84] But what praise does he deserve who is not touched by such feelings? I call the instinct of nature a supernatural power created by God. At this point Clichtove will ask me whether John the Baptist, John the Evangelist, and Paul were not human beings, or good citizens, or whether they were stones. Did you expect me to cite such examples in a declamatory exercise? In the Scriptures even stones are praised,[85] and it merits praise to rebel against nature, but what does this have to do with the person whom I depict as shunning marriage out of human sentiments? And he restricts the question to those who are not influenced by human feelings. But a certain Parisian theologian[86] of some renown wonders whether the mother of Jesus felt the first stirrings of nature, especially before she gave birth to Christ, although in my opinion it would have been more seemly not to raise this question. Josse admits that those whom he named struggled against the promptings of nature. If this is true, they were influenced by them. He adds, 'corrupted'[87] nature, but I posit that the stimulus to procreate comes from nature understood in an absolute sense, as thirst and hunger by nature stimulate us to preserve nature, although rebellion may rise from the corruption of nature, about which there will be opportunity to say more later on. Again in this instance I use the word 'seem,' playing the part of one who is discussing, not asserting as a fact. Despite all this, Josse concludes by saying that all these statements are undeniably impious and thoroughly detestable.

He takes offence at another passage: 'But nowadays conditions and times are such that you would not find anywhere a less defiled purity of morals than among the married' [CWE 25 137]. The declamation talks about impurity, which Josse says does not exist, and for that reason cannot be adduced to vilify religious orders, as if it were prohibited to say anything

* * * * *

84 Matt 11:12
85 Isa 28:16; Matt 21:42
86 Probably Pierre Cousturier (d 1537), a controversial Carthusian monk from the monastery of Vauvert-lez-Paris, who wrote a treatise against the detractors of the Blessed Virgin Mary, *Apologeticum in novos anticomaristas praeclarissimae beatae Virginis Mariae laudibus detrahentes* (Paris 1526)
87 *Propugnaculum* 122r

on a fictitious subject that was not absolutely verifiable. Would that Clichtove could have said with complete certainty, 'The declamation is shamefully lying.' Perhaps he has spent all his life among pure virgins, male and female, but for those who have lived in various regions it is more than apparent that what the declamation says is true. I won't mention here the bands of prostitutes of both sexes who are supported in some places by leading men of both the religious and the secular sphere. I won't mention the monasteries of men and women where all discipline has collapsed, which are openly nothing else but brothels. Those who are occupied in hearing the confessions of religious relate these things as certain facts, even in the case of well-reputed monasteries, cloistered nuns, and boarding-schools, in which the young are trained under a rigid regime – stories such as any religious person could not hear without feeling great chagrin. These things are not said to cast aspersion on religious orders; I merely touch on them lightly and in a general way since the case required it. I do not see how they could have been referred to more briefly or in a more seemly fashion. But if whoever makes general observation on men's morals is considered offensive, who is more offensive than Jerome,[88] who scours monks, virgins, clerics, and bishops with caustic wit?[89] Who is more rude than Bernard,[90] who vents his rage against the corrupt morals of the Roman Curia and the monks themselves? 'Where?' you ask. In innumerable passages, but especially in the books to which he gave the title *De consideratione* and also in his *Meditations*. Josse objects[91] that I do not compare one set of morals with another, one state of life with another. Then why did I use the words 'nowadays conditions and times are such' [see 134 above]? That statement clearly precludes, unless I am mistaken, any accusation that I appear to prefer marriage to continence in absolute terms.

This phrase from the declamation also irritates him: 'For the others will seem to have been interested in leading a pure life; you will be judged the murderer of your line, because, when you were able to have offspring by honourable wedlock, you allowed it to die out through vile celibacy' [CWE 25 143–4]. Here the speaker is arguing from the standpoint of what is considered praiseworthy, and is not expressing his own opinion, but what the masses

* * * * *

88 As in Jerome's letters to Eustochium PL 22 394–425 and to Heliodorus PL 22 347–54
89 Horace *Satires* 1.10.4
90 Bernard of Clairvaux (1091–1153) also speaks out against the abuses of the clergy in the fourth book of *De consideratione* PL 182 727–807, and in the *Meditationes piissimae de cognitione humanae conditionis* PL 184 485–507.
91 *Propugnaculum* 122v

would say. In his eyes celibacy is vile not for anyone at all but for one who, not through love of a more perfect way of life but through hatred of marriage, allows his race to die out. Clichtove's subsequent statement is amusing: 'The sublime herald of the Lord, John the Baptist, was not the murderer of his race.'[92] Perfume on the lentils,[93] as the proverb goes. I resolved this difficulty earlier, for a little before this passage I admit that celibacy is fitting for apostles, bishops, priests, and monks, so why would I condemn it in John the Baptist, the precursor of the Lord?

He goes on to make further references to the declamation: 'Some indulgence should be granted to her sex and her years. The girl did wrong because she was overcome with grief; at the instance of foolish women or foolish monks she threw herself into it headlong' [CWE 25 144]. Here Clichtove constructs a syllogism: 'If a girl who professes the monastic life commits a sin, then the profession of continence is a sin.'[94] And at this point my good friend Josse shouts at the top of his voice that nothing more impious, more detestable could be uttered. But he does not advert to the fact that there are various kinds of sins. A person with a fever who does not abstain from wine sins against the art of healing; one who does not propagate his race is guilty of a sin against the political order. Lastly, a girl who throws herself headlong at the instigation of foolish men and women into an unfamiliar kind of life, while not even being sufficiently aware of who she is herself, sins against Sacred Scripture, which says that a faithless and foolish promise is displeasing to God.[95] The declamation illustrates in the case of this girl that it is a grave offence to make a difficult and indissoluble vow rashly. How impudent of Clichtove to accuse me of impiety for saying this in a declamatory exercise, when if it were said in a sermon, all would agree that it is a salutary admonition, especially in this age, when so many young girls are caught in a trap who will afterwards, but too late, repent of their way of life. Then my gentle adversary rebukes me for having exposed a girl to derision in my composition. How can I do that, my good sir, if I do not disclose the name of any young man or any girl; on the contrary, when the whole situation is fictitious, as befits a declamatory exercise, in which even if I had wished to use names, I would have had to use fictitious ones, as I do in other letters?

At the end of this chapter[96] he concludes: 'He should have commended marriage in such a way as to give primary importance to celibacy and

* * * * *

92 *Propugnaculum* 123r
93 *Adagia* I vii 23
94 *Propugnaculum* 123r
95 Eccles 5:4
96 *Propugnaculum* chapter 31, 123r

to confess candidly that celibacy is preferable to marriage.' So says Josse. Actually I do just that in more than one place in the declamation itself, but I argue from the circumstances that marriage is more suitable for the person concerned. What kind of an orator would I have been if I had convinced him that celibacy was preferable, when I am overtly persuading him to marry? So often does Clichtove din into our ears that celibacy means chastity, that if he continues to misuse a Latin word it would almost become a fixed rule and henceforward speaking Latin would be forbidden, because by his repeated solecisms he cleared a path for calumny.

In the next chapter he has the effrontery to say that after citing passages from Scripture, I added the following statement in denigration of continence: 'What do we read like this concerning celibacy anywhere in the sacred writings? Wedlock is called honourable, and the marriage-bed undefiled by the apostle Paul,[97] but celibacy is never even named there ... But if the law condemns and stigmatizes a barren marriage, it has condemned the unmarried much more severely' [CWE 25 132]. First of all he joins my sentences together incorrectly through carelessness or, more probably, through malice. The sentence beginning 'What do we read like' depends on what precedes it. '"Marriage is a great sacrament," says Paul, "in Christ and the church"'[98] [CWE 25 131]. Obviously Paul is here commending marriage because it is an image of that ineffable union by which Christ is joined to his spouse the church, and the union in him of divine nature with human nature. From this follows the statement 'What do you read like this concerning celibacy?' And I use the word celibacy according to good Latin usage in its simple connotation of a manner of life that is free from marriage. After the citation of that passage, another one from Paul follows: 'Wedlock is called honourable, and the marriage-bed undefiled. Not even virginity is ever called a great sacrament in Christ and in the church' [CWE 25 132, not exact]. This does not mean that marriage is superior to virginity in absolute terms. I admit this, but it belonged to the other part of the declamation. In the passage in which Paul pays homage to marriage he does not mention celibacy, since celibacy is diametrically opposed to marriage. But Josse distorts my words, as if I wrote that nowhere in the sacred writings is there honourable mention of a life free from marriage. He says, 'But in many other places virginity and continence are praised.'[99] Who does not know that? But here I am using the word celibacy in an absolute sense, debating with one who perhaps avoids having a wife not through love of piety but through dislike of marriage.

* * * * *

97 Heb 13:4
98 Eph 5:32
99 *Propugnaculum* 123v

But suppose I understood the word 'celibacy' to mean 'chastity,' would it have been appropriate for me as an orator to mention things that are opposed to my case, and suddenly turn from being an opponent of celibacy into its advocate? The fact that the law says, 'Cursed is he who has not left his seed in Israel';[100] that it relates that he who spilled his seed upon the ground was gravely punished by God; that women who did not give birth were thought of as disgraced, since the common people thought that this was a manifestation of divine wrath; that those who had offspring after a long sterility give thanks to God for having taken away the disgrace they brought upon Israel; that among the Mosaic blessings the fruit of the womb is mentioned while sterility is counted as a curse; that David calls down as a great curse upon Michol,[101] the daughter of Saul, that no man would see offspring from her – all of these examples were sufficient for the declaimer of the speech to prove that the law condemned a sterile marriage. 'Cursed' sometimes denotes abominable, hateful, and shameful. I leave it to him to consider the value of John Damascene's commentary.[102] We are not bound to any particular interpretation of Scripture, especially in a declamatory exercise.

What follows is equally unabashed: 'Besides, it is not one who lives unmarried who makes himself a eunuch, but one who in chaste and holy fashion carries out the duties of wedlock' [CWE 25 137]. My copies, three in all, each a different edition, read as follows: 'Not *only* he who, etc.'[103] I mean that chastity can be achieved to a large degree also in marriage, if one is not a slave to lust, but only desires offspring so that they may be brought up for the sake of Christ, and if one suspends the exercise of the marital right at times in order to pray.

He does not like this argument of the declamation: 'If it was rightly said that God and nature do nothing in vain, why did nature assign us these reproductive organs and these incitements, if celibacy in itself is to be considered praiseworthy?' [CWE 25 136, not exact]. As long as the theologians in the schools base their arguments on the authority of Aristotle, they are

* * * * *

100 Gen 38:8–10, the curse against Onan, quoted by Erasmus (CWE 25 138)
101 2 Sam 6:20–3
102 John Damascene (c 645–750) comments on this passage in his *Theologia* PG 94 1210–11; Clichtove elucidates Damascene's commentary in his edition *Theologia Damasceni, quattuor libris explicata et adiecto ad litteram commentario elucidata* (Paris 1519) fols 188–9.
103 The adverb *modo* is in the text of *De conscribendis epistolis* but not in the *Encomium matrimonii*.

considered learned, but is it unlawful for the declaimer of a speech to reason in the same way? 'But the argument is invalid,'[104] he will say. I agree, if by invalid we mean that which can be refuted. But if I were to resolve all the issues, what would the speaker on the opposing side have to say?

I must say repeatedly that I am dealing here with one who shrinks from marriage not through pious zeal but for other reasons, like the widows whom Paul[105] wishes to be married and procreate children. If the Apostle recommends this, is it a crime if a declaimer makes the same recommendations? In such cases, at least, marriage is preferable to celibacy. That I am not making this up is revealed in my words, which Josse neglected to cite: 'In all other respects one who follows the law of nature and procreates children is to be preferred to one who perseveres in the single state simply in order to have a more independent life' [CWE 25 132].

He criticizes this passage also: 'I have no patience with those who say that sexual excitement is shameful and that venereal stimuli have their origin not in nature, but in sin. What is so far from the truth?' [CWE 25 136, not exact]. Some were offended in this passage by the word 'shameful,' as if I meant that all sexual intercourse was dirty and illicit. I use the word 'shameful' to mean something of which we are ashamed, just as Paul calls those parts of the body shameful[106] not because they are by nature more shameful than other members, but because it is considered indecent to expose them. I readily admit that the rebellion of those members had its origin in sin, but the stimuli themselves I consider as merely natural, and that they would have existed in our first parents even if they had never sinned. For how could the function of marriage be carried out without them? I do not deny that rebellion and baseness would not have been present, but let Clichtove himself discover by what authority he asserts that natural instincts[107] would not have been present. There are many things that Augustine[108] and other ancient writers mention about the state of our first parents if they had persevered in their innocence, which we are not obliged to believe as articles of faith. I know that a distinction is made between created nature and fallen nature, but it is

* * * * *

104 *Propugnaculum* 124r
105 1 Tim 5:14
106 1 Cor 12:23 (*inhonesta*)
107 Clichtove *Propugnaculum* 124v argues that Adam and Eve were not ashamed of their nakedness and thus were not subject to the promptings of the flesh until they had disobeyed the divine command.
108 Clichtove cites Augustine *De civitate Dei* 14.17, which supports his view of the innocence of the first parents, 'clothed in grace,' as Augustine says, before their disobedience.

still called fallen *nature*. Paul says, 'We are children of wrath by nature.'[109] Indeed, rarely is the nature of man understood otherwise in the Christian writers, unless they make a distinction because of some additional factor. I understand the word nature in an absolute sense, that is, common to us with other animals. For I am writing a declamation, not teaching theology. Indecency did not originate with nature, but the sexual stimulus that is now judged to be shameful did come from nature. My additional remarks that indecency arises more from men's imagination than from reality, I confess to be not a very good argument, not even in a declamation, yet it is not altogether false. A great part of this sense of shame rises out of men's words, when they shout at their children: 'Aren't you ashamed? Cover yourself!'

There has been no lack of philosophers who taught that what was not shameful in itself was not shameful when done in public. I do not approve, however, of the shamelessness of the Cynics,[110] but in a declamation everything is turned to the uses of persuasion. Consider for a moment Clichtove's dialectical skill. He taught that at the beginning of the human race before the fall there were no illicit instincts rebellious to the spirit, and from this assertion he infers that Erasmus' contention that these instincts were instilled in us by nature and not from the sin of our first parents is weakened. Which instincts did he mean? Those that arise against the will of the spirit? That is not what I said. I spoke of purely natural instincts. When nature instigates us to procreate, it performs its natural function. It incites us to self-propagation just as it incites us to self-preservation through hunger and thirst. But man is hungry and thirsty even when he does not wish to be. Is that a consequence of sin? The fact that we resist these impulses with difficulty and are often mastered by them is due to the weakness of our reason. It is clever of him to call an excerpt from a declamation an opinion of Erasmus, of which I also strive to persuade others. By the same token, when Thomas[111] argues that simple fornication is not a sin, because to wipe one's nose is not a sin, he calls this a belief of Thomas. But that is more than enough concerning sexual appetites and natural instincts.

When I say that opposition to nature is not a virtue, he says that I should have distinguished between created and fallen nature. Of course that distinction would have been very useful in a fictitious composition! For the

* * * * *

109 Eph 2:3
110 The works of Aphrodite could be performed in public according to the Cynics. Cf Diogenes Laertius *Lives of the Philosophers* 6.69.
111 See n36 above. This is stated as an objection in II-II q 154 art 2, which is then refuted.

purposes of declamation it was sufficient to make use of the Stoic teaching that the essence of virtue is to live according to nature. But the fundamental role of nature is to preserve itself and propagate its kind. These things are good in themselves, but can become shameful in particular situations.

The declamation introduces the example of the daughters of Lot, whose sexual intercourse with their father Josse calls monstrous,[112] I know not on whose authority. It is quite plausible that those young girls had been brought up with upright morals by an upright father. He says that I 'subinsinu-ate'[113] that they either did not sin or could readily be forgiven. What is this Lynceus[114] not capable of seeing? On the contrary, the declaimer of the composition neither 'subinsinuates' nor 'superinsinuates' that they did not sin. He merely introduces an example of an action by which to show how great is man's natural desire to propagate his kind. And if they did sin gravely, it serves so much the more as an example for the development of the argument. They preferred to preserve future generations through a wicked deed rather than let the race perish. These young girls were convinced that the whole world had been destroyed by fire and that there were only three survivors. Origen[115] extenuates and excuses this deed in various ways. At the beginning of the world brother reproduced from sister without guilt because necessity so required. Perhaps necessity could also excuse the incest of these girls. What wrong proposition did Erasmus put forth this time? This is Josse's conclusion after careful reasoning: 'Erasmus should not have proposed this example of a monstrous crime for the purpose of recommending a good action.'[116] No one called this a monstrous crime before Josse. But even granted that it is, whence does he produce this rule that one ought not make use of a lowly example to recommend something good? Why does Christ use the example of the thief in the night[117] to teach holy vigilance, or the treacherous steward[118] to teach pious generosity? When the declamation reasons from the standpoint of that which gives pleasure, he says that I describe the pleasure of the marriage act in words that are so sexually arousing[119] and titillating that he was afraid to quote them, no doubt to have the reader think

* * * * *

112 The adjective in Latin is *infandum*; *Propugnaculum* 126r. The passage is found in Gen 19:36.
113 *Propugnaculum* 126r
114 *Adagia* II i 54
115 Origen *Contra Celsum* 4.45 PG 11 1102 and *In Genesim homilia* 5 PG 12 190–4
116 *Propugnaculum* 126v
117 Luke 12:39
118 Luke 16:1–8
119 *Propugnaculum* 126v

that my words contained excessive obscenity. But the fact is that the declamation so treats this subject that it could hardly be treated with more modesty by a virgin theologian. When it compares the friendship of marriage with other friendships, it says, 'For while we are linked with other friends by benevolence of mind, with a wife we are joined by the greatest affection, physical union, the bond of the sacrament, and the common sharing of all fortunes' [CWE 25 139]. Moses spoke with less modesty when he said, 'And they shall be two in one flesh.'

The declamation continues: 'If you are at home, she is there to dispel the tedium of solitude; if abroad, she can speed you on your way with a kiss, miss you when you are away, receive you gladly on your return. She is the sweetest companion of your youth, the welcome comfort of your old age' [CWE 25 140]. Is this prurient? What Hippolytus[120] could speak more chastely? It goes on: 'I should not presume at this point to set before you those pleasures, the sweetest that nature has bestowed upon mankind, which men of great genius, for some reason or other, have chosen to ignore rather than despise' [CWE 25 140]. These presumably are those prurient words that Clichtove found titillating. When I mention licit sexual intercourse, that is, existing within marriage, what could have been stated with more modesty? There is not a word there on the pleasure of the marriage act. What can be the purpose of those who publish such things in defamation of their neighbour?

He also thinks that another statement of the declaimer of the speech is worthy of censure, namely, that one who is not attracted by this type of pleasure seems more like a stone than a human being. He asks me whether the saints,[121] who perhaps by a special gift of God did not have these feelings at all, should be called stones. If he wants a humorous answer, I shall say that they were stones, but special stones for the building of God's house, and they were not men in the sense of Paul's words 'Are you not men?'[122] but through their extraordinary virtue angels or gods. If he wants a serious answer, I shall say that the declamation does not deal with those few who were raised above the condition of mankind, if indeed they did exist, which is uncertain. I always make exception for Christ and his most holy mother.

One terrible passage is left: the speaker, not Erasmus, wishes 'that those who indiscriminately encourage to celibacy those who are not mature enough to know their own minds should direct similar efforts to presenting a picture of chaste and pure matrimony' [CWE 25 138]. I refer to those who by

* * * * *

120 Chaste son of Theseus, liege of Diana
121 *Propugnaculum* 126v
122 1 Cor 3:4

improper exhortation constrain young girls and boys to enter the monastic life, and I add the word 'indiscriminately' because not all are suitable for this type of life. Does Clichtove approve of such individuals? I don't think so. But Augustine, as he says,[123] and Jerome encourage few people to the married life. My declamation encourages only one person. But if highly esteemed, learned men encourage some persons to a life of continence with due deliberation and prudence, are we to give immediate approval to those who do this today rashly and unadvisedly? The declaimer does not wish them to spend their efforts exhorting everyone to embrace the married state, as Josse falsely interprets, but to present a picture of chaste matrimony. Since there is a great multitude of married people, the masses think that it is licit to gratify their lust in marriage. If the image of a chaste marriage were depicted for them, we would have more chaste marriages. What the declaimer wishes to be changed is something worthy of denunciation; what he prefers to take its place is holy and virtually necessary; yet the defender of the church takes offence.

One finishing touch remains to be added to this theological declamation. Despite the fact that it is a declamation; that it is the first part of a set theme to which an opposing argument must be made; that these things are said not by Erasmus, but by a young layman; that they are addressed not to everyone, but to one individual; that a virtuous action is being recommended and one that in a certain way is necessary for him; that there is not a licentious word in the whole speech; that even in theological disputations it is permitted to use false reasoning in order that the listeners may learn how to refute it; despite all this, listen, I beseech you, to what my friend Clichtove has to say in his *Bulwark of the Church*. 'To utter freely at long last,' he says, 'what I feel, I should wish that all books that are redolent of Venus and incite the unwary minds of the readers to her through the deadly poison of their words, such as this little treatise of Erasmus, of which we are speaking, as well as the *Facetiae*[124] of the Florentine, Poggio, and the first two books of the *De voluptate*[125] of Lorenzo Valla, which advocate adultery and fornication and condemn celibacy in those dedicated to God in the monastic life, and

* * * * *

123 *Propugnaculum* 127r
124 A collection of anecdotes, mostly salacious, and not sparing in their castigation of monks and clerics, written by Poggio Bracciolini (1380–1459) when he was papal secretary under Pope Martin v
125 The first two books of this treatise, written in 1431, expounded the views of Epicurean philosophy in the person of Antonio Beccadelli, il Panormita, whose own life accorded well with the views he is made to represent.

some other books published by Christian writers, should be consigned to fire and brimstone as they deserve.'[126] Were you sober when you wrote this, Clichtove? If you mean by Venus illicit intercourse, there is not a syllable in my declamation that is redolent of such a Venus. If you mean licit intercourse, is it not permitted even in a declamation to urge this or that individual to enter into a chaste marriage? And do you judge that this 'little treatise,' in which there is not a single lascivious word, is to be compared with the filthy witticisms[127] of Poggio and the books of Valla that patronize whoring and adultery, as you say?

Paul rightly said, 'Evil conversations corrupt good morals,'[128] but do not those who defame their neighbour with such calumnies publicize evil conversations? If similar impartiality is used in making judgments by those whose verdicts determine whether men are to be burned at the stake, what are we to say? And although they publish books of this kind, they still wonder that there are some who do not immediately regard whatever has been said or written by theologians as oracular. I could amplify this point with many words, but I prefer to make allowance for Clichtove's ingenuousness.

I do not think it necessary to refute his accusations against my letter on the choice of foods. I think sufficient answer was given to them in the notes[129] I added to the letter. But I will touch selectively on a few of his points. His list[130] includes 'Erasmus attempts to advise against the practice of the law on priestly continence.' What is the practice of the law but continence itself? Does Erasmus ever advise against that? Or does he not strongly endorse it on various occasions throughout his writings and in that very epistle which Josse condemns? But he harps on these same words at the beginning of his discussion. He says that if permission to marry were granted to priests, a vile disgrace and a dire contagion of more grievous crimes would be visited

* * * * *

126 *Propugnaculum* 127r
127 Cf Ep 182:99–101. Erasmus calls Poggio's writings 'filthy, pestilent, godless stuff' in Ep 337:352–3.
128 1 Cor 15:33
129 In answer to the objections of Clichtove voiced in the third book of the *Propugnaculum* and to other critics, Erasmus published a revised version of his essay on fasting, *De interdictu esu carnium*, appending to it a series of scholia which elucidate no fewer than fifty-seven points. The full title of the work is *Epistola de delectu ciborum, cum scholiis per ipsum autorem recens additis*. It was published together with the *Dilutio* and an answer to Alberto Pio. The work was included neither in the 1540 Froben edition nor in Leclerc. A critical edition of the text has now been published by C. Augustijn (ASD IX-1 65–89).
130 *Propugnaculum* 169r

upon the church. What crimes is he prophesying to us in these words? As if both the eastern and the western church did not permit marriage to priests and deacons for several centuries. He does not wish the weeds[131] to be pulled out lest the wheat also be uprooted at the same time, as if the result would be that if marriage were permitted to the incontinent, no one would live a continent life, but everyone would immediately be corrupted by the admixture of wedded priests. And now are none corrupted by the admixture of those living with concubines? not to mention more obscene things.

He says that the mysteries of the altar are too exalted to be performed by married men. Therefore Paul sinned in admitting not only married deacons,[132] but married bishops[133] to celebrate the mysteries of the altar. I shall not make reference here to the fact that Peter was married, or that Philip was a deacon. The church was shrouded in deep darkness when for so many centuries it did not see that it was wrong to entrust the ministry of the altar to those who were married. What is the opinion of the synod that pronounces anathema upon those who refused to receive communion from the hands of married priests?[134] What of the fact that today very few priests minister at the altar but attend to those sacred duties through the intermediacy of others while they themselves hunt, wage wars, gamble, and administer worldly affairs?

Again he concludes: 'Since,' he says, 'once this breach was made, the status of the whole ecclesiastical class would appear excessively degenerate and would be defiled by an ugly disfigurement.'[135] Thus speaks Josse. Such must have been the Greek church at one time and such it must be today; such also was the Roman church for several centuries. Is he not aware that this language verges on gross slander of the Catholic church? Is it defiled by marriage but not defiled by harlots and other lusts not to be mentioned here?

'But,' he says, 'these evils would not be lacking in the clerical order even if marriage were permitted to them.'[136] To prevent these evils an ancient

* * * * *

131 Matt 13:26
132 1 Tim 3:12
133 1 Tim 3:2; Titus 1:6
134 In Ep 1039:138–48 to the Bohemian nobleman Jan Šlechta, Erasmus cites Augustine on Ps 10:6 that the gift of God conferred through the sacraments is not vitiated by the morals of the minister. The belief of the Donatists that the validity of the sacraments depended on the worthiness of the one who administered them was condemned at the Council of Arles in 431.
135 *Propugnaculum* 121r
136 *Propugnaculum* 121v

law[137] would be revived. An adulterous priest would be punished by death, one who consorts with prostitutes or possesses a concubine would be deposed from his office; or if leniency is recommended, the adulterer would be forced to do public penance and would afterwards be numbered among the laity. A priest or deacon guilty of impure actions would be debarred from wealth and office. But what hope would there be for putting an end to evils of this kind or how would religious leaders have the courage to correct these abuses when they themselves admit indiscriminately into the ecclesiastical order ignorant young men who betray their immorality in their whole bearing and are already plainly contaminated by these very vices?

In the third book, after reviewing Luther's opinion[138] that bishops and priests have the right not to prescribe but only to encourage, he adds that he was quite astonished that Erasmus was tainted with almost the same idea, because I wrote somewhere[139] that it seemed to me that Christianity would be more unadulterated if no particular kind of food were prescribed.

Can we be said to be tainted with the same ideas if one of us refuses all validity to papal constitutions and the other hopes for such spiritual vigour in the church that no one will have need of such prescriptions, but the faithful will withdraw themselves far from any type of Judaism[140] by observing a simplicity of diet voluntarily and with lifelong frugality? And he ends his speech in this way: 'Erasmus should follow the opinion of the universal church in this regard, publicly approved by the consent of the Christian people, and confirmed by long practice, rather than depart from it, relying on his own opinion, which is contrary to it.'[141] Where does Erasmus depart from the opinion of the church? Does he advocate that the general practice of the church should be violated? He teaches the very opposite. And what

*****

137 Penalties were imposed on uncelibate clerics and their offspring were deprived of civil status by Pope Benedict VIII at the Synod of Pavia, 1020, and these pronouncements were enacted as the law of the empire by Henry II. At the Synod of Tournai in 1520 statutes were published by Bishop Louis Guillard, a disciple of Clichtove, assigning severe penalties to priests living with concubines. Sessions 29, 21, 22, and 25 of the Council of Trent were dedicated to the eradication of this abuse. Cf Karl Joseph von Hefele *Histoire des conciles d'après les documents originaux* trans Dom H. Leclercq (Paris 1907–) x.

138 *Temporal Authority: To What Extent It Should Be Obeyed* (1523) 45 117–18 and *The Sacrament of Penance* (1519) 35 12–17 in *Luther's Works* ed Jaroslav Pelikan and Helmut T. Lehmann 55 vols (St Louis 1955–86)

139 Ep 916:164–6, dedicatory letter of the *Paraphrasis in Corinthios* LB VII 851–2

140 That is, empty religious formalism. Cf *Enchiridion* CWE 66 127 and Ep 541:149n.

141 *Propugnaculum* 131r

of his desire that such ardour for true spiritual piety should return that men will not have need of prescriptions of this kind? I think this has always been the wish of pious men. Of course, my opponent sings a palinode for having written that certain words that the church recites in the consecration of the paschal candle, 'O happy fault,[142] which earned us such a great Redeemer,' should be suppressed. But what does this have to do with my wish, which, unless I am mistaken, I hold in common with the church?

A little further on, when he says that my complaints were designed to reject fasting and abstinence, it is manifestly false, since in the same letter[143] that he criticizes, I reproach those who without necessity violate such constitutions of the church. And yet he insists on this reproof in other passages also. If he had said that my complaints aimed at changing obligations into exhortation, his speech would have been at least plausible, if not true. I do not complain there of constitutions, but of the preposterous judgments of men, who give such importance to these external matters that in deference to them they neglect what is more directly concerned with evangelical piety.

And if one were to complain of the immoderate number of such constitutions, what crime would there be? Does not Jean Gerson[144] complain of the great number of feast days? Does he not complain of the excessive quantity of constitutions, by which he says the 'vigour of the spirit is impeded, men's consciences are ensnared, and Christ's sweet yoke becomes iron-clad'?[145] And he makes these complaints about the prescriptions not of just anyone, but of bishops, popes, and even synods, recognizing that the hierarchy often abuse their power. As for what Josse asserts, that if the obligation should be removed no one would fast or abstain from sumptuous foods, to put it frankly, he has a dull imagination.

* * * * *

142 In his commentary on John Damascene's *De fide orthodoxa* (Paris 1512) Clichtove had rejected the phrase *O felix culpa* of the Easter hymn *Exsultet*, considering it to be a late interpolation. He preferred to substitute (more prosaically) *O magna misericordia, quae talem nobis miseris dedit salvatorem* (fol 181r). Following Duns Scotus and Bonaventure, the Sorbonne theologian argued that Adam's sin was not necessary to bring about the Incarnation, but that Christ would have become man to bring his creation to perfection. In the wake of much criticism he retracted this opinion in *De necessitate peccati Adae et foelicitate culpae eiusdem apologetica disceptatio* (Paris 1520). He does so once again in the *Propugnaculum* 132r.

143 Ep 916 criticizes those who violate the church's constitutions.

144 Jehan Charlier, born in Gerson (1363–1429), chancellor of Paris. In his *De potestate ecclesiastica* he complains of the multiplication of feast days; in *Oeuvres complètes* VI 239 (see n46 above).

145 Gerson *De vita spirituali animae* in *Oeuvres complètes* III 129 (see n46 above)

And here I should warn the reader not to imbibe unwarily the deadly poison that lies hidden under these honied words. Were you sober, Clichtove, when you committed this to writing? He does not see that I am merely engaged in debate in my treatise, stating nothing categorically, but deferring judgment to the leaders of the church. He considers that it is forbidden to discuss established practices. None at all? Is there any constitution of the church which teaches that the obligation concerning the choice of foods will last forever? I don't think so, but I do teach that a law must be observed as long as it lasts. And furthermore, in the entire discussion in which he praises Christian fasting, he calls me his adversary, as if I spoke ill of fasting; and lest anyone should think that this attack was directed against others, he reminds the reader in the table of contents, 'I have refuted Erasmus in the third book.'

He culls certain phrases of mine and constructs verbose syllogisms out of them, vindictively stating such premises for the purpose of calumniating me in this way: 'Discrimination in food is close to Judaism; therefore, the constitution must be abolished.' 'Christ made no prescription about discrimination in food; therefore the law should be abrogated.'[146] The letter does not follow this form of reasoning, but by collecting various reasons in the figure of speech called συναθροισμός[147] it urges bishops to consider whether in the present circumstances it would not be expedient to change the obligation of the law into an exhortation. But if he had set forth the argument in a proper manner, there would have been no opportunity for his hateful vituperations, which he did not want to lose at any cost. Clichtove would have given a better example of a theologian's integrity if he had used the same scrupulousness in refraining from calumny and impudent words against his brother as he did in proclaiming fasting and abstinence from forbidden foods to us. That is a much more grievous offence than breaking a fast or partaking of an egg against the practice of the church. And as certain men now praise the scrupulous spirit in which he humbly asked pardon for having rashly attacked a chant of the church which is not even taken from divine Scripture, so many more would praise the man's integrity if he would retract the many slanderous things he wrote against his friend. May the Lord grant us all a mind worthy of him.

* * * * *

146 *Propugnaculum* 130r ff
147 συναθροισμός, 'accumulation'; mentioned also in *De conscribendis epistolis* CWE 25
   93. Cf Quintilian *Institutio oratoria* 8.4.26.

THE REPLY OF ERASMUS TO
THE DISPUTATION OF A
CERTAIN PHIMOSTOMUS ON DIVORCE

Responsio ad disputationem cuiusdam Phimostomi de divortio

translated and annotated by ANN DALZELL

In 1532 Johann Dietenberger published an attack on the doctrines of the reformers entitled *Phimostomus scripturariorum*, 'A Bridle for the Scripturalists.'[1] To this he appended a 'special treatise' on the subject of divorce.[2] He had been working on this for some time, ever since he had discussed the subject with Valentin von Tetleben, the archbishop of Mainz. Tetleben had shown some sympathy for the view of Erasmus that the laws governing divorce might be relaxed, given certain circumstances.[3] Erasmus had argued this point in a lengthy excursus on 1 Corinthians 7:39: 'The wife is bound by the law as long as her husband liveth; but if her husband be dead, she is at liberty to be married to whom she will; only in the Lord.'[4] Dietenberger did not see Erasmus' work until 10 October 1531, but once having read it he took up his pen and finished his treatise.[5] He reviewed the passages in the Bible that state the conditions for divorce,[6] then listed and attempted to refute sixty-one points in Erasmus' excursus to which he took exception.[7] Erasmus' *Reply*[8] first appeared on 19 August 1532, and in the following month was published at Freiburg im Breisgau together with the *Epistolae palaeonaeoi* of Joh. Emoneus Iuliacensis.[9] The work was written hastily. The style is unpolished and the arguments not always clearly presented. Erasmus did not choose to spend more time in refuting Dietenberger's attack than he had to, and further, because Dietenberger had misrepresented Erasmus' position on confession (176), it was essential to correct his allegations speedily before they could harm Erasmus' reputation for orthodoxy and sound doctrine. He directed his defence to Tetleben (see 177) but did not address him by name.

The exchange between Erasmus and Dietenberger was the subject of a paper entitled 'Erasmus and Dietenberger on Divorce' by Dr Edwin Rabbie, presented at a colloquium, 'Erasmianism: Ideal and Reality,' organized by the Royal Netherlands Academy of Arts and Sciences and held in Amsterdam, 19–21 September 1996. Dr Rabbie's paper is published in the proceedings of the conference, edited by M.E.H.N. Mout, H. Smolinsky, and J. Trapman.

The text of the Leiden edition (LB), with a few minor corrections, has been used for this translation. The corrections are indicated in the notes where

* * * * *

1 Cologne: P. Quentel
2 Dietenberger 211–52
3 Dietenberger 212
4 *Annotationes in Novum Testamentum* LB VI 692D–703C
5 Dietenberger 212
6 Dietenberger 213–26
7 Dietenberger 226–52
8 *Responsio ad disputationem de divortio* LB IX 955A–965D
9 Dietenberger 211 n1

they occur. Discussions of technical terms are also to be found in the notes in their appropriate place. I have translated biblical texts by the Authorized Version wherever possible. When the Vulgate does not correspond to the text used for the Authorized Version, I have followed the Douai-Rheims Bible. Occasionally – where, for example, Erasmus has provided his own Latin translation – I have modified the English version in order to make his point clear.

AD

THE REPLY OF ERASMUS TO
THE DISPUTATION OF A
CERTAIN PHIMOSTOMUS ON DIVORCE[1]

ERASMUS OF ROTTERDAM TO THE MOST DISTINGUISHED ..., DOCTOR
OF CANON AND CIVIL LAW

I have been reading a tract on divorce written by a man who in my opinion
makes his points quite well and reveals a more moderate attitude of mind
than some whom we see contending in this arena. Yet he is not entirely dis-
pleased with himself. You can see this from his title page, which rattles its
'bridles' and 'bits' at us, arrogant words indeed! Now why he thought that he
would insult his opponents by calling them Scripturalists I do not know.[2] He
might with more justice have called the others Rationalists, for they ignore
the Scriptures and apply secular criteria to their study of the Gospels. Or if
they introduce anything from Holy Writ, they do so from convention rather
than conviction and often with little point, so you know that their knowledge
of Scripture is superficial.

It was my critic's intention to refute the remarks which I made some
time ago in my annotation on chapter 7 of the First Epistle to the Corinthians.[3]
My sole purpose was to provide the authorities of the church with an opportunity for considering whether there is any way to ensure that marriages
are not undertaken so rashly; or if undertaken rashly, whether they could be

* * * * *

1 Dietenberger's attack on Erasmus was appended to his *Phimostomus scripturariorum*, published by P. Quentel in Cologne, 1532 (Dietenberger 211–52).
Phimostomus (bridle) is part of the title, not a name for the author as Erasmus
pretends. Dietenberger returned to the image at the conclusion of the treatise: *frenum istud*, 'that bridle,' and *freno rectitudinis catholicae*, 'with the bridle of
Catholic rectitude' (Dietenberger 210).

2 Scripturalists (*scripturarii*): see Dietenberger 210: 'those who boast that they do
everything according to the Scriptures'; and 'the thrice and four-times damned
heresy of the Scripturalists.'

3 1 Cor 7:39. A brief note in the first edition (1516) was greatly expanded for
the second edition (1519). Further revisions were introduced in the third and
fourth editions (1522 and 1527), but these were not used by Dietenberger.

dissolved by an ecclesiastical court, given good and sufficient grounds.[4] His first move was to establish certain criteria as foundation blocks on which the structure of his whole argument might rest, but some seem to me so shaky that they need other pillars to support them! He wants the words *divortium* and *repudium*,[5] when used in Holy Writ, to be understood always as 'the termination of cohabitation without the termination of the marriage bond,'[6] whereas I use these words throughout the whole of my discussion with a broader meaning;[7] and he limits the term 'divorce' to those unions in which sexual intercourse has taken place.[8] Then, he says that he does not choose to discuss what the pope or the church can do by way of loosening or tightening the bond of matrimony,[9] although this topic forms no small part of my discussion; for its purpose is to urge that some consideration be given for those who are unhappily married, or if this is impossible, that at least some consideration be given in future to ensure that marriages are not contracted so easily.

Now who has given him the authority to impose on me new restrictions affecting the meanings of words? Even a betrothed woman[10] is 'divorced':

* * * * *

4 *Annotationes in Novum Testamentum* LB VI 692F

5 '*divortium* and *repudium*': ie 'divorce.' *Divortium* is not found in the Vulgate. 'Divorce' is expressed by the verbs *dimitto* and *discedo*, and the bill of divorce authorized in Mosaic law by *libellus repudii*.

6 Dietenberger 212: 'I do not understand divorce to mean the dissolution of the marriage bond'; and Dietenberger 216: 'not complete freedom from the authority of the husband, but the dismissal merely of the wife from her husband's house.'

7 *Annotationes in Novum Testamentum* LB VI 697E: 'I mean by divorce – true divorce, that is, and the only form known to that age – a form of divorce by which it was lawful to marry a second wife after divorcing the former wife. For what our generation understands as divorce, namely "the termination of cohabitation without the termination of the marriage bond," what ancient theologian or legal authority ever meant that by divorce?'

8 Dietenberger 214: 'The law of divorce has reference only to a marriage that has been consummated and that has been lawfully undertaken in other respects.' All authorities agreed that consent was the essential condition of a valid marriage, but not all believed that the marriage must be consummated before being considered valid; see Gratian *Decretum* pars 2 C 27 q 2, and Peter Lombard *Sententiae* book 4 dist 27 cc 3–5, who cites authorities on both sides. See F. and J. Gies *Marriage and the Family in the Middle Ages* (New York 1987) 136ff.

9 Dietenberger 212: 'I do not presume to set out here what the pope and the church can do regarding the termination of a marriage.'

10 'Betrothed woman' (*non iam ducta*) denotes a woman whose marriage has been contracted, but who has not yet moved from her father's to her husband's house. In the Palestine of the Bible betrothal was a solemn contract. The betrothal was the more important part of a Jewish marriage because the bride was 'consecrated' to her husband at that time. She normally remained in her father's

when her intended husband withdraws from the contract, a divorce takes place; both the man who dismisses and the woman who is dismissed bring about a divorce even if sexual intercourse has not taken place. St Joseph, seeing that his 'wife' was pregnant, was about to arrange a divorce. (The same word, ἀπολύσαι, 'put away,' is used there and in Matthew 5 and in other passages where the Lord is speaking of divorce.)[11] Furthermore, divorce can take place between those who have not been married legally; if, for example, a man unknowingly marries a woman related to him in the second degree of consanguinity, or if a woman remarries, believing that her former husband is dead. If my opponent wanted to refute my arguments, he ought to have used words in the same way that I used them.

   Now what theologian has taught or what angel has revealed that the word *foeditas*, that is, 'foulness,' in Deuteronomy 24 means 'adultery' and nothing but adultery?[12] The translators of the Septuagint wrote ἄσχημον

* * * * *

house for a year, then the second part of the marriage was celebrated, the groom took her to his house, and the marriage was consummated. In the Europe of Erasmus also betrothal was a solemn contract, so much so that in some parts of Europe a betrothed couple were automatically regarded as married if they had sexual intercourse. Erasmus believed that Mary and Joseph were betrothed but not married when Jesus was 'conceived by the Holy Ghost' (Matt 1:18: 'When as his mother Mary was espoused to Joseph, before they came together'). Because she was formally consecrated to him, she was called his 'wife' in Matt 1:20 and 24, and when she appeared to be guilty of adultery, it was appropriate that Joseph arrange a 'divorce.' The expression 'espoused wife' (Luke 2:5) emphasizes the solemnity of the betrothal and indicates that the marriage had not been completed.

11 Matt 1:19 and 5:31–2
12 Deut 24:1; cf Dietenberger 215–16. Dietenberger cites as his authority for this interpretation Paul of Burgos (c 1353–1435), a converted Jew and exegete, who wrote approximately 1100 additional notes (*additiones*) for Nicholas of Lyra's great biblical commentary, the *Postillae perpetuae in universam S. Scripturam*, the first biblical commentary to be printed (Rome 1471–2). For the text of Burgos' *additio* on Deut 24:1, see Dietenberger 215 n17. Burgos stated that the Hebrew word translated in the Vulgate by *foeditas*, 'foulness,' would have been rendered more accurately by *turpitudo*, 'disgrace,' as in Lev 18:6–18, where it is used to denounce forbidden forms of intercourse: adultery, incest, and bestiality. The sexual connotation which it clearly bears in this passage must be understood in Deut 24:1; and Mal 2:15–16, 'When thou shalt come to hate her . . .,' quoted by Erasmus below, 159, should also be interpreted in this light: 'because she has broken the Mosaic law.' The Septuagint expression is broader in meaning. Erasmus translated it by *rem indecoram*, which may refer to either a physical or a moral blemish.

πρᾶγμα, that is, 'an unlovely thing.' The text of the Law is as follows: 'When a man hath taken a wife, and hath had her, and it come to pass that she find no favour in his eyes because he hath found some foulness in her, then let him write her a bill of divorcement, and give it in her hand, and send her out of his house.'[13] A man 'takes a wife' when he contracts a marriage; he 'has had' her when he has taken her to his house.[14] (The expression 'has had' is translated in the Septuagint by συνοικήσῃ, that is, 'lived in the same house.') It may happen at this point, because they are living together, that the husband discovers a hidden blemish of body or mind which he had not noticed before, even though intercourse does not take place. Now suppose that an illness attacked you: would anyone refer to it in such an imprecise manner as this if he knew that you suffered from one specific disease?

But if 'foulness' means solely and simply 'the adultery of the wife' as my opponent wishes, does he think that a 'suspicion of adultery' is meant, or 'known adultery'? Now within the limitations of human understanding no distinction can be made between a strong suspicion of adultery, which the Law calls 'the spirit of jealousy,' and an adultery which, though known, cannot be confirmed by witnesses. The words of the Law in the fifth chapter of Numbers make this clear: 'whether she is defiled or is charged on a false suspicion.'[15] Now the right to divorce his wife was not granted to a husband on the ground of a suspicion of adultery: another remedy was provided for that.[16] If the adultery was detected and could be proved – and there is no other ground on which it is lawful to divorce – then by giving a bill of divorce, a man delivers up his wife to stoning.[17] (I speak of Jewish divorce.) That accomplished, it will be perfectly lawful for the husband to marry another woman; but who would want to take for his wife a woman who had been divorced on the ground of adultery and was subject to capital punishment?

Furthermore, it is agreed that the Law ordained the giving of a bill of divorce as a kindness to the woman in order that she might marry whom she

* * * * *

13 Deut 24:1
14 Dietenberger (213–14) understood 'has had her'(*habuerit eam*) to mean 'She has become his as a result of sexual intercourse.' Erasmus refers the two verbs, 'has taken' and 'has had,' to the two parts of a Jewish marriage.
15 Num 5:14: 'And the spirit of jealousy come upon him [the husband], and he be jealous of his wife, and she be defiled: or if the spirit of jealousy come upon him, and he be jealous of his wife, and she be not defiled.'
16 A wife's integrity could be ascertained by the drinking of 'bitter waters' (Num 5:18–24).
17 Deut 22:20–1

chose after she had been released from the authority of her former husband. But what kindness does an adulteress deserve?

Again, it is unlikely that the reason for a divorce was normally added to bills of divorce; that was a matter for the families. According to Josephus, through this document the husband gave up the right to reclaim his wife against her will;[18] or if she had married a second husband and had been divorced by him as well, or if she were freed from her second husband by his death, her former husband could not marry her[19] because it would seem that he had rashly divorced a woman who later came to please him. And this was done to show disapproval of the divorcing husband and good will to the wife who was divorced. And the divorcing husband is ordered to give the bill of divorce into the hand of his wife for the following reason, so that she may have the means of finding a husband and of demonstrating that she is completely free.

The clause that follows, 'send her out of his house,'[20] is designed to protect the woman's reputation, for if she lived in the man's house after she received the bill of divorce, people would suspect that she had intercourse with him after the divorce. But our Theologian imagines it to be obvious from this clause and, as they say, as clear as day that the right to remarry is denied to the woman. 'Do you understand?' he says. 'It does not mean that he will release her from the bond of matrimony, but from cohabitation.' And here you have one of the principal foundations of his argument. Pure straw!

Divorce is a matter not of law but of privilege. Even so, the manner of divorce, by giving a bill of divorce and by dismissal, is a matter of law, for divorce by any other means is unlawful. It was a law of great humanity: it took into account the husband's passionate nature and aversion and the wife's right to freedom.

But if divorce in that text is interpreted simply as 'separation from bed and board,' why does it happen in our day that men who have divorced their wives are not told to get them out of the house? What interpretation can be more cruel or absurd than this?

* * * * *

18 Josephus *Antiquities* 4.8.23
19 Deut 24:2–4
20 Deut 24:1. Dietenberger (216) understood 'out of his house' as a restricting clause (*clausula ... restrictoria*): 'not to send his wife from him altogether, but from the house only.' He maintained that the Mosaic law of divorce and the Christian law were the same, and he had, therefore, to explain Deut 24:1–4 in the light of Jesus' teaching as recorded in eg Mark 10:11–12: 'Whosoever shall put away his wife, and marry another, committeth adultery against her. And if a woman shall put away her husband, and be married to another, she committeth adultery.'

Our alert and penetrating Investigator should at least have noticed the phrase that follows immediately in the Law, 'and when she has left and married another husband.'[21] This is the reason she is sent from the house, that she may go lawfully to the house of a second husband. But this Phimostomus of ours interprets the phrase to mean 'She should *not* marry a second husband'!

Again: it says in the same passage, 'She is defiled and become abominable before the Lord.'[22] The word 'abominable' is used not because the woman committed a sin by marrying a second husband; but just as 'cursed' is used of a sterile woman, and 'unclean' of a menstruating woman, and 'accursed' of a man hanging on the gibbet, so in the same way 'abominable' is used of a divorced woman. (And indeed she ought to be abominable in the eyes of her former husband, for this will prevent him from taking her back after she has had intercourse with her second husband.) It is the alternation of marriages and the intermingling of semen that is abominable, not the woman herself, divorced for some physical blemish. Here you have one foundation pillar that cannot stand.

The second pillar is that Christ, when speaking of divorce in Matthew 5 and 19, Mark 10, and Luke 16,[23] does not introduce a new law, but merely explains what Moses meant: what Moses calls 'foulness' Christ calls 'fornication.'[24] But why is this so clear? Did Moses lack words for naming the heinous crime of adultery? He names it in many other places. Now the Lord did not reply to the Jews who cited the Mosaic law: 'Moses and I mean the same thing. He permitted divorce for some foulness which I define as fornication, and men who divorced their wives in his day were just as guilty of adultery if they married again as they would be today under the law of the gospel.' But as if he were offering a more perfect law Jesus said, 'But I for my part say unto you.'[25] Also, my critic claims that when the Jews replied, 'Moses made it lawful to divorce a wife by a bill of divorce on other ground than that of adultery,'[26] they did not state the meaning of the Law,

* * * * *

21 Deut 24:2
22 Deut 24:4
23 Matt 5:31–2 and 19:3–9; Mark 10:2–12; Luke 16:18
24 Dietenberger 215–16. Dietenberger accepted the interpretation of Paul of Burgos, 'basing his argument on the text of the Law and confirming it by the words of Christ.'
25 Matt 19:3–9. In his translation of Matt 19:9 Erasmus emphasized the contrast between 'Moses' and 'I': *Ego autem dico vobis*, cf Vulg *Dico autem vobis* (= λέγω δὲ ὑμῖν).
26 'on other ground than that of adultery': translating *ob aliam causam* rather than *non ob aliam causam* as printed in LB IX 957B

but rather the interpretation of it given by the Pharisees.[27] But what he claims must be proved. For the Lord himself did not say in his reply, 'The Pharisees misinterpreted the Law to you for the following reason,' but he said, 'Moses permitted you.'[28] Now what my critic attributes to Christ is of no importance. The only thing that matters is what is expressed in the Gospel.

Evil is permitted, my critic says, lest a greater evil ensue.[29] I grant that this statement is valid under human law, which permits public brothels in order to prevent rape and adultery. (Yet permits them to this extent only, that it does not punish them severely, for it does punish them to a degree.) But divine law does not permit evil that good may ensue, although sometimes it grants to frail humanity a less than perfect way lest it fall into sin; as when Paul, for example, permits widows to marry again.[30] Adultery, however, is listed not among imperfections but among serious crimes, punished among the Jews by stoning, among the Romans by decapitation. How, then, is it reasonable to suggest that such a crime was permitted by Moses?

Furthermore, since there is no passage either in the Law or in the Prophets which states that the expression 'foul thing' means 'adultery,' and 'divorce' means 'the termination of cohabitation without the termination of the marriage bond,' what a trap would have been laid for the Jews through not understanding the Law! what a great, open pit for falling into adultery! The Law, which is binding on all, ought to express clearly what it means. Moreover, since the Law requires that an adulteress be put to death by stoning – and by this interpretation a divorced woman who marries again clearly commits adultery – such a woman ought to have been punished, according to the Law; nor would there have been need for a trial in this case,[31] since according to my critic adultery consists in this very thing, that is to say, in marrying a second husband.

Now it often happens in Scripture that a point which has been expressed somewhat obscurely in one passage is clarified in others; but the second chapter of Malachi provides not even a glimmer of light by which we may conclude that adultery was the only ground for divorce permitted to the Jews

* * * * *

27 Dietenberger 217: 'but because it was commonly said by Jews who were under the influence of the teachings of the Pharisees that a wife could be dismissed for any cause whatsoever'
28 Matt 19:8
29 Dietenberger 218: 'But I think that reconciliation on account of the weakness of the flesh was admitted lest they be tempted by Satan after their separation.'
30 1 Cor 7:8–9
31 Ie the trial 'by bitter waters,' Num 5:18–24

and that after divorce a wife could not lawfully marry a second husband.
The text is as follows: ' Despise not the wife of thy youth. When thou shalt
come to hate her, send her away, saith the Lord the God of Israel.'[32] What
is the meaning of 'Despise not'? 'Do not send her off in a way that would
cause her shame and disgrace, like a servant or a slave,' as Abraham sent
Hagar away, with no provisions apart from a loaf of bread and a bottle of
water, Genesis 21.[33] But if you have conceived an aversion towards her, send
her away with humanity so that she may marry again in accordance with the
Law, and return her dowry so that she may find a husband, and abjure the
right to claim her again once she has been sent away.

Now aversion does not arise from adultery alone. Moreover, the entire
twenty-fourth chapter of Deuteronomy records laws whose generosity reveals an admirable humanity. For example: Do not require military service
of a man during the first year of marriage. Do not take the millstone as security. Receive security outside the house. Return security before sundown.
Pay labourers each day for the work of that day. Do not take a widow's cloth-
ing as security. Leave the gleanings for strangers and paupers; and do the
same when harvesting the grapes and olives.[34]

My critic cites Burgos as his authority for maintaining that in Deuteronomy the expression 'foul thing' denotes the adultery of the wife. I do not
know if Burgos says this, for I have not yet found the reference and I can
hardly persuade myself to believe it. But granted that this was said by him,
he is not an irrefutable Doctor of the church. When I cite in my note the distinguished Doctors of the church, Ambrose, Origen, and Tertullian, my critic
says that it makes no difference what this one or that one has said, but only
what Scripture says.[35] It would be more appropriate for me to say this to him
when he introduces Burgos. However, Cardinal Cajetanus, in his commentary on that passage of Deuteronomy, states on the authority of the Hebrew
that by the expression 'foul thing' any physical blemish is meant which ought
to be hidden on account of its ugliness; and he states categorically that a
woman does not sin if she has married again after being divorced, and that a
man does not sin if he has married again after divorcing his wife.[36]

* * * * *

32 Mal 2:15–16. See n12 above.
33 Gen 21:14
34 Deut 24:5–21
35 Dietenberger 231: 'I do not ask here what this one or that one has written about
    divorce, but what God has taught and ordained in his Holy Word.'
36 Cajetanus, like Burgos, based his interpretation on the Hebrew text, but he un-
    derstood Deut 24:1 to mean that a previously known condition or circumstance

Phimostomus says that permission to remarry was granted to a husband not because he had divorced his wife, but because Jews in antiquity were permitted to have a number of wives at the same time.[37] If this is true, Christ spoke to no purpose when he said in Matthew 19, 'Whosoever shall put away his wife, except it be for fornication, and shall marry another, committeth adultery,'[38] assuming that Christ teaches nothing new in this text but simply expounds the meaning of the Law. It seems likely in fact, that the concession of which certain patriarchs and kings availed themselves, perhaps under the inspiration of the Spirit, had been withdrawn long before the coming of Christ because the Israelites had already become a sufficiently populous nation. For there is no text in the Old Testament which sanctions polygamy. There are only a number of examples, a small number, among its holy men.

My critic does not take up this argument of mine: If divorce as defined in the Law consisted of nothing more than the termination of cohabitation, why do Leviticus 21 and Ezekiel 44 state, 'A priest is forbidden to marry a widow or a divorced woman'?[39] 'Even such a woman was permitted to marry,' the Law says, 'but as one defiled.'[40] If a divorced woman commits adultery when she takes another husband, on what ground is she said to marry? For 'marry' is a word used of matrimony, not of harlotry. A divorced woman is called defiled in the same way that a widow is called defiled, because she has had sexual intercourse with her husband. A woman who has had sexual intercourse is in some measure defiled, and for that reason a priest is forbidden to marry her; not because she is unworthy of a husband, but because it is appropriate to the priestly office that he marry an unsullied virgin. For virginity, even among the heathen, has always had its own honour and grace.

A further point: why were the children of a later marriage held to be legitimate if the marriage was adulterous?

* * * * *

(res) was revealed to the husband. It was a condition by its very nature hateful, but not defined in the Law. He did not state that the blemish was physical, but may have meant to describe it as such when he said that it was 'in the woman herself.' Cajetanus' commentaries on the Pentateuch were first published in 1531, at Rome. Erasmus was availing himself of the most recent scholarship on the subject.

37 Dietenberger 236: 'not under the law of divorce, but because a husband was permitted at that time to have several wives – a concession now totally withdrawn'
38 Matt 19:9
39 Lev 21:14; Ezek 44:22
40 Deut 24:4

And so, if it is by no means clear either from the words of the Law or from the words of the Prophets that the true meaning of 'some foul thing' is 'adultery,' and that the true meaning of 'divorce' is 'the termination of cohabitation without the termination of the marriage bond,' and if the words of Christ mean exactly the same as those of the Law (except that while he relaxes in some measure the first law given in the Garden of Eden,[41] he grants less latitude to Christians than Moses had granted to the Jews because he restricts the grounds for divorce to one), what other type of divorce could the Jews understand – or the disciples, for that matter, who at that time were no different from Jews – except what they had learned from the Law?[42] Moreover, the Lord does not indicate to them by any word that the form of divorce which he favours here was the only form of divorce among the Jews. In fact, the disciples say, 'If the case of the man be so with his wife, it is not good to marry.'[43] The estate of matrimony does not appear forbidding to them because a man may not remarry after he has divorced his wife, but because divorce had been permitted for one cause only while the Law had permitted it on many grounds; and many women are possessed of faults no less distressing than adultery.

But if we insist on that well-known ordinance 'What God hath joined together, let not man put asunder,'[44] not even the form of divorce which today the church permits on numerous grounds will be found acceptable. For God so joined man and woman in the beginning that the two were 'one flesh'.[45] (Bodily union, as they explain it, makes one flesh.)[46] But men who divorce their wives today deprive themselves of this union; and so those who live apart and do not share a bed do so in defiance of the commandment of the Lord; and this is clearly true because the expression 'put asunder' properly expresses the dissolution of conjugal relations (for Matthew

* * * * *

41 Gen 2:24: 'and shall cleave unto his wife: and they shall be one flesh'
42 What the disciples learned from the Law is implied by their reply to Jesus, Matt 19:10: 'If the case of the man be so with his wife, it is not good to marry.' They understood from Jesus' teaching that he greatly restricted the freedom to divorce which had been permitted by the Mosaic law, and they were shocked by the limitations that he imposed. If the disciples had interpreted the Mosaic law in the same way as Dietenberger, they would have expressed surprise that Jesus admitted divorce on any grounds.
43 Matt 19:10
44 Matt 19:6
45 Gen 2:24
46 Dietenberger 214: 'But how will they be "in one flesh" or "one flesh" unless sexual intercourse has taken place?'

says χωριζέτω);[47] even as 'will cleave unto' (προσκολληθήσεται) and 'joined together' (συνέζευξεν) express an indissoluble union.[48]

My opponent takes refuge in the apostle Paul, 'the interpreter' of the mind of the Lord,[49] who writes to the Romans in chapter 7, 'The woman is bound to her husband as long as her husband liveth,' etc.[50] First of all, it is recognized that the Apostle is not concerned in this passage with the question of divorce, but that he is drawing an illustration from the Law in order to prove that those who profess the gospel are no longer bound by the usages of the Law. Now it is recognized that an illustration used to make a point need not be applicable in every detail: it is enough if it applies to the point it was chosen to elucidate. For example, the Lord compares his coming to a thief in the night.[51] Now 'the law of the husband' is Paul's term for 'the right of the husband.' The right of the husband is his authority over his wife and his power to exact her obedience. But this right is lost in this new kind of divorce; so according to Paul, even this kind of divorce would not be lawful. This text, therefore, presents two difficulties: the first is that it is an illustration; the second is that if we are restricted by its words, even divorce understood as 'separation from the marriage bed' will be unlawful.

But if my opponent says, 'One must understand in this text "except on the ground of fornication,"' there will be two difficulties. One is that the exception does not square with the point Paul is making, for he wants to show that the law which he calls 'the law of the husband' is dead, not that it is vexatious. The second is that if the death of the husband and divorce on the ground of adultery have the same force, it will be lawful in our day too for divorced women to remarry.

A further point: in that text the Apostle speaks about the woman, not about the man, for the Law did not grant to the wife the right to divorce but granted it to the husband only. In my opponent's argument, on the other

* * * * *

47 Ie 'put asunder,' Matt 19:6
48 Matt 19:5 and 19:6. Jesus is describing marriage as ordained by God in the Garden of Eden.
49 Dietenberger 217: 'St Paul, the divine interpreter of passages of Holy Writ whose meaning is obscure'
50 Rom 7:2–3: 'For the woman which hath an husband is bound by the law to her husband so long as he liveth; but if the husband be dead, she is loosed from the law of her husband. So then if, while her husband liveth, she be married to another man, she shall be called an adulteress: but if her husband be dead, she is free from that law; so that she is no adulteress, though she be married to another man.'
51 Matt 24:43; Luke 12:39; cf Rev 3:3.

hand, the same regulation is applied to both, but nowhere is this set out in Holy Writ. I shall speak about this soon in some detail.[52]

There remains the passage in First Corinthians, chapter 7: 'And unto the married I command, yet not I but the Lord, Let not the wife depart from her husband: But and if she depart, let her remain unmarried, or be reconciled to her husband: and let not the husband put away his wife.'[53] In this passage Paul admits no exception, although the Lord, whose precept he cites, made an exception for adultery. But Ambrose says that we should understand here 'except on the ground of adultery.'[54] Suppose I grant the point, even so, the exception is to be understood with the last clause only, 'and let not the husband put away his wife,'[55] because nowhere does Christ permit or does the Law permit a wife to divorce her husband on the ground of her husband's adultery. Ambrose explains this point clearly in the same note,[56] since my opponent hounds me with the authority of Ambrose. Now when the Apostle says, 'Let not the wife depart from her husband,' he speaks of a divorce arranged by a wife who has been distressed by her husband's conduct; otherwise there would have been no point in his adding, 'and let not the husband put away his wife,' for he would be saying the same thing

* * * * *

52 165 below
53 1 Cor 7:10–11; cited and discussed by Dietenberger 217–18. In his Latin trans-
    lation of the New Testament Erasmus placed a full stop after verse 10, 'Let not
    the wife depart from her husband.' The Vulgate (and English translations) carry
    the sentence over into verse 11: '(10) ... depart from her husband: (11) But and
    if she depart ...' If verses 10 and 11 are taken together, the authority of the Lord
    applies to both. If they are taken as two sentences, verse 11 need not carry the
    authority of the Lord. This point is significant for the discussion that follows.
54 Ambrose *Commentarium in epistolam B. Pauli ad Corinthios primam* 7:10–11 PL 17
    230: '"Except on the ground of fornication" is understood.' Cf Dietenberger
    218: 'except on the ground permitted by the Lord, which Ambrose said was to
    be understood.'
    Erasmus questioned the authenticity of this commentary in 1527 and suggested
    that it be referred to as the work of 'Ambrosiaster.'
55 'Ambrosiaster' introduced the exception under the lemma 'And let not the
    husband put away his wife' (PL 17 230). Erasmus is following this interpretation
    of the passage, not suggesting one of his own.
56 Ambrose *Commentarium in epistolam B. Pauli ad Corinthios primam* 7:10–11 PL 17
    230: 'And he did not add, as he did of the wife, "But if he depart, let him remain
    unmarried," because it is lawful for a husband to marry if he has dismissed an
    adulterous wife. The husband is not restricted by the law in the same way as is
    his wife, for "the husband is the head of the wife" (Eph 5:23).' And cf under the
    lemma *Aut viro suo reconciliari*, 'or be reconciled to her husband' (1 Cor 7:11):
    'The same law does not apply to the inferior person as to the superior.'

twice, since the rejected wife 'departs' and the rejecting husband 'puts her away.'[57] But we do not read anywhere that a wife was permitted to dismiss her husband. On the basis of this passage, the only one adduced, it cannot be proved conclusively.

And so the Apostle proposes in the name of the Lord what was a counsel of perfection, namely, that there should be no separation at all, not even on the ground of adultery, because such a sin does not occur between those who have been made perfect; but that the bond should remain unbroken, even as it was in the original institution of matrimony.[58] (For the Lord did not command that the husband repudiate his wife if she committed adultery; rather he granted this concession in recognition of our infirmity. It is Paul who calls this a 'commandment' of the Lord.)[59] But if the woman leaves her husband – and if she does, she goes beyond the concession permitted – then the Apostle advises her on his own authority to remain unmarried;[60] or if she cannot endure the single life, to forgive her husband and return with him to a loving union. And Ambrose calls this the 'advice' of the Apostle, namely, that it is better for her to live alone in the hope of a reconciliation than to live with a second husband in an adulterous relationship. Again, the author of the commentaries on all the Epistles of Paul which we read under the name of Jerome supports the same interpretation and adds, 'This is better.' The passage from Ambrose is as follows: 'This is the advice of the Apostle, that if she has left as a result of her husband's bad conduct, she should now remain unmarried.'[61] The words of the commentator are as follows: 'If she has left for any cause, let her not marry another; or if she desires to marry

* * * * *

57 The words 'depart' and 'put away' can refer to one divorce, for when the husband 'puts away' his wife, she must 'depart' from his house. But they can also distinguish two divorces, the one in which the wife takes the initiative and 'departs,' the other in which the husband takes the initiative and 'puts away' his wife. If Paul meant the former, he repeated himself unnecessarily, but if the latter, then he introduced a concept not found in the teaching of Christ or the Law. But according to Dietenberger, the Apostle's teaching cannot differ from that of his Master, 'since we submit that the Apostle, in whom Christ speaks, is in complete accord with Christ' (Dietenberger 217).

58 Gen 2:24; Matt 19:3–6 and 8

59 1 Cor 7:10: 'And unto the married I command, yet not I, but the Lord.'

60 Erasmus has just shown that the Mosaic law does not permit the wife to arrange a divorce and that Jesus did not enlarge the concession granted by the Law. Therefore Paul could not invoke the authority of the Lord for the advice offered in 1 Cor 7:11: 'But and if she depart . . .'

61 Ambrose *Commentarium in epistolam B. Pauli ad Corinthios primam* 7:10–11 PL 17 230

again, let her be reconciled, for this is clearly better than for her to marry again.'[62] Ambrose calls this addition 'the advice of Paul'; and he does not say 'on the ground of adultery,' but 'as a result of her husband's bad conduct,' an expression open to broader interpretation. Likewise, the other commentator says 'for any cause,' which implies 'for many causes'; and he says 'it is better,' not 'it is necessary.'

On the other hand, the Apostle does not command the husband to remain single if he does not desire to be reconciled to his wife, because he may lawfully dismiss his wife for adultery. Many reasons can be adduced to explain why greater rights were granted to the husband than to the wife, but it is not necessary to consider them in this discussion. I know that some authorities regard husband and wife as equal in the legal aspects of matrimony, but Paul considers them equal only within the estate of matrimony when he says, 'The husband hath not power of his own body, but the wife, and likewise also the wife,' etc.[63] This does not apply to the right of divorce. In other respects he wants the wife to be subject to her husband[64] and calls the husband 'the head of the wife.'[65] And Peter summons wives to follow the example of Sarah, who called her husband 'lord.'[66] So far are they from being considered equal.

But let us grant to the wife the right of divorcing her husband on the ground of adultery, if after the divorce the bond of matrimony remains unbroken; how then can Paul[67] describe her as ἄγαμος, that is, 'unmarried,' if she is still bound to her husband? Or how can Ambrose describe as 'advice' a commandment which cannot be contravened?[68] From this text, therefore, it cannot be proved conclusively that a woman who has been dismissed in accordance with the terms permitted by the Law and the concession granted

* * * * *

62 *Expositiones XIII epistularum Pauli* PL 30 736, usually ascribed to Pelagius.
   The quotation as given in LB IX 959F (and in Froben's 1540 edition of Erasmus' *Opera omnia*, volume IX) makes poor sense. As given in PL it says, '. . . or if she desires, let her be reconciled to her husband; for this is clearly better than for her to marry a second husband.'
63 1 Cor 7:4
64 Eph 5:22; Col 3:18
65 Eph 5:23
66 1 Pet 3:6; cf Gen 18:12
67 Reading *a Paulo* for the *Paulo* of LB IX 960B
68 Ambrose understood 1 Cor 7:11, 'But and if she depart, let her remain unmarried, or be reconciled to her husband,' as Paul's advice to a woman who had left her husband, contrary to the Law and the teaching of Christ. Dietenberger interpreted this as part of the injunction introduced in 1 Cor 7:10 with the words 'I command, yet not I, but the Lord,' and therefore as the teaching of Christ.

by the Lord, cannot lawfully marry again. And so it is abundantly clear that Paul speaks in this passage of a woman who has left her husband unlawfully, since a woman does not have the right to go her own way. Otherwise he would have required of the husband too that he remain single or be reconciled to his wife.

Furthermore, the clause of exception is not without difficulty;[69] and although my critic declares that he will dispel this difficulty, he does not do what he promises – through forgetfulness, I imagine. The ancient Doctors of the church take 'except it be for fornication'[70] as referring to the whole sentence. In that case the meaning will be that the husband is permitted to take another wife without incurring the sin of adultery, and that the wife may marry again without incurring sin.[71] But St Augustine refers the phrase 'saving for the cause of fornication'[72] only to the clause that reads, 'he causeth her to commit adultery'; for a husband who dismisses an adulterous wife does not make her an adulteress. On the contrary, he rejects a wife who has already committed adultery.[73] Augustine devised this interpretation lest it appear from the Lord's words that it is lawful to marry again after divorce. I say that such an interpretation is more to be praised for its intellectual subtlety than for its truth. For the words of the evangelist in chapter 19 have a different meaning: 'Whosoever shall put away his wife, except it be for fornication, and shall marry another, committeth adultery.'[74] Here the position of the exception, placed in the middle, shows that it is to be understood with both parts of the proposition 'shall put away his wife

* * * * *

69 Ie 'Whosoever shall put away his wife, saving for the cause of fornication, causeth her to commit adultery' (Matt 5:32); and 'Whosoever shall put away his wife, except it be for fornication, and shall marry another, committeth adultery' (Matt 19:9)
70 Matt 19:9
71 Although she is an adulteress
72 Matt 5:32
73 Augustine *De coniugiis adulterinis* 1.2.2 PL 40 452, commenting on Matt 5:32: 'How are we to understand the text otherwise than as prohibiting a husband from divorcing his wife except on the ground of fornication? And the explanation is given: lest he "cause her to commit adultery"; for even if she has not divorced her husband but has been divorced by him, she will be an adulteress if she marries. Therefore, in order to prevent so great an evil, a man is not permitted to divorce his wife except on the ground of fornication; for in that case he does not make her an adulteress by divorcing her; rather he divorces a woman who is already an adulteress.'
74 Matt 19:9

... and shall marry another.' Certainly it cannot be taken only with the second part. And so the evangelist means: a man who divorces his wife for other than the legitimate cause provides her with the circumstances for committing adultery; and a man who marries a woman who has been divorced for other than the legitimate cause commits adultery, because he sleeps with a woman who belongs to another. From this it follows that a man who has divorced his wife for the reason named by the Lord and has married another does not himself commit adultery, and he does not provide his wife with a cause for adultery because it is lawful for a woman who has been divorced on lawful grounds to marry again if she cannot contain herself.

Where, then, is this new kind of divorce clearly approved, in which a husband and wife live apart, but the Hercules-knot remains?[75] Nothing can be proved from the passage in Paul except that a wife does not have the right to divorce her husband if she is the injured party and has left him, lest she contract a marriage with an adulterer.[76] It is different if she has been divorced by her husband in accordance with the Law.

At this time I omit what the orthodox Fathers have written about marriage, for my critic cares nothing for their authority except when they support his point of view. Perhaps he will reject Origen and Tertullian:[77] but everyone grants that they surpassed Ambrose and Augustine in their understanding of the Scriptures. With regard to the matter in hand, they were never censured by the church; and censured they certainly would have been if they had been found in error. If they have departed from the norm in anything, their lapse is explained by their antiquity, for in their day many doctrines had not yet been formulated. The errors of Origen have been carefully censured, but on this subject he was never reproved. That Tertullian did not agree with the perverse doctrine of Montanus is made clear by the fact that he soon left that sect.[78] He has been criticized because he condemned second marriages.[79] He was

* * * * *

75 *Adagia* 1 ix 48: 'Hercules-knot ... a fastening that is very tight and difficult to undo' (CWE 32 7)
76 Matt 5:32: 'and whosoever shall marry her that is divorced committeth adultery'
77 Dietenberger 299: 'I do not ask what Origen "was not inclined to doubt," but what the law of God ordained concerning divorce.' Cf Erasmus *Annotationes in Novum Testamentum* LB VI 693ff (on 1 Cor 7:39).
78 Tertullian remained faithful to Montanist teaching much longer than Erasmus realized.
79 See Tertullian *De monogamia*, a Montanist work. The Montanists, contrary to the teaching of the church, forbade a bereaved spouse to marry.

never reproved for permitting a husband to remarry after he had divorced his wife.[80]

There remains, then, the interpretation, or rather the ruling, provided by the church. I follow where my critic calls, although he declared that he did not wish to employ human arguments to support his position, but would demonstrate clearly, on the evidence of the canonical books of the Bible taken in their literal senses, that it is not lawful for a husband to marry again if he has divorced his wife on the ground of fornication, and that it is not lawful for a woman who has been divorced to marry again.

My critic refers me to the decisions of the Fathers, *causa* 32, *quaestio* 7; and there I find men cited whose authority he does not accept.[81] Moreover, even an opinion cited in the *Decretum* is not a law of the church, since it often happens that the opinions of the ancient authorities cited there are diametrically opposed to one another. Some are even heretical, should anyone care to examine them. Now in this *quaestio* Augustine takes first place;[82] and I grant that everywhere he teaches what the church now follows. But it is not an act of impiety, I believe, to question the opinion of Augustine in some instances. Gregory is cited there,[83] and he does not allow a woman who was divorced on account of adultery to marry again even after the death of her husband, although Paul does not deny her this privilege. When the texts of those authors are cited by us, when this author and that are named, when they are cited in the *Decretum*, do they suddenly become lawgivers?

'But Gratian decides.' Does he, indeed! 'It is clearly demonstrated by these authorities,' he says, 'that whoever has divorced his wife on the ground of fornication will not be able to marry another while she is still alive, and if he marries, he will be guilty of adultery.'[84] But immediately he adds, 'To these the following reply is given: these authorities speak of those whose chastity is not hindered by infirmity of the flesh and of those who have made themselves unfit for union with others because they were responsible for the separation.' A fine decision! Let Phimostomus enjoy it, and let him admit that those who cannot live chastely after divorcing their wives do not sin

* * * * *

80 Tertullian *Contra Marcionem* 4.34.5–6, a Catholic work; quoted by Erasmus *Annotationes in Novum Testamentum* LB VI 693F

81 Dietenberger 222. See Gratian *Decretum* pars 2 C 32 q 7 C 3: 'If a man who has divorced his wife on the ground of fornication can marry again while his wife is alive.' Erasmus' title for Gratian's work is *Decreta*.

82 *Decretum* pars 2 C 32 q 7 C 1: 'The bond of matrimony cannot be dissolved by fornication' (*De bono coniugali* 7 PL 40 378–9).

83 *Decretum* pars 2 C 32 q 7 C 18

84 *Decretum* pars 2 C 32 q 7 C 16

if they marry again. Again, what are the *Decretals* but papal rescripts and episcopal decisions? And yet I find nothing there which properly pertains to this question.

Now I have shown that archbishops and Roman pontiffs have held different opinions, not only about matrimony but about other serious matters as well, and that an earlier opinion has been corrected by later reflection. The same thing has happened with regard to numerous decrees of the early councils.[85] The church has never been without the spirit of her Bridegroom, but it has seemed good to him to defer the clarification of certain matters until his own good time. I believe that the spirit of Christ was with the apostles, yet Peter was criticized by Paul,[86] and dissension rose between Paul and Barnabas,[87] although the Spirit itself never disagrees with itself. It is probable also that the Spirit did not desert the sacred Doctors of the church, but sometimes they falter and from time to time they oppose one another violently. It is also possible that the Spirit is with the Roman pontiffs, and yet a decree of Celestine [III] was rescinded by Innocent III,[88] one of Pelagius [II] by Gregory [I],[89] a decree of the church of Modena by Innocent [III],[90] *placita* of John XXII were condemned by Nicholas,[91] and these dealing not with trivial matters but with fundamental ones, pertaining to the substance of the sacrament; unless, perhaps, there is no difference between a husband and an adulterer, between marriage and adultery.

Formerly it was not thought wrong to believe that the Holy Spirit proceeds from the Father only; now it is explained differently.[92] Formerly it was acceptable to believe that the body of the Lord is present through the act of consecration performed by the priest; later, transubstantiation was discovered. Formerly the whole church, and especially the western church, believed that when an infant is baptized, the washing with water does not assure salvation unless the body and blood of the Lord are administered immediately. The church thought that it was bound to this interpretation by

* * * * *

85 For examples, see *Annotationes in Novum Testamentum* LB VI 695 and 696.
86 Gal 2:11–14; see *Annotationes in Novum Testamentum* LB VI 697C.
87 Acts 15:36–9
88 *Annotationes in Novum Testamentum* LB VI 696F
89 *Annotationes in Novum Testamentum* LB VI 696F–697A
90 *Annotationes in Novum Testamentum* LB VI 697A–B
91 *Annotationes in Novum Testamentum* LB VI 696E–F. Nicholas is not identified by Erasmus; probably the antipope Nicholas V, installed by Louis of Bavaria in 1328, during the pontificate of John XXII.
92 Ie the *filioque* dispute. The word was added to the Nicene Creed at Rome in 1013 and had been used elsewhere before that date.

the words of the Lord in John 6: 'Verily, verily, I say unto you, Except ye eat the flesh of the Son of Man, and drink his blood, ye have no life in you.'[93] The church now understands that text in a different way.

Well, then, does not this text support my argument? The Apostle urges a believing wife to remain with an unbelieving husband provided that he does not seek a divorce.[94] But today the church forbids this. If people say in reply that Paul advised but did not command this,[95] it will be correct to say the same thing of the verse that immediately precedes it.[96]

But if the church on so many occasions and in matters of such grave import has corrected earlier judgments by later, why are we to think that now 'the Lord's hand is shortened'?[97] And why does my critic think that it was improper for me, although I introduced my remarks so circumspectly, to examine an issue on which lawyers of the highest reputation freely express their doubts and also their decisions? on which the distinguished and early Doctors of the church hand down divergent opinions? on which the Lord so spoke that his words incline more to the view which some of the earliest interpreters advanced? especially since no error is imputed to the church in this discussion. For the church does not by her law abrogate the commandment of the Lord. She too is opposed to divorce and narrows the concession granted by the Lord even as the Lord restricted that of Moses.

Moreover, it is agreed that the Roman pontiff, or certainly the church, can interpret the canonical Scripture, can expand and contract. By interpretation he shows that the Scripture has a meaning different from the one formerly accepted. By expanding, he grants what divine law did not expressly grant; permits divorce, for example, on the ground of heresy or apostasy or entrance into the religious life. By contracting, he subtracts from its concessions, as when he forbids marriage between persons related by degrees of consanguinity permitted by the Old Law and not forbidden by the New, and likewise on the ground of spiritual affinity; again, when he terminates a valid marriage for the sake of a religious profession; when he takes from

* * * * *

93 John 6:53 (= Vulg 6:54). The text has been understood as referring exclusively to the sacrament, and with wider reference as in Augustine *Tractatus in Ioannem* 26.15 CCSL 36 267–8: meat and drink are the fellowship of his own body and members, which is the Holy Church.
94 1 Cor 7:13: 'And the woman which hath an husband that believeth not, and if he be pleased to dwell with her, let her not leave him.'
95 1 Cor 7:12: 'But to the rest speak I, not the Lord.'
96 1 Cor 7:12: 'If any brother hath a wife that believeth not, and she be pleased to dwell with him, let him not put her away.'
97 Isa 59:1: 'Behold the Lord's hand is not shortened, that it cannot save.'

a husband the right of divorce if he too is guilty of adultery, or if he has prostituted his wife, or has had sexual relations with her after he has suspected her of infidelity, or has kept her when she was publicly playing the harlot. But if the pope has so much authority over the sacraments of the New Law, which Christ alone could institute, and over matters pertaining to the substance of the sacrament, much greater will be his power over the decrees of general councils, whose authority some people regard as equal to that of the Gospels, but only, I believe, if they show clearly that what they decree is in accordance with canonical Scripture. But let no one so take matters into his own hands that he behave as if it were right for a private individual to despise or rescind the decrees of councils. If a matter has been established by the corporate authority of the church, it is appropriate for it to be changed by the same authority; but let the greater good of Christ's flock require it.

At this point I am going to be told that the church has no position on divorce apart from that expressed by Moses, by the Lord, and by the Apostle. As far as Moses is concerned, it seems to me that my opponent is suffering from the same misfortune as the dog in Aesop's fables, who, while he was trying to seize the shadow of the meat, lost the real meat that he was holding in his mouth.[98] Thus while my critic shamelessly attempts to equate the law of Moses with the teaching of Christ, despite the authority of all the ancient commentators, he loses credibility in his other arguments as well. As far as the passage of Paul is concerned, if the Apostle in writing to the Corinthians thinks that divorce takes place only on the ground of adultery, he says nothing that differs from the teaching of the Lord. He wants everyone to be perfect so that divorce need not occur. If this cannot be achieved, he advises the wife not to marry again,[99] but to leave an opportunity for a return to favour. This would be impossible if she had had intimate relations with another husband after the divorce. For as long as the husband who divorced her did not marry again, there is hope of a reconciliation provided that the woman restrain her desires. The command which Paul addresses to the wife has, then, a practical value, for the concession granted by the Lord does not allow her any ground for leaving her husband and marrying another man; nor does the Old Law, unless her husband initiate the divorce. For a similar reason Paul urges a Christian wife not to leave a non-Christian husband,[100] because one may hope that a man who does not shrink from the society of a Christian woman will some day be converted through the effort of his wife. But if we are concerned

* * * * *

98 No 133 in *Aesopica* ed B.E. Perry (Urbana 1952)
99 1 Cor 7:11
100 1 Cor 7:13

with the usual kind of divorce, which comes about because women, offended by the conduct of their husbands, recoil from marital intimacy, this text does nothing to help my opponent's argument, for a husband too, if he rejects his wife on similar grounds, is forbidden to marry again.[101]

Now if divorce is permitted on the ground of adultery because adultery is such a heinous offence, there are other more serious crimes, such as unnatural vice, which Paul detests equally in men and in women,[102] infanticide, poisoning, abortion induced by drugs. But if the reason is that adultery is particularly damaging to the marriage bond, does the wife who makes her body available to another deal a more deadly blow to that bond than the wife who contrives the murder of her husband or who destroys their child either after or before its birth? For the marriage bond is not based solely and simply on the mutual enjoyment of bodies, since coitus is not an essential element of marriage,[103] but rather on unbroken, lifelong partnership and on mutual support, whatever fortune brings. Truly a woman who sins against their child sins against the bond of matrimony in a particularly devastating way.

But the church grants a wife separation from her husband's bed and board if he demands from her the use of her body in ways other than nature has decreed. The church, in fact, grants divorce for many reasons other than that of adultery, the only reason which the Lord approved. But my critic does not allow that the church deviates a straw's breadth, as they say, from the literal meaning of Scripture.

With regard to apostasy or lapse into heresy, they offer a tropological explanation, that this is spiritual adultery. But what texts of Scripture make this clear? When one argues that every sin is an adultery of the soul committed against Christ the Bridegroom, they admit that this is true, 'but not to the same extent,' they say. This interpretation does not, I think, satisfy everyone. What they say about affinity is similar.

When one argues about a wife who has been abandoned in favour of a profession to the monastic life, they value this so highly that they think it right for a girl who has been publicly married to be torn from her husband against her will and protesting, and to remain alone until he, after a year and a half (which is the period assigned for probation) makes his profession. But if, before the completion of this period – or after its completion even –

* * * * *

101 Since adultery is the only exception granted by the Lord as a ground on which a husband may lawfully initiate a divorce
102 Rom 1:26–7
103 154 above, and 173 and 175 below

he transfers to another monastery and must again put in a year of probation, or if he does it a third time, his deserted wife is told to wait until he is professed as a monk. Where does Holy Writ permit this? They offer us the following text: 'But if her husband be dead, she is loosed from the law of her husband so that she is at liberty to marry whom she will.'[104] 'Profession of the monastic life is the death of the secular life,' they say. But where do the canonical Scriptures teach this? Are not all Christians dead to the world, and are they not all buried with Christ through baptism?[105] And yet Paul does not desire that a baptized wife leave an unbaptized husband unless he rejects their union.[106] But if Paul understood both deaths, the physical and the spiritual,[107] why does the physical death so free a woman that it is lawful for her to marry a second husband after a marriage that has been consummated? And why does the same law not obtain for secular death, that is, death in a spiritual sense? Why do we make a distinction that Paul and the Lord did not make? And who does not perceive that this is a human argument devised in support of the monastic life? But human institutions should be fostered in such a way that no harm is done to what God has established and the Apostle confirmed. If I should at this point raise the case of certain gentlemen who have arranged for wealthy abbacies before receiving the cowl, and in the name of religion desert the wives with whom they had contracted legal marriages and from which they had perhaps taken every pleasure except coitus,[108] my opponents will say that what often happens is of no concern, only what ought to happen. The gospel calls us to perfection, I admit; but even as perfection exists beyond the monastic life, so it is possible for it to exist within marriage also. Even if perfection were not found in marriage, perfection is a matter of practice rather than of profession. And if profession is attractive, then the step should have been taken when it was honourable, and when it could be taken without injuring anyone. But let others see to the privilege of monastic life.

I strongly approve the fact that the church permits the dissolution of conjugal union when the offences are intolerable; but it does this through the power entrusted to it of granting dispensations, and not from the clear teaching of Scripture; yet my critic maintains that everything is done in accordance with the literal meaning of Scripture.

* * * * *

104 Rom 7:2 and 1 Cor 7:39
105 Rom 6:3–4
106 1 Cor 7:13
107 Rom 6:3–4
108 Cf LB IX 964C (175 below: 'Monastic profession dissolves a marriage,' etc).

My critic's entire argument, then, rests on extremely shaky foundations; and yet, as if he had proved his case in every detail, he passes on to his epilogue. There he sets out a number of short passages taken from my annotation, and he refutes them,[109] all of which is right and good for him if I concede that Moses in Deuteronomy, the Lord in the Gospels, and Paul in the Epistles did not know of any ground for divorce except adultery, nor any form of divorce except that which breaks off the conjugal union without terminating the marriage bond; if I granted that the Lord expressed by the word 'adultery' both physical and spiritual adultery; if I granted that the Apostle clearly expressed by the word 'death' both secular death (that is, death by monastic profession) and physical death; finally, if I admitted that the pope and the church can make no decree except in accordance with what has been expressed in Holy Writ.

My critic argued against certain matters which he did not understand, as in the rehearsal of the law in the fifth chapter of Numbers.[110]

I had mentioned in my annotation that Origen had written that there were some bishops who permitted wives separated from their husbands to marry again, and that Origen admitted that they did this contrary to the teaching of the Lord and Paul, but that even so he did not condemn what they did.[111] My critic says in reply that he does not see how Origen can fail to condemn what he admits to be at variance with the commandment of the Lord and the Apostle. But if he had followed that passage in the annotation for some lines further, he would have seen that Origen was referring there to husbands who had divorced their wives on other grounds than that one ground which the Lord permitted. 'Why, then,' he will say, 'does Origen not condemn this action of the bishops?' I shall explain in a few words: because they did not know if it was lawful to reject wives on grounds as serious as adultery or even more serious. For the Lord appears to mention fornication by name, not because it is quite simply the most wicked of all sins, but because it is a far more serious sin than those for which Jews, and gentiles too, used to divorce their wives. Perhaps those appalling crimes[112]

* * * * *

109 Dietenberger 226–52. Dietenberger took issue on sixty-one points.
110 Ie Num 5:11–31 (155 above), the trial by bitter waters, used to prove the innocence or guilt of a woman suspected of adultery. This passage was discussed neither by Erasmus in his annotation nor by Dietenberger.
111 LB VI 693A; Dietenberger 229; Origen *Commentarium in Matthaeum* 14 PG 3 1245A–B
112 Origen noted poisoning, murder of an infant during the absence of its father (the husband), other forms of murder, and the dispersal of the household during the husband's absence.

are passed over in silence because Christians were not expected to commit them. Similarly the gentile who founded jurisprudence did not establish a penalty for parricide.[113] In fact, this line of reasoning – 'If it is lawful to divorce a wife for adultery, it is even more reasonable to do so for poisoning or sorcery or infanticide' – is a somewhat more acceptable argument than that other: 'She is ordered to leave the house, therefore it is not lawful for the divorcing husband or the divorced wife to make a new marriage'; and 'It is lawful to divorce on the ground of heresy, for that is spiritual death'; and[114] 'Monastic profession dissolves a marriage which is lawful and solemnized but not consummated, because religious profession is secular death.'

In commenting on the thirty-first passage, where I had written that among the gentiles, let alone among the Jews, a marriage was not valid unless ratified by the authority of parents or older relatives, although both societies permitted dissolution of marriage given sufficient ground, my critic makes a wonderfully witty remark. 'Until this moment,' he says, 'I did not know that the law regulating marriage for Christians had to be drawn up in accordance with the customs of gentiles and Jews rather than in accordance with the law of God.'[115] But if something is done well by the gentiles, why would it be absurd to adapt it to the practice of Christians? What passage of Scripture would be attacked if dependent sons and daughters could not marry without the consent of their parents? Their legal status is like that of bondsmen, for they are under the authority of another. Why does he fuss about the Jews, when he himself, throughout the whole of his disputation, twists the teaching of Christ and the Apostle into conformity with the Mosaic law?

In discussing the thirty-fourth passage, my critic 'frankly admits' that the church is right to dissolve a marriage 'contracted when wine has drained away the use of reason.'[116] But I ask him if a young man, after passionate fondling, embracing, and kissing, inflamed by wine and love in equal measure, with his male organ already at the entrance to the girl's private parts and their naked bodies touching one another, has the use of his reason? The penniless girl, instructed by the procuress, sees that the young man is not in control of himself and says, 'I will not permit intercourse unless you are willing to marry me.' He replies, 'I will marry you,' not realizing that by their

* * * * *

113 Solon. See Diogenes Laertius *Lives of the Philosophers* 1.2
114 'and': reading *Ac* rather than *At* as printed in LB IX 964C
115 Dietenberger 239; cf *Annotationes in Novum Testamentum* LB VI 698D.
116 Dietenberger 241; cf *Annotationes in Novum Testamentum* LB VI 698E. Erasmus mentions not only drunkenness in this passage, but youth, sin, rashness, ignorance, and the influence of pimps and bawds.

sexual union a future promise becomes a present vow.[117] And yet marriages of this kind are called legitimate, and we have drummed into our ears, 'What God hath joined together, let not man put asunder.'

In commenting on the twenty-ninth passage, in which I show that it was lawful among the Jews for a divorced woman to marry a second husband, and base my argument on the fact that a priest is forbidden to marry a divorced woman, my critic replies as follows: 'But not everything that was at one time lawful for Jews is lawful for Christians today.'[118] But throughout the whole of his disputation he was concerned to show that in the matter of divorce, Jews had not been permitted a hair's-breadth more latitude than the Lord and the Apostle permitted to the Christians. What he repeatedly called adultery before, he now says was lawful.

On the final passage, when I had introduced the example of Fabiola[119] and said, 'Perhaps Paul in that instance would have interpreted his own words with more humanity than we have done,' he wittily replies, 'Rather, Paul would have said, "What I have written, I have written." '[120] But I said not a word about changing Scripture, only about interpreting Scripture.

I have gone over these points in the hope of arousing that distinguished scholar to a more rigorous defence of his arguments; arguments which he thinks he has made so clear that no place is left for uncertainty. In other respects, I think he is a good man. So much for his treatise on divorce.

Now at the beginning of his disputation he calls me 'his friend';[121] yet as if it were an honour he names me in his list of 'Scripturalists,' in the company of excellent men, beginning with Arius and Sabellius going on to Martin Luther. In this venerable company he mentions Erasmus between Karlstadt and Zwingli with this comment: 'Erasmus of Rotterdam questions whether

* * * * *

117 Consent was recognized as the basis of matrimony, but lawyers argued as to what forms of consent were legally binding. Peter Lombard *Sententiae* book 4 dist 37 c 3 distinguished between 'words of the future' (*verba de futuro*), 'I will take you as my husband,' which do not constitute a binding contract, and 'words of present' (*verba de praesenti*), 'I take you as my husband,' which do; but coitus, the distinctive act of marriage, was recognized as converting the nebulous future, 'I will take you as my wife,' to the factual present, 'I am taking you as my wife' (here and now).

118 Dietenberger 242–3; cf *Annotationes in Novum Testamentum* LB VI 698E

119 St Fabiola (d 399). *Annotationes in Novum Testamentum* LB VI 701E; cf Jerome Epp 64, 77, 78.

120 Dietenberger 252; John 19:22

121 Dietenberger 212: *doctrissimus Erasmus noster Rhoterodamus*, 'my learned friend, Erasmus of Rotterdam'

the sacrament of confession practised in the church is ordained by God and is necessary for salvation; but he is wrong because he disagrees with the decree of the church.'[122]

What a lot of nonsense! and in so few words! First: Nowhere does Erasmus question whether a sacrament of confession was practised in the church, for the sacraments of baptism and penance cannot be separated from confession; but he does somewhere question whether the form of confession which is now used in the church was instituted by Christ as part of the sacrament.

Nowhere in his discussion does he express doubt in these words, 'whether it is ordained by God.' It may be that 'divine law' is a wider term and that many things come under the divine law which were not instituted by Christ.

Far less does he question whether it is necessary for salvation. For if it had only been introduced by a general decree of the church and approved by use over many years, I would still think it necessary for salvation.

But my critic will perhaps say in excuse that he has not read my works; and what he says comes close to the truth, for he thanks the Carthusian Lambertus[123] most generously because through him he happened to read the annotation of Erasmus which he criticizes. And yet he seems not to have read it with due attention.

But let him show me that decree of the church which states clearly that the form of confession which we now practise was instituted by Christ. Indeed the serious nature of theological dispute requires that one examine closely what one criticizes before sending such a damaging statement in a letter.

I thought that I should address this little reply to you because my critic had addressed his treatise to you. Then if you think fit, you can act as adjudicator and mediator between us. Best wishes.

Freiburg im Breisgau, 19 August 1532

* * * * *

122 Dietenberger 50–1
123 Lambertus Pascualis, moderator and rector of the Carthusians at Koblenz

WORKS FREQUENTLY CITED

SHORT-TITLE FORMS
FOR ERASMUS' WORKS

INDEX

WORKS FREQUENTLY CITED

This list provides bibliographical information for publications referred to in short-title form in introductions and notes. Erasmus' letters are cited by epistle and line number in the CWE translation except where Allen or another edition is indicated. For Erasmus' other writings see the short-title list following.

Allen   P.S. Allen, H.M. Allen, and H.W. Garrod eds *Opus epistolarum Des. Erasmi Roterodami* (Oxford 1906–47) 11 vols, plus index volume by B. Flower and E. Rosenbaum (Oxford 1958). Letters are cited by epistle and line number.

ASD   *Opera omnia Desiderii Erasmi Roterodami* (Amsterdam 1969–)

Bedouelle *Lefèvre d'Etaples*   Guy Bedouelle *Lefèvre d'Etaples et l'intelligence des Ecritures* (Geneva 1976)

Bedouelle *Quincuplex psalterium*   Guy Bedouelle *Le Quincuplex psalterium de Lefèvre d'Etaples: un guide de lecture* (Geneva 1979)

CCSL   *Corpus christianorum, series Latina* (Turnhout 1954–)

CEBR   *Contemporaries of Erasmus: A Biographical Register of the Renaissance and Reformation* ed P.G. Bietenholz and T.B. Deutscher (Toronto 1985–7) 3 vols

CSEL   *Corpus scriptorum ecclesiasticorum Latinorum* (Vienna and Leipzig 1866–)

CWE   *Collected Works of Erasmus* (Toronto 1974–)

Dietenberger   Johannes Dietenberger *Phimostomus scripturariorum* (Cologne 1532) ed E. Iserloh and P. Fabisch (with J. Toussaert and E. Weichel) Corpus catholicorum 38 (Münster 1985)

LB   J. Leclerc ed *Desiderii Erasmi Roterodami opera omnia* (Leiden 1703–6) 10 vols

Massaut *Clichtove*   Jean-Pierre Massaut *Josse Clichtove: l'humanisme et la réforme du clergé* (Paris 1968) 2 vols

Massaut *Critique et tradition*   Jean-Pierre Massaut *Critique et tradition à la veille de la Réforme en France* (Paris 1974)

PG   J.P. Migne ed *Patrologiae cursus completus ... series Graeca* (Paris 1857–1912) 162 vols

PL   J.P. Migne ed *Patrologiae cursus completus ... series Latina*
                            (Paris 1844–64) 221 vols

Propugnaculum   *Propugnaculum ecclesiae adversus Lutheranos, per Iudocum*
                            Clichtoveum Neoportuensem, doctorem theologum, elaboratum et
                            tres libros continens (Paris 1526)

Reeve   *Erasmus' Annotations on the New Testament*, a facsimile of the
                            final Latin text (1535) with all variants. I *The Gospels* ed Anne
                            Reeve, introduction by M.A. Screech (London 1986); II *Acts,*
                            Romans, I and II Corinthians ed Anne Reeve and M.A. Screech
                            (Leiden and New York 1989); III *Galatians to the Apocalypse* ed
                            Anne Reeve, with an introduction by M.A. Screech (Leiden
                            1993)

Rummel *Catholic*   Erika Rummel *Erasmus and His Catholic Critics* (Nieuwkoop
    Critics   1989) 2 vols

Telle *Dilutio*   *Erasmus Roterodamus. Dilutio eorum quae Iodocus Clithoveus*
                            scripsit adversus Declamationem Des. Erasmi Roterodami
                            suasoriam matrimonii ed Emile V. Telle (Geneva 1968)

Telle *Erasme*   Emile V. Telle *Erasme de Rotterdam et le septième sacrement*
                            (Geneva 1954)

WA   *D. Martin Luthers Werke, Kritische Gesamtausgabe* (Weimar
                            1883–)

WA *Briefwechsel*   *D. Martin Luthers Werke, Briefwechsel* (Weimar 1930–78) 15 vols

SHORT-TITLE FORMS FOR ERASMUS' WORKS

Titles following colons are longer versions of the same, or are alternative titles. Items entirely enclosed in square brackets are of doubtful authorship. For abbreviations, see Works Frequently Cited.

Acta: Acta Academiae Lovaniensis contra Lutherum *Opuscula* / CWE 71

Adagia: Adagiorum chiliades 1508, etc (Adagiorum collectanea for the primitive form, when required) LB II / ASD II-1, 4, 5, 6 / CWE 30–6

Admonitio adversus mendacium: Admonitio adversus mendacium et obtrectationem LB X

Annotationes in Novum Testamentum LB VI / CWE 51–60

Antibarbari LB X / ASD I-1 / CWE 23

Apologia ad Caranzam: Apologia ad Sanctium Caranzam, or Apologia de tribus locis, or Responsio ad annotationem Stunicae ... a Sanctio Caranza defensam LB IX

Apologia ad Fabrum: Apologia ad Iacobum Fabrum Stapulensem LB IX / ASD IX-3 / CWE 83

Apologia adversus monachos: Apologia adversus monachos quosdam Hispanos LB IX

Apologia adversus Petrum Sutorem: Apologia adversus debacchationes Petri Sutoris LB IX

Apologia adversus rhapsodias Alberti Pii: Apologia ad viginti et quattuor libros A. Pii LB IX

Apologia contra Latomi dialogum: Apologia contra Iacobi Latomi dialogum de tribus linguis LB IX / CWE 71

Apologia de 'In principio erat sermo' LB IX

Apologia de laude matrimonii: Apologia pro declamatione de laude matrimonii LB IX / CWE 71

Apologia de loco 'Omnes quidem': Apologia de loco 'Omnes quidem resurgemus' LB IX

Apologiae contra Stunicam: Apologiae contra Lopidem Stunicam LB IX / ASD IX-2

Apologia qua respondet invectivis Lei: Apologia qua respondet duabus invectivis Eduardi Lei *Opuscula*

Apophthegmata LB IV

Appendix de scriptis Clithovei LB IX / CWE 83

Appendix respondens ad Sutorem LB IX

Argumenta: Argumenta in omnes epistolas apostolicas nova (with Paraphrases)

Axiomata pro causa Lutheri: Axiomata pro causa Martini Lutheri *Opuscula* / CWE 71

Carmina LB I, IV, V, VIII / ASD I-7 / CWE 85–6

Catalogus lucubrationum LB I

Ciceronianus: Dialogus Ciceronianus LB I / ASD I-2 / CWE 28

Colloquia LB I / ASD I-3 / CWE 39–40

Compendium vitae Allen I / CWE 4

Concionalis interpretatio (in Psalmi)

Conflictus: Conflictus Thaliae et Barbariei LB I

[Consilium: Consilium cuiusdam ex animo cupientis esse consultum] *Opuscula* / CWE 71

De bello Turcico: Consultatio de bello Turcico (in Psalmi)
De civilitate: De civilitate morum puerilium LB I / CWE 25
Declamatio de morte LB IV
Declamatiuncula LB IV
Declarationes ad censuras Lutetiae vulgatas: Declarationes ad censuras Lutetiae vulgatas sub nomine facultatis theologiae Parisiensis LB IX
De concordia: De sarcienda ecclesiae concordia, or De amabili ecclesiae concordia (in Psalmi)
De conscribendis epistolis LB I / ASD I-2 / CWE 25
De constructione: De constructione octo partium orationis, or Syntaxis LB I / ASD I-4
De contemptu mundi: Epistola de contemptu mundi LB V / ASD V-1 / CWE 66
De copia: De duplici copia verborum ac rerum LB I / ASD I-6 / CWE 24
De esu carnium: Epistola apologetica ad Christophorum episcopum Basiliensem de interdicto esu carnium LB IX / ASD IX-1
De immensa Dei misericordia: Concio de immensa Dei misericordia LB V / CWE 70
De libero arbitrio: De libero arbitrio diatribe LB IX / CWE 76
De praeparatione: De praeparatione ad mortem LB V / ASD V-1 / CWE 70
De pueris instituendis: De pueris statim ac liberaliter instituendis LB I / ASD I-2 / CWE 26
De puero Iesu: Concio de puero Iesu LB V / CWE 29
De puritate tabernaculi: De puritate tabernaculi sive ecclesiae christianae (in Psalmi)
De ratione studii LB I / ASD I-2 / CWE 24
De recta pronuntiatione: De recta latini graecique sermonis pronuntiatione LB I / ASD I-4 / CWE 26
De taedio Iesu: Disputatiuncula de taedio, pavore, tristicia Iesu LB V / CWE 70
Detectio praestigiarum: Detectio praestigiarum cuiusdam libelli germanice scripti LB X / ASD IX-1
De vidua christiana LB V / CWE 66
De virtute amplectenda: Oratio de virtute amplectenda LB V / CWE 29
[Dialogus bilinguium ac trilinguium: Chonradi Nastadiensis dialogus bilinguium ac trilinguium] Opuscula / CWE 7
Dilutio: Dilutio eorum quae Iodocus Clithoveus scripsit adversus declamationem suasoriam matrimonii CWE 83
Divinationes ad notata Bedae LB IX

Ecclesiastes: Ecclesiastes sive de ratione concionandi LB V / ASD V-4, 5
Elenchus in N. Bedae censuras LB IX
Enchiridion: Enchiridion militis christiani LB V / CWE 66
Encomium matrimonii (in De conscribendis epistolis)
Encomium medicinae: Declamatio in laudem artis medicae LB I / ASD I-4 / CWE 29
Epistola ad Dorpium LB IX / CWE 3 / CWE 71
Epistola ad fratres Inferioris Germaniae: Responsio ad fratres Germaniae Inferioris ad epistolam apologeticam incerto autore proditam LB X / ASD IX-1
Epistola ad graculos: Epistola ad quosdam imprudentissimos graculos LB X
Epistola apologetica de Termino LB X
Epistola consolatoria: Epistola consolatoria virginibus sacris, or Epistola consolatoria in adversis LB V / CWE 69

Epistola contra pseudevangelicos: Epistola contra quosdam qui se falso iactant
  evangelicos LB X / ASD IX-1
Euripidis Hecuba LB I / ASD I-1
Euripidis Iphigenia in Aulide LB I / ASD I-1
Exomologesis: Exomologesis sive modus confitendi LB V
Explanatio symboli: Explanatio symboli apostolorum sive catechismus LB V /
  ASD V-1 / CWE 70
Ex Plutarcho versa LB IV / ASD IV-2

Formula: Conficiendarum epistolarum formula (see De conscribendis epistolis)

Hyperaspistes LB X / CWE 76–7

In Nucem Ovidii commentarius LB I / ASD I-1 / CWE 29
In Prudentium: Commentarius in duos hymnos Prudentii LB V / CWE 29
Institutio christiani matrimonii LB V / CWE 69
Institutio principis christiani LB IV / ASD IV-1 / CWE 27

[Julius exclusus: Dialogus Julius exclusus e coelis] *Opuscula* / CWE 27

Lingua LB IV / ASD IV-1A / CWE 29
Liturgia Virginis Matris: Virginis Matris apud Lauretum cultae liturgia LB V /
  ASD V-1 / CWE 69
Luciani dialogi LB I / ASD I-1

Manifesta mendacia CWE 71
Methodus (see Ratio)
Modus orandi Deum LB V / ASD V-1 / CWE 70
Moria: Moriae encomium LB IV / ASD IV-3 / CWE 27

Novum Testamentum: Novum Testamentum 1519 and later (Novum instrumentum
  for the first edition, 1516, when required) LB VI

Obsecratio ad Virginem Mariam: Obsecratio sive oratio ad Virginem Mariam in rebus
  adversis LB V / CWE 69
Oratio de pace: Oratio de pace et discordia LB VIII
Oratio funebris: Oratio funebris in funere Bertae de Heyen LB VIII / CWE 29

Paean Virgini Matri: Paean Virgini Matri dicendus LB V / CWE 69
Panegyricus: Panegyricus ad Philippum Austriae ducem LB IV / ASD IV-1 / CWE 27
Parabolae: Parabolae sive similia LB I / ASD I-5 / CWE 23
Paraclesis LB V, VI
Paraphrasis in Elegantias Vallae: Paraphrasis in Elegantias Laurentii Vallae LB I /
  ASD I-4
Paraphrasis in Matthaeum, etc (in Paraphrasis in Novum Testamentum)
Paraphrasis in Novum Testamentum LB VII / CWE 42–50
Peregrinatio apostolorum: Peregrinatio apostolorum Petri et Pauli LB VI, VII
Precatio ad Virginis filium Iesum LB V / CWE 69

Precatio dominica LB V / CWE 69

Precationes: Precationes aliquot novae LB V / CWE 69

Precatio pro pace ecclesiae: Precatio ad Dominum Iesum pro pace ecclesiae LB IV, V / CWE 69

Psalmi: Psalmi, or Enarrationes sive commentarii in psalmos LB V / ASD V-2, 3 / CWE 63–5

Purgatio adversus epistolam Lutheri: Purgatio adversus epistolam non sobriam Lutheri LB X / ASD IX-1

Querela pacis LB IV / ASD IV-2 / CWE 27

Ratio: Ratio seu Methodus compendio perveniendi ad veram theologiam (Methodus for the shorter version originally published in the Novum instrumentum of 1516) LB V, VI

Responsio ad annotationes Lei: Liber quo respondet annotationibus Lei LB IX

Responsio ad collationes: Responsio ad collationes cuiusdam iuvenis gerontodidascali LB IX

Responsio ad disputationem de divortio: Responsio ad disputationem cuiusdam Phimostomi de divortio LB IX / CWE 83

Responsio ad epistolam Pii: Responsio ad epistolam paraeneticam Alberti Pii, or Responsio ad exhortationem Pii LB IX

Responsio ad notulas Bedaicas LB X

Responsio ad Petri Cursii defensionem: Epistola de apologia Cursii LB X / Allen Ep 3032

Responsio adversus febricitantis libellum: Apologia monasticae religionis LB X

Spongia: Spongia adversus aspergines Hutteni LB X / ASD IX-1

Supputatio: Supputatio calumniarum Natalis Bedae LB IX

Tyrannicida: Tyrannicida, declamatio Lucianicae respondens LB I / ASD I-1 / CWE 29

Virginis et martyris comparatio LB V / CWE 69

Vita Hieronymi: Vita divi Hieronymi Stridonensis *Opuscula* / CWE 61

Index

This book

was designed by

VAL COOKE

based on the series design by

ALLAN FLEMING

and was printed by

University

of Toronto

Press